X2/50

JPR

an Autobiography

Contents

Illustrations

Foreword

JPR is a man after my own heart, simply because he is never less than completely honest and forthright in his views. He follows the advice given in Shakespeare's *Hamlet*: 'To thine own self be true' – a remarkable philosophy which is usually alien to politicians, even rugby politicians.

Longfellow's lines also come to mind:

> *—I shot an arrow into the air,*
> *—It fell to earth I know not where.*

JPR knows his little patch of earth well; it is in Bridgend, Wales, where his roots are firmly embedded despite his London Welsh connections. He has never been afraid, unlike so many other public and rugby figures, to shoot his arrows from well behind the shoulder. And to rub shoulders with him has always been for me a unique privilege, so I'm delighted that in this autobiography John has decided to put on record his views on the current scene as well as his views on a decade or so of a golden era of Welsh and Lions rugby, successful, though not without blemish.

He played an important part in the success of the 1971 and the 1974 Lions tours. Knowing him, I think that even in the hour of success he was always aware of the chinks in his own armour. Like a forest animal he was blessed with a sixth sense for the presence of danger, an element which he often sought, and loved. Fearless. Uncompromising. The competitor of competitors. Early on he won the Junior Wimbledon. The following year he lost and I for one shall never forget the anguish as he hid his face with his two hands to conceal the disappointment which he felt so bitterly. The champion had lost. He had let his parents and his younger brothers down, he

9

had let Wales down, or so he felt. But the true champions always come back and so did J. P. R. Williams, the very same young lad who was even then playing rugby for his country with Phil Bennett, Derek Quinnell and Allan Martin, at the start of an illustrious career.

The private views of a well known person, I find, are always fascinating. With JPR this is particularly so, for his courageous, extrovert displays are a front for a sensitive nature. Welshmen, and this is a weakness in us as a nation, are given to please. To outsiders we may appear charming but somewhat insincere, but I don't think you'll find JPR guilty on this count.

When he was awarded the honour of being chosen as Rothman's player of 1976–77, I wrote at that time of the Twickenham match: 'John Peter Rhys Williams, a doctor himself, had seven stitches inserted to patch a facial injury. He had gone on to the field with seven others, acquired in a previous match. To Welshmen along the centuries the figures three and seven are nothing if not mystical. The figure of Williams in the distance, long hair flying in the wind, may remind us of Pwyll, Prince of Dyfed, riding majestic and mysterious in the mists of the Mabinogi; but a closer look reveals the stark realism of a warrior fully committed to battle. And at Twickenham, that day, in the cold January air, rivulets of blood congealed below his high cheek-bones. What a sight he made on television immediately after the match! The gory, victoriously happy sight of a man who had scored two winning tries – both initiated from a wheeled scrummage!'

And the figure seven struck again. Pinned down at the bottom of a ruck in the first few minutes of the All Blacks match at the Brewery Field, his unprotected face was trampled upon by a vicious prop. Before leaving the field to have another seven stitches inserted he paused and gave instructions to his men. A lesser mortal would never have returned to the field of play. Characteristically, he did.

Bridgend, Millfield, London and Old Deer Park, every famous rugby stadium in the world, the joys and tribulations of long tours, Wimbledon, hospital wards, famous players, fifty caps culminating in the captaincy of his country; and like a thread running through the fascinating tale which he tells, there is always the influence of his family and his charming wife. I found JPR's story compulsive reading, and so will all Welshmen, all rugby fans and players, and all who share a love of sport.

CARWYN JAMES

Introduction

The roads became narrower and narrower, and the hedgerows began to close in on us as we turned yet another sharp bend, each one taking us deeper into the heart of the Glamorgan countryside. As each bend unfolded, with still no sign of the cottage we were looking for, anticipation began to mount. We were in the middle of the weary process of house-buying. For weeks we had stood outside estate agents' windows, seeing something suitable and letting our imagination run wild. Then we would pluck up courage to go in and ask, only to have our hopes dashed with the inevitable letters splashed across the file: SOLD SUBJECT TO CONTRACT . . .

But this one was to be different – they hadn't even got as far as taking the photograph. 'You'll fall in love with it,' warned the estate agent. We did.

I took one look at the hillside opposite, with its ancient quarry turning back to grass, and decided this was it: ideal for incline training, ideal for speed bursts, and miles and miles of country lanes to run along to my heart's content, with no cynics watching. I doubt whether the same thoughts were going through my wife's mind! She was probably far more impressed with the roses rambling up the front of the cottage, the little arched windows and the thick walls which had obviously stood firm for hundreds of years.

Still, that settled it. We were twenty-five minutes from Cardiff, where I was to work at the University Hospital, twenty minutes from the hospital where my wife Scilla was to take up a short post and, most important, only fifteen minutes from Bridgend, my home town. Here I would be re-starting a rugby career after almost nine years' absence playing and living up in London. It was no mean task, for I knew I would have to put that little bit extra into my game if I was to counter the inevitable critics.

So, as I recount later in the book, just over two years ago, in August 1976 – only hours after I had walked off a plane from the States – we packed up our little house in Teddington and made the momentous journey back to Wales. It was momentous for many reasons, not least of which was the feeling which ran through my mind that this was to be another milestone in my life. Yet to begin with everything went wrong: I had been touring with London Welsh in the States,* and the flight back was delayed by twenty-four hours, with none of us getting any sleep. And the longer the delay the sadder I became at leaving all my friends. For some reason Scilla was also late getting back from her holiday, and we ended up packing the entire contents of our London house in four hours, ready to meet the removal van. In the end I have never been so pleased to see the Red Dragon and 'Croesi y Cymru' as we passed the border at the Severn Bridge leaving England behind us.

I always knew that I would come back to Wales; it was just a question of when. In fact, as I played my last game for Bridgend in 1968 before leaving to take up medical studies in London, I had promised my team-mates then that I would finish my playing career with them.

I had decided that the right time to move would be when I had passed the primary examination necessary to pursue a career in surgery. I knew that all the other candidates for the job I wanted would certainly have passed that exam. But I'd been involved in medicine and rugby long enough to know that people would be quick to suggest I had only been given the job because of my rugby status, and I needed the necessary qualifications to make sure I was taken seriously.

In spite of this I still found I had to prove myself for the first six months, because people in Wales didn't seem to accept

* I describe this tour fully in Chapter 8.

the idea that I could be anything other than the full-back they were used to seeing on the TV in their front room. Certainly, many of the small boys I came across in the hospital expected me to have a big '15' printed on the back of my white coat!

I never really had the same problem in London. I suppose the consultants and the rest of the hospital had seen me go through my years of medical school just like the other students – well, almost. The other factor was that England just is not like Wales as far as anything connected with rugby goes.

The fanaticism of the Welsh for rugby is exceeded only by that in New Zealand, although New Zealanders do not demonstrate their love for the game in quite the same way. The Welsh have more of a passion for it, and it is this passion which is unleashed in full Celtic fervour at the National Stadium, Cardiff Arms Park – the rugby shrine of the world. To play a home International there, and especially against the English, is an unbelievable experience. The expectations and tensions of the occasion are channelled by the crowd into musical form, and this alone is worth a good few points on the board in our favour before the game even starts. Surely only the Welsh could design a stadium where the acoustics are so arranged that the noise from the crowd is actually amplified on to the pitch? That sums up all that is Welsh.

I had not realized just what Welsh rugby meant to me until I was in South Africa. Long after the matches I had played in for the Lions I saw a film of a game played at the Arms Park: that of the Barbarians playing New Zealand. By the end of the film I had tears rolling down my face. It was not because I had seen a re-run of one of the greatest games I have ever played in; it was because of the atmosphere at the Arms Park – the singing, the emotion, the sheer elation of people who knew they were seeing something spectacular. There had been nothing like that during any of our matches on tour. It was then I knew I would have to return.

Playing rugby for my country has been at the centre of my life – my ambition when a schoolboy and for the last ten years the cause of any fame I have achieved. Of the nine years I spent away from Bridgend most were spent at St Mary's Hospital Medical School, one of the London teaching group. To the rest of the world St Mary's is renowned for the discovery of penicillin by Alexander Fleming; to those in Wales it is better known as a rugby establishment. That it attracts many Welsh schoolboys each year is probably related to the latter, but the old joke is that the train would pull into Paddington Station and the naïve Welsh lads, fresh from the valleys, would get lost within a hundred yards of the station and end up on the doorstep of St Mary's. They would then stay for seven years.

In spite of being based in London with the main objective of becoming a doctor I cannot deny that there was plenty of room for other diversions. Most of these were inevitably connected with rugby, but they were as varied as manning a train up-country in Sri Lanka, flying over Alaska, coming face to face with an original Zulu warrior and wearing a skirt in Fiji.

I managed to fit in most of my activities between courses, on weekends off or occasionally on official holidays. I obviously needed special permission to delay my training for the long tours. These included the Welsh tour to New Zealand in 1969 and the very much more successful Lions tour back down under in 1971.* This meant that all in all I ended up six months behind my contemporaries – which wasn't such a sacrifice, all things considered. I always found it wiser to explain my comings and goings to our clinical tutor beforehand. I could not just disappear for the odd few days as did the other lads, with the inevitable rugby reports, however small the print, telling of my antics the next day.

The facilities at London University were fantastic for all kinds of sport, but I mainly confined myself to rugby and tennis, with a little squash later on. I had been playing tennis

* Described in Chapter 5.

seriously every summer since I was about eleven and had reached my peak at the age of sixteen by winning the Junior Wimbledon Championships of Great Britain. At that time tennis was my first love, and the day of winning the Championship seemed the most important day of my life. Since then there have been other days to equal the satisfaction of achievement, but not over tennis. I was still enjoying playing, but by the time I reached St Mary's I had decided that tennis was not to be the sole object of my existence. I continued to play whilst at St Mary's both for the hospital and for the University where I went on to gain my 'colours'.

Music was the one hobby I could not continue as well as I would have liked; although my hands are better known catching a ball, swinging a racquet or even, in later years, wielding a scalpel, at one time they had tripped along the piano in gay abandon and produced vibrato on my old violin. I had played in the Glamorgan Youth Orchestra as a first violin and had experienced a great thrill when we performed well . . . or even just when we all finished on the right note – especially after many hours of rehearsal. It was rather like training hard for an International and running off winners. It's the team spirit and sense of achievement which are common to both and I wished I could have repeated some sort of musical achievement when I was up in London.

As it was, I had to content myself with singing. Each year, St Mary's would put on a light opera, usually by Gilbert and Sullivan. This was a great excuse for a continuous party, with the necessary beer to lubricate the vocal chords and for matchmaking activities between the basses and the sopranos.

My musical activities are now confined to listening. It's a marvellous way of relaxing, to come home after a heavy day in the operating theatre and wind down with a bit of Mozart in the background. He is my favourite composer. One day, I will probably find that I take up the piano and violin again, if only to keep one step ahead of my little daughter Lauren, should she decide she wants to play.

It was very lucky that I was able to play top-level rugby at such an early age when apart from my medical commitments I had no real responsibilities. To visit New Zealand at the age of twenty-two on a Lions tour would seem every young enthusiast's idea of heaven. It was rather like that for me in 1971, and to end the tour, having won the Test series for the first time ever, was the icing on the cake. It was the experience of a lifetime and, as shown in 1977, not one to be easily repeated. We had such a marvellous collection of players, who were not only talented sportsmen but great characters and consequently great tourists. As I describe later in this book, it was a happy tour, not just because we were successful but because we were brilliantly coached, managed and captained – by the trio of Carwyn James, Doug Smith and John Dawes. It was a similarly successful, though contrasting, experience to tour South Africa with the 1974 Lions.* There was much more at stake, both in the rugby and politically, and for this reason – a different line of approach both in coaching and captaincy was necessary. Syd Millar and Willie-John McBride fulfilled these posts admirably. It is difficult to think of any one man in the world of rugby who could command as much respect as Willie-John.

I also feel very privileged that I played for Wales at a time when we had so many outstanding players in their particular positions. I could not help but be influenced by such people as Gareth Edwards, Gerald Davies and Barry John, nor help develop playing under the astute captaincy of John Dawes. Add plenty of ball, won for us by stalwarts like Mervyn Davies, and we had a winning potential.

It all started when I was playing for London Welsh. I was able to expand my game as an attacking full-back, only because the rest of the side was so strong and we were playing so confidently. Then, with so many of the same players playing for Wales at the same time, I was able to continue attacking in

* I describe this tour fully in Chapter 9.

the same way. Confidence is the key to being able to run the ball out of defence, and knowing that the other backs are able to carry on a move is a prerequisite to deciding not to kick or run to touch. It was a marvellous era which we enjoyed playing in as much as spectators enjoyed watching.

But it is not just top level rugby that's enjoyable. It is far more than just a game and probably involves more people in the social side of things than any other sport. I often think that the top rugby players get a totally different view of the game as a whole from other people, and it is not until we are invited to the smaller clubs that we get to the heart of what rugby is all about in its broadest sense. One of the lessons I have learnt is that, no matter how large or small the local player's aspirations, he is no less fanatical in his pursuit of them as we are (or like to think we are). We certainly get little insight into the activities involved in, say, a weekend trip to Paris to watch the France *v* Wales match. (Since Max Boyce has put so many supporters' experiences into words we are getting a much truer picture!) It's a sobering thought to see all the Welshmen in their thousands in Edinburgh or Paris and to remember that many of them have been saving for the trip for the two years leading up to it. The thought terrified me when I was up in Scotland for my first senior cap. I felt a sudden pang of responsibility and thought for a moment that the prospect of playing and letting them all down was too great. Luckily that particular moment soon passed, but not without leaving a definite impression in my mind of the true meaning of the words 'to represent Wales'. It's not really the country but the people that makes playing for Wales so different from playing for England or Scotland or Ireland.

With the accountability of the player to the Welsh people goes the understandable feeling that the top players are public property and expected to behave in rather the same way as the Royal Family. Certainly we are treated like royalty most of the time, but there are inevitable pressures which coincide with this elevated position. I had known of the pressures on players who had become personalities and had felt extremely lucky that I was somewhat sheltered from similar pressures whilst in London compared with those players who were in the thick of it in Wales. When I did move back to Wales I felt I was much more experienced, less shy of my position and more able to cope with the pressures and criticisms. The more I was criticized for being 'not the player he was', 'past his best', and the rest, the easier it was for me to get down and accept the challenge.

With such high stakes at International level some of the enjoyment of 'pure' rugby is lost. I used to make up for this by playing in some of the Sunday games which were organized by a few of the star socializers at London Welsh. Often I would play flanker, since it is quite obvious that this would be my position by choice if I had my time over again. In fact, had the kicking to touch laws not changed as they did in the '60s I would certainly not have wanted to stay at full-back.

I used to try and emulate my hero, albeit also my contemporary, Jean-Claude Skrela. I am sure that if I had known I would one day run on to the field and take my position on the flank for Wales, as I had occasion to in Australia in 1978, I would have tried a little harder!

Although I was very proud to play on the flank, the situation leading up to that desperate move was one I hope never to see repeated on a rugby tour, in any country. The number of injuries incurred by one touring party was incredible. As a medical person with special interest in sporting injuries, I had a field day. As a player, I found it a nightmare.

I did not go into medicine with the specific intention of specializing in either orthopaedics or sports medicine, but knew only that I wanted to become a surgeon. They were subjects from which I just couldn't escape. Before long I was being consulted off the field, invited to 'take a look at this, Japes,' in the dressing-room, and asked 'Do you think it's broken?' in the bar. The one thing I am reluctant to do now is to make decisions concerning players on the field. Obviously, if an injury seems serious or life-threatening, I step in; any doctor would. But to decide whether a key player in the opposition should leave the field is asking too much of my impartiality.

I do remember, however, being involved in an incident not so long ago when I was playing for Bridgend against London Welsh, who included in their team both my brother Chris and an old friend, Jim Shanklin. Jim was playing in the centre, and had been involved in a hard tackle and was convinced that he had broken his jaw. He had done exactly this only a few months before, and I had every right to believe that he had done it again. I examined him, and thought that it was wisest for him to go off. This produced a great roar from the crowd, because they knew that I knew that one of my other brothers, Mike, was subbing on the bench, the official reserve for centre. It looked like a contrived move to make it a one-family show! Still, it must have made my parents very proud to see three of us taking part.

During my time in London I was so heavily committed to my medical duties, with nights on call in the hospital, that unfortunately I had to refuse many invitations to clubs and charitable functions. This led some people to believe that I was difficult to approach, or was being mean with my time, but I don't think they realized the responsibility I had to the hospital and to the patients. I would like to feel that in writing this autobiography I am sharing my time and my life with all those people who have been sufficiently interested in me to invite me to their functions, and who have had to suffer disappointment.

The book itself I would like to dedicate to my parents.

When I was young I used to think I would never forgive them for burdening me with a mouthful of Christian names. John was all right, so was Peter, even Rhys come to that, but all three together was just too much. It seemed so unfashionable to have *three* when my friends had only one, or two at the most. I used to get so embarrassed to have to stand up in class and recite a sentence, when all the teacher had asked was 'Name please?' Now of course the initials 'J.P.R.' have stuck firmly as my nickname, even my trademark, and have been my passport to rugby friendship throughout the world.

Often I have written the plain words 'John Williams' in autograph books, only to have angry small boys rushing back and saying, 'You *are* J.P.R., aren't you? Then why haven't you gone and *put* J.P.R.?'

So *J.P.R.* it is.

I

Four of a Kind

I was almost born on St David's Day.

In fact I was a few hours late. Considering the importance of St David to Wales, I was to regret those few hours' delay in arriving. He is the patron saint of the Welsh people, and much revered as the great deliverer from the enemy – usually the English. Despite my unpunctuality he must have had some influence on my life; at least, English players defending their line at Twickenham would believe so!

As it was I was born a rather large baby, to two not-so-large parents, on 2 March 1949. My father was away in Germany for all but a few days of my early life, since he was serving as a surgeon in the army. That March he arrived back in Wales to spend some hours catching a glimpse of me – and a lot more hours out celebrating with all his old medical school friends in Cardiff. 'Well,' he would explain later, 'everyone celebrates their first-born, don't they?'

My mother was a doctor too, and as 1949 was right at the beginning of the National Health Service and most local practitioners were still in the forces, she was required to return to work in general practice as soon as she – and I – could manage it. My early days, and certainly most of my first year, were thus spent in a carry-cot in the back of my mother's car. As it proved, the work done by my mother was the foundation of what has now become a large family practice in the town of Bridgend and the surrounding Vale of Glamorgan, and I

23

became well known to many of our patients long before I was known to the rugby world.

For instance, to Nurse Jones in the dispensary (nicknamed 'La' by me) I was a real menace. ''Sciption, please,' I would say, just as she had reached a tricky stage dressing a wound or giving an injection. Then I'd hand in my crumpled prescription, on which I'd printed my request: ONE PACKET OF CIGARETTES. These were of the chocolate variety, needless to say, and 'La' needed a fair supply of them to keep me out of trouble.

Early photos show me complete with the most innocent of smiles, but it certainly hid a strong streak of mischief. Pram trips to town, for instance, proved particularly profitable. Whilst my mother was up at the till, paying for her shopping, I would carry on with my own. Only on our return home would she discover that the weight of her pram was not just due to her bouncing son. There under the pram cover were the fruits of my outing: the morning paper, the latest *Beano*, a nice variety of sweets and groceries – in fact, anything within arm's reach. I didn't let anything slip through my hands, even in those days . . . Unfortunately it did not do for the local doctor to return red-faced to the grocer to pay for her son's misdemeanours, and it was not long before shopping became a much colder business than before – I still accompanied my mother, but without the shelter of my accomplice in crime, the pram cover.

However, at about this time I discovered that the contents of a soap-flake box were very similar to the contents of cereal boxes, and I spent many happy hours mixing up a bit of this with a bit of that, playing at being grocer. The trick was to mix them *in* their boxes . . . then wait to see my father's reaction at the breakfast table. Mind you, that was nothing to my mother's reaction after she'd poured half a box of cornflakes into a week's load of washing!

I remember little of my first home. It was at Ogmore by Sea, a delightful village situated directly on steep cliffs and leading down to the sea, and so receiving the brunt of the south-westerly winds. Such was my lust for adventure it was probably a safe move which took us to Coity Road, in Bridgend itself. It seemed a huge house – so much so that all the furniture we possessed fitted into one room. But we were not there long. In 1952 we moved to Ashfield, in Merthyrmawr Road, and so my parents came to live in the house adjoining the surgery premises. This was an ideal move, since they were looking after the practice between them at the time when the family was beginning to grow. I was to be the first of four brothers. Phil was the next to arrive, in 1951, and was to be my sparring partner until Chris and Mike appeared on the scene, within the next five years. Four was an ideal number, because we could always divide up into two teams for any battle or game. Being all boys, and having a sporting bias from both parents, we were never at a loss for things to do. Mind you, we didn't always divide up very fairly. More often than not in the early years it was Phil and I against the other two. Games were easily improvised, and we were lucky in not only having plenty of company but also having a large garden in which to play. This included conveniently spaced fir trees – for placing dropped goals – and a grass tennis court, which was usually badly scarred by our penalty attempts. Sadly, the court was soon to be wrecked in a much grander fashion – by the bull-dozers making way for the inner by-pass of Bridgend.

With Phil's birth I adopted the older brother role. This was the new, serious John – all of two years old. We spent a lot of time together in those early days, especially as our parents were so busy in their ever-demanding jobs as family doctors. After five years under the new National Health Service patients were beginning to take advantage of all the medical services available to them, and as this was long before the days of the appointments system it was not uncommon for patients to arrive as late as 8 p.m.

In 1955 Chris was born, and it was not long before he was included in most of the antics with Phil and myself, since there

were only four years between us. The one side of our life from
which he tended to be excluded was Donna Gonna. How this
special bed-time-story figure originated no one remembers, but
Donna Gonna was a fictitious golly who popped up each night
out of my imagination – initially, I think on my part, as a way
of sending Phil to sleep, but soon for both of us the means by
which we set off on all kinds of adventures. Phil and I shared
a room together, and by the time Donna Gonna was on his
way home Phil would usually have fallen off to sleep. In the
morning he would want to find out what he'd missed, as too
would Chris, who would wander into our room and was always
most upset that he never knew anything of what had happened
to our little golly the night before. In comparison with our
Donna Gonna we found the Robertson's variety of golly
very tame stuff.

Mike arrived on the scene in 1956. Our immediate reaction
to the news that it was 'another boy' was great delight; now
there would not have to be an odd one out.

I had been given my first rugby ball when I was six months
old. It is perhaps symbolic that it came from Dr Jack Matthews,
one of the hardest tackling three-quarters the game has ever
seen. He and my father were great friends together at medical
school in Cardiff, and played together for the Cardiff Medicals,
with my dad outside him on the left wing. Jack Matthews
then went on to play for Wales.

In those days the Medicals were among the top clubs in the
country, with St Mary's fractionally ahead. With all the
rugby influence in my life there was no way I could have not
played the game. For those first few years I was rarely seen
without my leather companion, tucked carefully under my
arm. I spent hours playing with it on my own, with Phil
napping in his cot. But soon Phil, and the others, were old
enough to join me, and they did so without a second asking.
Saturday morning visitors to Merthyrmawr Road would see
a parade of two, then three, then four small boys, all dressed
in blue and white, busily engaged at 'playing for Bridgend':

there was no greater ambition in those days. We would cross the River Ogwr, and run over to Newbridge Fields, young Mike bringing up the rear. He was only just able to walk by the time I was eight (and a very 'senior' player), and he would struggle behind us wearing a rugby shirt so large that the sleeves had to be rolled up six times to let his hands out. In his own way he must have been the keenest of us all. Our efforts at kicking between the fir trees were now directed to real posts, and we thought we were playing for Wales.

By this time I was attending Trelales Primary School at Laleston, a tiny village just outside Bridgend. It was the only school to accept four year olds, and so it was there that I had started in 1953. One of the teachers there was a certain Mr W. Morgan, better known as Billy Morgan, the full-back for Bridgend. His enthusiasm for the game was infectious, and not surprisingly he became my hero. On Saturday afternoons we would watch him and Bridgend play down at the Brewery field.

Once, as a rare treat, I was taken to an 'away' match at Cheltenham. I remember that day clearly for in that match the ultimate disaster occurred: Billy Morgan was sent off. Retaliation? I can no longer remember nor do I have any other recollection of the rest of the game, but it left a deep impression on my young mind. It is a very disturbing experience, seeing one's No. 1 hero diminished by such treatment.

I suppose I was seven, and at school, when I first played in a proper game of rugby with fifteen players on either side: there was no such sophistication as mini-rugby then. I was meant to be out on the left wing, but in fact spent the entire game chasing after the ball, as all youngsters do. We used to play on a Friday afternoon, and I looked forward to the game all week. After a few games I was 'promoted' to fly-half for one year, but in my last year Mr Morgan suggested that I should move to his own position – full-back. The disgrace! In those days that was next to being out of the team altogether.

I was very upset and, trying not to hurt Mr Morgan's

feelings, made it quite clear that this just wasn't on. As top try-scorer, even at the tender age of ten, I was cheeky enough to think I had a say in the selection. He allowed me to air my views, and eventually, after much debate, I was persuaded by his belief that the full-back should in the future adopt an attacking role to give the new position a go. This was very advanced thinking at the time, since the 'kicking to touch' law was not to change for another ten years. I am indebted to Billy Morgan for his foresight, because with the fly-half factory in Wales stepping up production I would never have progressed further than the Laleston side had I stayed at No. 10.

One of my closest friends, dating back to those Laleston days, was Rob Leyshon. He was not from the school itself but from one of the opposition teams. In fact he was a fly-half himself, and we had many battles together on a Friday afternoon. Our paths crossed frequently from this time on: as fellow schoolboy trialists, as violinists in the Glamorgan Youth Orchestra and then, since he was a year ahead of me, the same Rob Leyshon was there to meet me on my first day at St Mary's. We are now on the same surgical rotation back in Cardiff.

Although I was mad keen on rugby at Laleston the physical contact side of my game had not yet developed: far from it. I was involved in fewer of the usual schoolboy fights than most, and particularly remember one fight that never was – although the rest of the school was behind me, and wanted it to take place. It all involved a difference of opinion with the school 'tough guy', who had the unlikely name of Billy Dainty. Dainty he certainly was not, but for some reason he declined my puny challenge. I was very small for my age in those days, and probably had something of a complex about it. I often wonder if my attitude on the field has anything to do with this: it could be a legacy of constantly having to prove I was not as puny as I looked!

I stayed at Laleston until I was ten, then transferred to the local preparatory school. My parents, in typical post-war fashion of wanting the very best for their offspring after all the years of hardship, had put my name down for Epsom College, famous for its medical connections. The idea was to prepare me for the Common Entrance exam, and to this end I was put down for tuition from Bryntirion Preparatory School. After a few months of Latin – and very little rugby – I became wary of what was in store for me. I was old enough to realize that public school didn't appeal to me one bit, and refused to take the exam. Instead I took the Eleven Plus, and got a place at Bridgend Grammar School.

The one thing that the year at prep school taught me was to play soccer. This came in useful at St Mary's, when in 1972 I was forced to 'retire' from rugby for five weeks, whilst my jaw was wired up after a fracture. Although I enjoyed playing and even appeared in a hospital cup match, I fear I was only running off the ball for ninety minutes, just to maintain fitness. It must have looked like the early rugby games at Laleston, when I was a very roving wing three-quarter.

Music plays an integral part, along with the inevitable rugby, in the lives of most Welshmen, and I was no exception. Everyone is familiar with the magnificent male voice choirs which have come from the mining valleys, mainly in the Rhondda. This is often a lad's first introduction to music, and I was seven when I became a chorister at Nolton Church. We were a large choir, with about twenty men and twenty boy sopranos under the direction of a great character nicknamed 'Boss Rees'. The church was literally at the bottom of our garden, and although the inner by-pass was soon to separate us it was still almost next door. Most days during the week, at four o'clock, I would run across the road to choir practice. We enjoyed singing the Sol-Fa system long before we could read a word of music, but obviously needed some added incentive to get us to practise regularly. This took the form of small payments, as is the rule, and treats like outings to the coast. These would probably have provided a great attraction for choristers living up the valleys, but most of our group lived no more than five miles from the sea, so beach expeditions were

29

not much of a success. It almost always rained anyway.

Not the best, but the most unusual bait, was a large cricket bag containing all the necessary equipment for a formal game. This was kept locked up in the rectory, and was for use in the summer after the choir sessions. We all tramped down to Newbridge Fields, including some of the much older bass members. No one really knew where the bag had come from, nor when it had arrived in the rectory, but it certainly served its purpose of getting us along to practise when we were much more tempted to play about outside.

After a couple of years' apprenticeship I was given my big chance. This was the solo rendering of the first verse of 'O Little Town of Bethlehem' in the Christmas service of lessons and carols. To be singing in front of a congregation of five hundred at the age of nine seemed a great ordeal. Ten years later it was no less of an ordeal to be singing *Mae Hen Wlad Fy'Nhadau* for the first time in front of fifty thousand fanatics at Cardiff Arms Park . . . albeit with a much deeper voice!

Anyway, my début as a solo soprano must have been adequate, as I was repeatedly asked to sing at other services. By special request, I would even sing at weddings – at least, until my voice broke. High up in my repertoire (in more ways than one) was 'Oh for the Wings of a Dove', which even I had to hear on tape to be convinced that I could sing. It still brings nostalgic tears to my parents' eyes whenever the tape is dug out of the family archives.

In addition to singing in the choir I also took part in other church activities, including becoming a server and helping out with the bell-ringing. We had mechanical bells played on a sort of keyboard, rather than true campanologists' bells, so it was something of a one-man show. It wasn't like playing the piano: we had to hit the keys so hard with the edge of the palm it was more like a karate chop.

All these activities were supervised by the fatherly figure of the Rev. Canon Haydn Rees. He was a close friend of the family, and we spent a lot of time with him and his wife, Auntie Rees, and shared many a laugh and serious rugby conversation together. He came from a mining valley in the Rhondda, so his passion for rugby was not unusual. He would watch any glimpse of it on the television, even on a Sunday afternoon, when most of his fellow clergymen were busy preparing their evening sermon. Blessed with a warm and understanding personality, he had a profound influence on my life. Against the odds of failing health he even made a four hundred mile trip to Derbyshire and back so that he could officiate at my wedding. And not just officiate. Half an hour before the service began he took charge of the rugby-playing guests from London Welsh. As they were poised to dive into the pub across the road from the church he delivered a short sermon: 'All these people up here know that you're Welsh and expect you to sing. So get in there and have a couple of pints, then go into that church and *show 'em*. Don't you dare let me down!' They didn't.

His fight against ill health finally ended in October 1977, leaving a great gap in the community of Bridgend. I have rarely been so moved as when, with my brothers, I acted as pall-bearer at his funeral. On leaving the church, with the poignant singing of 'Ton Lief' in the background, in spite of the weight on my shoulders, I broke down. Tears were pouring unashamedly down my face. It was then I realized the effect that his life had had on mine.

The weekend rugby did not finish on a Saturday night for us, though it was long before the days of Sunday squad training and Sunday rugby viewing. We had family sessions on Sunday afternoons, when my father took us all out to Porthcawl in the car. Not to be left out, my mother would come along with our little dog, Michelle. Porthcawl is a seaside resort on the 'Welsh Riviera', further east than the Gower peninsula, and is well known for its golf course and strong breeze. Here we learned many of the rugby basics, under the patient eye of my father, who could have been at home with his feet up in front of the

31

fire, reading the Sunday papers.

Up on Lock's Common the wind is at its strongest; this is where dad chose for his barrage of up and unders for us all to catch. He kept us under pressure, one by one, and really stretched our catching ability. It became a question of pride for us. However strong the wind, however far we'd have to run, we would not let that ball touch the ground . . . And it paid off. By the time I was starting representative schoolboy rugby it looked as though I was a natural fielder of the ball. But there's only a certain amount of natural talent available to any one person; the balance of what makes one athlete differ from the rest is mostly hard slog, persistence and an underlying belief that anything is possible.

We carried on these Sunday afternoon sessions for many years, becoming more and more competitive with each other to field every ball. It was at one such session that we realized that Phil was very seriously ill. It was 1967, and I had just spent my first term at St Mary's. I was back in Bridgend playing against the local schools with the St Mary's 'schools side'. This was a team of mixed talents which travelled over England and Wales, playing the first XV of various schools, ranging from Oundle to Pontadawe Grammar, and was mainly a recruiting exercise to encourage schoolboys of noted rugby ability to apply for St Mary's.

That same weekend Phil, now aged sixteen, was playing as fly-half for Bridgend Grammar School against Millfield. During the game he had fallen backwards and banged his head. The ground was very soft, so he thought nothing of it and carried on. The following day he felt dreadful, had persistent head-aches, and complained he couldn't concentrate on his studies. He was preparing for his 'A' levels at the time. Some of the St Mary's students were staying with us, and since it was a fine windy day we decided to go out to Porthcawl to kick the ball about. My dad thought that the fresh air and a break from studies would help Phil, and encouraged him to come along too.

So there we were, back to the up and unders again. When the first high ball came his way Phil just stood there, holding his head in his hands. It was then we realized that something must be seriously wrong: he would never have done that in normal circumstances, not even with a headache or if he was feeling low. Luckily my father assessed the severity of the situation and was able to get Phil admitted to the Cardiff Royal Infirmary for observation. He underwent the various unpleasant tests involved in diagnosing a brain haemorrhage, but all these came back negative.

Phil was still getting severe symptoms, so finally the consultant neuro-surgeon involved, Mr Bob Weeks, decided to operate to get to the root of the problem. It turned out to be a small sub-dural haemorrhage, which is just on the outer membrane of the brain, and Mr Weeks was able to evacuate the clot. Since then he has used his surgical expertise on other rugby enthusiasts, none of greater stature than the captain of the Welsh team which won the Grand Slam in 1976, Mervyn Davies.

Phil has been fine ever since. Luckily Mr Weeks did not forbid rugby completely, knowing Phil may have been inclined to play. But he did have to give up playing for a couple of years. It was a great loss to rugby, since he was an excellent fly-half, and he is the only one of the four of us not to be playing regularly for a first-class side. He did venture once on to the rugby field when at St Mary's. Ironically, he was filling in for me as a referee for the St Mary's 'B' side. One of the players didn't turn up, as often happens in the 'Bs', and Phil offered to play. He ended up back in St Mary's Casualty Department with a fractured tibia and fibula.

Now he plays well home and away, both vocally and with his right arm! I have never heard him speak resentfully about his injury – in fact he never mentions it. Yet there must be a great temptation to explain his position when strangers ask him why he doesn't play like his brothers. He usually just shrugs his shoulders.

Despite Phil's injuries, it is amazing how all four of us have in fact followed in each other's footsteps: all playing for Bridgend at under-15 level in rugby, all becoming Welsh Junior Tennis Champions, and finally all being accepted by St Mary's to study medicine. At the same time we have all developed our own particular trademarks. Chris gained his Welsh secondary school's cap before going on to become a rugby Blue at Cambridge for three years running; he is also the star on the piano. Phil is the extrovert, and the quickest with a joke, while Mike's talents include mastering the Welsh language, the ski slopes and, last but not least, championing the cause of CAMRA (Campaign for Real Ale). It cannot have been easy for them to overcome the perpetual comparisons, not only with me, but with the next brother up.

The way that they have risen above this without any jealousy or resentment on their part, makes me just as proud of them as they are of me. They are my most loyal supporters. Many is the time that news has filtered back to me that they have been involved in heated arguments over me. I often wonder how I would have reacted in their place with so much to live up to.

My parents were great believers in treating us all the same. So, although I had attended a primary school in the next village, because they could take me at an early age, my brothers followed me there rather than attend a different school. After the mistake with the prep school, that idea was not suggested to the other boys and fortunately we all passed our Eleven Plus. I have a feeling that I was a bit of a 'test case' as most first children are, and when I seemed to be making progress in both studies and sport, my parents were happy to continue with the other brothers as they had with me. Certainly the rugby sessions at Porthcawl had proved helpful to me as well as being enjoyable, and so my father made sure that all the boys were given the same chance. It was the same with tennis. My father had spent a lot of time with me, on the other side of the net, feeding me with balls to either my backhand or forehand. He did the same with the others, and consequently our strokes were pretty similar.

Later on, when I was old enough, I took lessons from the coach at the tennis club, as did my brothers, so our games were almost identical up to the ages of fourteen or fifteen. My real advantage came when I started to grow much taller. My serve improved so much that with a bit of work on it I found myself moving into more of a 'serve-volley' type of game.

The others boys did not shoot up as I had and remained very much the same heights as my parents. Consequently they did not improve their serves as much, although Phil still has a very useful one. This probably explains the reason why they all became junior champions in Wales, as I had, but were not able to go on from there. In some ways Mike has been the most remarkable of the lot of us. To follow on, after not one, nor two, but three had passed the same way before, must have subjected him to enormous pressure (unspoken of course). As if the Eleven Plus was not enough of a hurdle, he then had to go through 'O' levels, 'A' levels, university exams, then finals, knowing that we had all done it before him.

Mendel, the great geneticist, showed that if there was a freak gene present between two of the same human species, then one of their four offspring would be different from the other three. My brothers and I certainly are four of a kind: we speak the same, we laugh the same, we have the same red sideboards; but I think my brothers would agree that of the four, it was I who was the freak!

2

From Fly-half to Full-back

After passing the Eleven Plus examination at Bryntinian I spent most of my school life in Bridgend Grammar School. This was a particularly good school, both academically and in the sporting sphere, and I have many fond memories of my time there. My ambition when I started school was to become a detective, and I used to follow fervently the television series Dixon of Dock Green. My hero was Andy Crawford, Sgt Dixon's son-in-law. I was also very keen on Sherlock Holmes, although in retrospect I think I more resembled his assistant Dr Watson than the master-detective himself. After obtaining my 'O' levels I had to decide which 'A' levels to take. Because by that time I had chosen to study medicine I had to take physics, chemistry and biology, all of which I found boring. My best subjects at 'O' level were English, history and geography, and I always wish I had been able to continue with these.

There was great friendship between all the boys at the Bridgend school, and I can remember being thrilled to receive a telegram from my class before the Wales v England Under-15 International at Twickenham. Unfortunately, the school changed drastically when it became Brynteg Comprehensive in 1972 when my brother Mike was sixteen, and whereas in my day it was the players in the first XV who were the school heroes, the heroes became those who had spent time in Borstal or other institutions.

As a result the level of academic and sporting achievements

dropped quite considerably. Now, however, the standard is rising once again.

The keenness and success of the Bridgend Junior side was and is due entirely to the hard work and dedication of a number of interested school teachers. This had resulted in Bridgend frequently winning the Welsh knock-out cup at under-15 level, the Dewar Shield. I had started playing for the town at under-11 level. This was a great thrill at the time and I enjoyed the games very much, but in retrospect I doubt the wisdom of playing competitive rugby so intensively so early. It is much better to learn the skills involved in a variety of sports at that age rather than specialize in one or two – for instance, it is extremely useful to learn the ball skills involved in soccer as a grounding for future rugby. Gareth Edwards, Barry John and Phil Bennett were all good soccer players, whose prowess was sufficient for them to be offered professional terms with top clubs.

The one man who really stands out in my mind from these junior days is Illtyd Williams, the first and finest rugby brain I ever met. His involvement in Bridgend rugby as a whole has been immense. It was unfortunate that he had played rugby league at a time when players following the other code were made outcasts. They were not officially allowed near a rugby union ground. This seems ironic when one thinks of all the time he gave voluntarily to further the interests of Bridgend rugby. (I am glad to say that this biased attitude has changed a lot in Wales now, mainly due, I feel, to the influence of David Watkins who had played for Wales at outside half before turning professional. The success and interest that Watkins has brought to Wales for the league game has even resulted in a rugby league International being played at the Swansea Rugby Union ground (St Helen's). It has always seemed ridiculous to me that players should be ostracized for turning professional and making money out of their talents, if that particular talent happens to be rugby football. This is in complete contrast to so many other sports.)

Illtyd was the senior selector at Welsh under-11 and under-15 level in Bridgend, and taught me a lot about attitude and skills. He also coached the Bridgend senior side during their magnificent achievements in the '60s – although he was only coach unofficially, due to his background as a professional player. Home matches were played at Newbridge Fields either on the Bandstand field, which is where Bridgend Sports Club play, or on the adjoining field nicknamed the Cabbage Patch, complete with rather coarse grass and some very odd dimensions. One snag was that if one kicked the ball high over the goal line it went into a fenced-off tennis court. Whenever there was a conversion or penalty kick at goal, to retrieve the ball players had to climb up and over the fence and into the court. Many hours must have been wasted over the years. Fortunately there was no cup competition or national side at under-11 level in those days, so all the matches were 'friendlies' – though that term could hardly be applied to us, even as eleven-year-olds. We would play for the town in the morning and then go to watch the senior Bridgend side at the Brewery Field in the afternoon.

I made my entry into under-15 rugby in the third form at full-back – nobody else wanted to play there! Since Wales had a national side at this age group this was the start of the competitive trial system – and cup rugby. The under-15 level is perhaps the most enjoyable of all, as the players have become very skilled yet can still combine this with natural flair. In my final year in the under-15 side we had some memorable matches in the Dewar Shield. We eventually overcame Llanelli in an earlier round – after five matches! Everything happened in these games, including one match being abandoned because our coach, Illtyd Williams, shouted too much on the touchline. The Llanelli side that year contained Phil Bennett and Derek Quinnell, so it was quite an achievement to beat them eventually. We played Newport in the final on a home-and-away basis, and were on top for most of both matches. One player was to deny us our ambition, Allen Evans, who was captain of the Newport team and has been playing scrum-half regularly for Newport for many seasons since. He was a real thorn in our flesh, and was virtually responsible single-handed for our two 3–0 defeats.

A big year for me was 1964. At the beginning of it I was already being tipped for the Wales under-15 full-back position. I had great help from Grahame Hodgson at that time, who was Wales No. 1 full-back. Grahame taught PE at Heol Gam, a Secondary Modern School just down the road from Bridgend Grammar. He was technically one of the finest fielders and kickers to touch that I have seen, and also a most competent goal kicker. But the change in the kicking to touch laws which forbade players to kick directly into touch outside their own twenty-five yard line did not suit him. I remember him on several occasions kicking to touch in the dying seconds of the game when his side were losing. I also admired his courage and remember him playing a combined Neath and Aberavon team against the All Blacks in 1963/4, when he played virtually the whole match with concussion from an early contact and could not remember anything about the game afterwards.

At the same time as our battles with Llanelli in the Dewar Shield the trials for the Welsh under-15 team were also taking place. After several previous local trials we got to the last but one, with the Reds playing the Whites at Waunarlwydd, a place I had never heard of, let alone played at. I was in the Whites (Possibles) opposing a boy called Hywel Williams from Amman Valley who was much bigger than I. It was 25 January 1964; luckily I chose that day to produce one of my best performances and even though outplayed by the Reds we managed to keep the score down to 6–0 at half-time. I think I must have had some influence in this as I was changed into the Probables side for the second half.

I cannot remember a lot about the final trial except being convinced that I had lost my chance of making the Wales team by not playing particularly well. However, I was thrilled to learn after the match that I was one of the players picked to face the England Schools at Twickenham on 11 March 1964. This was one of the highlights of my life, and I can remember now the unbelievable excitement when I heard my name called, signifying that I was to represent my country at Twickenham.

We travelled up on the train on Tuesday night for the game on Wednesday afternoon. Lunch was at the Winning Post on the Chertsey road. Although I felt very nervous about the match strangely I did not worry about playing in the huge arena of Twickenham. Perhaps I knew that the wind would never be as strong as the Porthcawl! As it was the match went well, and we won 11–3, scoring eight points in the last ten minutes. Phil Bennett kicked a long dropped goal from nearly half-way out and Wilson Lauder converted a try from the touchline. These two players are still doing similar things today. Many of the Welsh players went on to win further honours in the game, Phil Bennett, J. J. Williams and Allan Martin, but of the English side only Tony Neary, from the De La Salle School at Salford, had further recognition in later years, and even then it was not as often as it should have been.

Our next match was against the South of Scotland at Galashiels, and we got home 9–0 in a tough game characterized by hard Scottish tackling. After the match, however, we got into deep water as we all had a few drinks, even though only fifteen years of age. Many of the team were big enough to pass as eighteen, but unfortunately did not hold their drink like eighteen-year-olds. Word got back to the officials, so when we assembled at Newport for our return match with England, those who had been drinking were asked to stand up. Everyone stood up, and I remember the Chairman saying, 'Not you too, John!' At the time I was the smallest member of the team and certainly didn't look older than fifteen. So we went to Newport looking for a hat trick of victories. This was a much harder game than our previous match at Twickenham, and we were very relieved to scrape home by six points to nil. Thus we ended the season unbeaten and since we had also played some very attractive rugby many critics were predicting a bright future in the game for a number of those in the team. Phil Bennett, Allan Martin and myself have been regular team-mates for the full Welsh side for the last few seasons or so, and I think this shows a good yield. It is this continuity that helps to keep Wales to the fore in international rugby, although it must be said that Wales starts off with some considerable advantages, for the travelling distances are small in comparison to the larger rugby-playing countries.

So the 1963/4 season came to a close and yet another transition had to be made – that from the under-15 to senior schoolboy rugby. I managed to get into the School 1st XV the following year, and again found a great difference between the two grades. Players were now men compared to the boys they had been before. To think I was smaller than Phil Bennett seems amazing when you look at us both now. People often accused my parents of putting me on a rack or on special tablets because the following year I grew a full five inches. I put this down to the great deal of weight training that I started under the watchful eye of Lynn Davies, our great long jump champion, who taught at Bridgend Grammar School for a year. One can get away with being small at junior level but it becomes increasingly difficult to make an impact as one climbs the ladder.

Lynn Davies and Cliff Daniels were a great influence on me at that time; I got very interested in the weights and spent a lot of time in the gym. This was combined with running exercises to keep up my speed. It was quite a sight to watch Lynn training, and I shall never forget seeing him hopping around the field with three hundred pounds on his back, as if there was nothing there. He was also a very fine rugby player and nearly played for Bridgend. Although there was an obvious danger of injury, he used to play with the senior boys in school and not hold back at all. All schoolboys like to have a go at their teachers when given the chance, but nobody got the better of Lynn. The other quality which impressed me at the time was how modest Lynn was. He had won a gold medal in the

1964 Tokyo Olympics the previous year and yet he had no pretensions and would get totally involved in whatever he was doing. But underneath his pleasant character, there was definitely that killer instinct which is so necessary for anyone striving for world fame.

I thought there had been a lot of trials at under-15 level but Secondary Schools trials (under nineteen) were unbelievable. In my first year – that is, the fifth form at school – I just got as far as the regional trials. The following year I played in ten trial matches and still did not get in the side. The one criticism I do have of the selection for Welsh junior teams is that you either have to have an influential person pushing you or you must have been around for several years in the trials. It is almost like an apprenticeship. I played three years at both under-15 and under-19 level and felt I only got there in the end for good service. Certainly in the Secondary Schools team, I had played better the year before I eventually got capped. I played in the final trial against Paul Wheeler, who later went on to play for Aberavon, when he was at senior level, and thought I had outplayed him. I was very disillusioned when I did not make the team. The following year I put up a far less convincing performance yet got into the side.

I found Secondary School rugby particularly well organized, especially in Wales. All sports at junior level reflect the strengths and weaknesses of their senior counterparts, but in spite of rugby being the national sport of the country, it did not always follow that Welsh Junior rugby was well organized at that time. It was played in all the schools, but there was rarely the national coaching pattern that is now practised in Wales.

After my first year in the sixth form I went to Millfield School in Somerset for one year on a tennis and rugby scholarship.* The idea behind the school was a revolutionary one, for in spite of the astronomical full fees there were many different people from different walks of life, ranging from

* I describe the importance of this for my tennis in the following chapter.

princes' to labourers' sons, and the fees each parent had to pay were in proportion to his income. Academic and sporting scholarships were plentiful. This was a great episode in my life and I am sure it taught me a lot and gave a far wider outlook on life.

Millfield had a great reputation for rugby, largely due to three Welshmen who had been there a couple of years before me: Gareth Edwards, Vaughan Williams and Nick Williams. The team at that time had carried all before them and also developed a keen interest in seven-a-side rugby. In fact, before Gareth and the others went there Millfield had always been prominent in the Public Schools VIIs held at Rockampton. The emphasis was always on attacking play and this had a great effect on my development as an attacking full-back.

The fact that I was still in school, albeit outside Wales, made me favourite for the full-back position for the Welsh Secondary Schools, but unfortunately fifteen-a-side rugby was only played during the Christmas term at Millfield. After that it was all seven-a-side, which did not help us a lot if we were involved in trials and internationals which generally took place in the New Year. We had a good fifteen-a-side team and managed to beat our old enemy Llanelli Grammar School 6–0 at Stradey Park. The terrible Aberfan disaster occurred that same weekend and I remember what a great effect it had on me.

My old Millfield schoolfriend, Wayne Lewis and I were only involved in the trials near the end, so it meant that we did not have to play in all the preliminary ones. Eventually I managed to be selected for the side to play the Yorkshire Secondary Schools at Otley, in the traditional annual match. This turned out to be a disaster both for the team and myself individually – quite the worse match I have ever played. The result was that we lost 3–0; it was a match which took place in the New Year after I had been playing tennis for five weeks over the Christmas holidays. This certainly contributed to my poor performance and in fact the team as a whole played very badly. The result of this was that most of them were relegated to the Possibles in the trial match following the Wales *v* Yorkshire match. In many ways this was a blessing in disguise for most of us were then forced to fight our way back into the side again.

I owed a great deal to Wayne Lewis in that trial, for early in the game he tackled the Probables full-back very hard, so much so that my rival took no further part in the match and thus had no opportunity to impress the selectors. This left the way open for me to fight my way back in.

Once again there were many players 'capped' that season who have gone on to make names for themselves in the first-class game. The team included Keith Hughes (London Welsh), John Bevan (Aberavon), Wayne Lewis (Cardiff and London Welsh), Ian Wagstaff (Neath and London Welsh), Bowen Thomas (London Welsh), Allan Martin (Aberavon) and Roger Lane (Cardiff). As can be seen it was a very good year for talent and this was the reason for our big disappointment in losing the first match.

Our next match was against the Welsh Youth at Stradey Park, Llanelli, and to face us at outside-half was Phil Bennett again. We were relieved to win 6–3 with a dropped goal from our outside-half, none other than J. J. Williams. It was very good to get back to a winning sequence and the same team was kept together to travel to Le Touqet to take on the French Schoolboys XV. We lost a very close game, one which could have gone either way. We had a couple of injuries with John Bevan hurting his shoulder, the first of many occasions during his career. John was playing in the centre then and later changed to outside-half, eventually being selected for the 1977 Lions Team to New Zealand. He is not to be confused with the winger of the same name who was such a star with the 1971 Lions Team to New Zealand before signing for Warrington in the Rugby League.

That weekend was very enjoyable after the initial disappointment of losing, as we did score and we spent most of the time with the French players, led by Claude Spanghero, one of the famous brothers of that name. He seemed to have the freedom of the town and was adulated wherever he went. There are five Spanghero brothers, and all of them had played for Narbonne, which is a fantastic record. Walter is the most famous and has played many times at No. 8 or second row for France, several times with his brother Claude in the same team.

Between the French game and the English game at Cardiff came a remarkable episode in which the Headmaster of Millfield, R. J. O. Meyer, confronted the Welsh Secondary Schools selectors. The conflict arose over the selection of Wayne Lewis and myself to play in the International against England the Saturday after the Public Schools VIIs at Rockampton. This seven-a-side tournament is a very popular and prestigious event in schools rugby, especially in England, and is held on three successive days of the week. That particular year it fell in the week preceding the schools International and we had applied to the selectors for special permission to be able to play in both. The same rules apply as for senior internationals, in that no players are allowed to play during the preceding week, but we had heard unofficially that we were going to be allowed to play in both. The week before the International a special meeting of Welsh schoolboy selectors had been called to discuss the matter and Meyer decided to go to the press. His remarks made big headlines and he was quoted to say: 'Who the hell do the Welsh selectors think they are, trying to take my players from me?' In actual fact nothing of the kind had happened and we were to be allowed to play in both events. However, this outburst finished any chances we had of that. The Welsh selectors informed us that we had to make the choice between playing for the school or for Wales. This obviously put us in a very awkward position and after much discussion we decided to play in the International match at Cardiff. Meyer never really forgave us for this, but the majority of teachers and pupils at Millfield understood the impossible situation we were put in. Colin Atkinson, one of the masters, who has since taken over

45

at Millfield as Headmaster, met us then and assured us that the masters were behind us and generally made us feel much easier. Whether I would have been discriminated against later on in Wales had I played for the school nobody can tell, but I would like to think not.

Wayne and I obviously felt under a fair bit of pressure for the game against England, as the incident had had a lot of coverage in the national press. We managed to hold on for a close win and both us of played our part, so things ended well for us, but it had been a difficult decision and one I believe we should not have been involved in, as schoolboy players. In fact I do not think any players should be put in the position of making such decisions.

I never really felt comfortable at Millfield after this and when I eventually left I was still under a bit of a cloud. I sat my 'A' level in physics, chemistry and biology and heard while in Canada playing tennis that I had gained a place in the medical school in St Mary's.

3

The Mighty Atom

'Forty–fifteen.'

'Forty–thirty.'

'Game, set and match to . . .'

It was the momentous final between Rosewall and Drobny at Wimbledon in 1953. I had been riveted to the television for two and a half hours, living every moment and hitting every stroke. I was four. When the match was over, I rushed outside and grabbed an old racquet of my father's. Banging a ball up against the garage door I was reliving those moments, pretending to be Drobny.

It wasn't until twenty years later, when I saw Drobny playing on an outside court – the same Drobny, playing at Wimbledon in the Veterans' Plate – that it suddenly occurred to me: I had relived his winning strokes on almost the same court in 1966. I had fulfilled my early dream of winning.

I wasn't allowed to join the Bridgend Tennis Club until I was ten, according to the club rules, so until then my only opposition was the faithful garage door . . . and of course the brothers three. My father had been a keen player at the club, and still was when I joined. He had won the championships on numerous occasions, and obviously delighted in my enthusiasm for the game. I took part in all the junior activities which included coaching by Doug Thomas, the club coach. We were a small club, but with some depth at junior level. We already had one outstanding youngster in Gerald Battrick, who went on to play on the professional circuit. He spurred the rest of us

47

along. We all had a goal – to be as good as Gerald.

I was happy playing tennis at the club, at school and at the various tournaments during the summer, and switching over to rugby in the winter months. There was no conflict between the two sports in those early days; in fact, at that time I was better known at school as a tennis player.

My first tournament was at Llanelli in 1961. Although more widely known as a rugby town, it staged the annual County of Carmarthen Tennis Championships. I had been on a junior coaching course the week before at Lilleshall, a beautiful country mansion deep in the heart of Shropshire which had been taken over by the forerunners of the Sports Council: the Central Council of Physical Recreation. It was a week of intensive coaching. I remember nothing of that, but I can tell you that the current number one in the hit parade was Elvis Presley's 'Wooden Heart' – the only hit that sank in! At any rate I must have emerged fairly well from that week, because, aged twelve, I was entered in the gentlemen's doubles with my father at Llanelli. The Welsh tournaments attracted mainly local entries, but there were always one or two national or international players there, having a bit of a rest from the big tournaments. My size – or rather lack of it – did not distract our opponents in the first round of the doubles, and we were beaten by the pair, who went on to win the prize money of £2 apiece – quite a lot in those days. My best performance of the week was in the mixed doubles at junior level, where my partner, six years my senior, carried us into the third round. It was a very generous move on her part.

Still, not discouraged, I entered the next tournament, both chronologically, and geographically, since Langland Bay is just round the Gower Peninsula. It is a charming little resort near Swansea, with the tennis courts set into an inlet in the cliffs. I have many happy memories of this tournament, because the atmosphere was so friendly, not just because of my success. In 1961 I was on my way. I reached the semi-finals of the boys' under-16 singles and the finals of the under-18 doubles. The next year I went on to win the boys' singles, and as a very tiny thirteen-year-old I was nicknamed 'The Mighty Atom' for beating my opponent, almost twelve inches taller than me, 6–0, 6–1. The next year was even luckier and I managed a hat-trick of titles. On the strength of this, and of winning the Welsh under-16 title, coupled with a place in the finals in the national youth tournament at Exmouth, I was accepted for a place at Junior Wimbledon.

Although I had proved myself in Wales, it was quite a different matter to compete against all the juniors in England. The strength of tennis in England compared with that in Wales is immense; the complete reverse of the positions of the two countries in rugby! But I got to the final at Exmouth, though I lost to John de Mendoza 7–5 in the third set, and this gave me the reassurance that perhaps I could, after all, hold my own against the National juniors, even though I was in their eyes, the little lad up from an unknown town in Wales.

During another visit to Lilleshall I came under the watchful eye of John Crooke, coach to the Welsh LTA. I was very impressed by his enthusiasm and his ability to get the best out of us, and I was lucky to continue to be coached by him on the odd occasions when he could spare a little time. Andy Evans was a friend at the Bridgend Club then and now; he and I used to go up to John Crooke's home in Shropshire at the odd weekends; he would coach us on a covered swimming pool in Dudley. He made me concentrate on my backhand, which was very weak, and gave me the confidence to put a topspin back-hand into effect, an ability I had always admired in the champions. I still enjoy seeing really top players in action on hard courts when they are able to spin their returns – men like Nastase, Borg and Panatta, the Italian. Crooke also helped me with my second serve, which was just a weaker version of my first. He encouraged me to vary it much more and to put a fair amount of spin into it, until it was quite different from my fast first serve.

All this time my father spent hours with me on the courts at the local club helping me to perfect my various strokes, feeding me balls from all angles, lobbing me from all heights, with the patience of Job. Without his encouragement I would never have progressed from Langland Bay.

By 1964 I was playing tennis matches outside Wales and as a family we were beginning to shape our summer holidays around the various tournaments. The other boys were getting old enough to enter the junior competitions, though Mike was still left out – he was only eight. Torquay and Exmouth were always popular, for they maintained a very high standard of tennis; many of the top players took part at senior level. So we had plenty to feast our eyes on, and plenty of technical expertise to aspire to.

By the time September had passed that year, Bridgend was no longer a little-known town in Wales. At Junior Wimbledon two of the semi-finalists had been produced by that little club. Gerald Battrick was one of them, I was the other. It was a great achievement, considering how much talent was available from the larger clubs in England. On my way to that semi-final, I had a pretty unnerving ordeal; I'm sure it would have upset me much more if I had not had a taste of Junior Wimbledon the year before. I had had to play the third seed, who completely lost his temper and started slinging his racquet about and shouting abuse at me. My compensation came in the third set, which I took 6–0; I had hung on patiently and let my opponent's temper make mistake after mistake.

A report which makes amusing reading now, over ten years later, is the one which appeared in the *Daily Mail* before I was due to meet David Lloyd in that semi-final. It says of me, 'he has this serene disposition, plus reliable ground stroking, that has already beaten two seeds'. 'Serene disposition'? Mention that in the rugby world these days and no one would believe you were talking about the same person!

By the time the covered court championships took place on New Year's Eve, 1964, rugby and tennis were beginning to clash in my life. I had played for the Welsh under-15 schoolboys' team three weeks before the championships and had fractured my left shoulder blade. Had it been the right one I would never have been able to play; as it was, it was likely to interfere seriously with my service action. I managed to reach the semi-final in spite of it, according to my seeding. At the time I was quoted as saying: 'I'm still mad about rugby, but I think I'll specialize in tennis eventually.' It was a decision I tossed back and forth in my mind from then on until the day I finally applied for medical school.

At the tender age of fifteen, one has very little idea of what life can be like ten years ahead. Many lads dream of becoming professional sportsmen at an age when their heroes are famous footballers, cricketers or tennis players. The thought of injury never enters their heads, nor what will happen when they grow old and are unable to make a living. It isn't easy for a youngster to think of providing for a family which doesn't exist yet.

But for about six months I lived with the dream of becoming a professional tennis player, or at least what was called 'full-time' player in those days. Theoretically Wimbledon players did not accept prize money and therefore had to live off private means. It was a 'shamateur' game. The professionals played openly for money in the 'open' tournaments whilst the 'amateurs' played for it under the table. 'Expenses' were very generous; prize money was often given in the form of vouchers which could be redeemed on the tennis circuit for equipment and so forth. This obviously had to change and in 1968 it did nearly everywhere, though Wimbledon did not come round to it until 1970. Since then prize money has spiralled; there is a lot of money distributed amongst the top twenty players, but it is still not easy to make a steady income on the circuit. Admittedly, the American Team Tennis has meant that more of the younger or lesser players get a share in the huge profits from the game but at the time when I had to make my decision there was little indication that this would happen.

The crunch really came for me when I had to think seriously about 'O' levels. It was inevitable that I should at least consider medicine, though medical qualifications had not been on my list of ambitions until quite recently and to be a doctor had meant just that to me – I never thought of all the things in between – 'O' levels, 'A' levels, applications to University, decisions and more decisions. My parents convinced me that I had the whole of my life to think about and not just the next ten or fifteen years. I was beginning to realize that I could still play rugby if I was to study medicine; come to that, I could play tennis in the summer as well. If I chose tennis I would have to exclude the other two completely. And so I chose the 'O' level course directed towards science subjects and the long journey had begun.

Meanwhile, I had to make the most of what was left of my tennis-playing days. 1966 was my big year. I started early in January in the West of England Covered Court Championships at Torquay. I had lost in the semi-finals of the Queen's Championships in the December of the previous year, so a win at Torquay was a very good omen for the New Year. Since I was not playing rugby at a higher level than the Bridgend District Team, I was able to concentrate more on my tennis during the winter months, and so when summer came I was in fairly good shape. I had won the men's singles at Newport and had been watched there by John Barrett, who was in charge of the 'Barrett Boys', a coaching scheme which took on talented youngsters and sponsored their playing on the circuit, both in Britain and abroad on a full-time basis. To be a 'Barrett Boy' was much coveted by British juniors. At Newport John Barrett had said he might consider taking me on if I could prove myself on the English circuit, playing at senior level.

I took his advice and travelled round a bit that summer. I ventured up to Scarborough in the North of England. There I got as far as the third round when I came up against Onny Parun, the New Zealander who is still playing well in all the big tournaments. I came fairly close that day. I had already played two junior matches in the morning which, on reflection, was a ridiculous way to prepare myself for big-time senior

tennis. Onny Parun took the first set and at 5–3 up in the second
he looked like a winner. Then I suddenly started up and took
the second set. I was leading 4–1 in the third when I got cramp
and that was it; I looked what I was, a junior playing senior
tennis. From Scarborough, I tried Budleigh Salterton in Devon
and again didn't do myself justice, coming unstuck this time
against a top Indian player.

So it was back to junior matches and another try at Junior
Wimbledon. This time I was seeded No. 3. David Lloyd was
eligible to play again since they had extended the age limit.

Lloyd, as the oldest player, was seeded No. 1. He had spent
all year playing full-time tennis as a Barrett Boy and had not
really wanted to return to junior level again. The other competitors were much the same year in, year out. They were
either children from wealthy families who had had fortunes
spent on their tennis, or they were the sons and daughters of
top British players. Many were sent to the school where there is
tremendous emphasis on sport, Millfield, by parents who could
afford the huge fees. There were not many like me, and I used
to feel quite inferior. The English juniors all seemed so self-
assured that I felt it was a strange reversal of roles for me;
at grammar school I had been teased, and sometimes envied,
because I was the son of the local doctor and therefore assumed
to be well off.

After I had played many consecutive weeks of tournaments
that summer, I had got a taste of the tennis player's life and I
came to the conclusion that I had made the right decision. In
those days only the very top players travelled abroad (for
Forest Hills and the Australian titles) and most of the English
players had to content themselves with tournaments in Britain
and perhaps the French and Italian Opens. The crowd was
always the same; it became very boring off-court. There would
be endless games of cards, and chit-chat which after a week or
so became predictable; whose form was good, who was going
off with whom, who had split up a mixed doubles partnership.
At the beginning of the season it was all quite exciting because

it was so unlike school, Bridgend and rugby, but as the summer drew to a close I sometimes used to think that I was only playing my hardest to get to the next round and not be left at the card table for the rest of the tournament. I knew that if I again got no further than the semi-finals at Wimbledon, people would always say that I couldn't make it in tennis and that was why I had given it up. I really had to pull something out of the bag if I were to prove myself.

I went to London and stayed for a week in Earl's Court with a few of the other competitors in motherly Mrs Weatherall's guest house. We used to catch the Tube to Southfields – always an adventure for me, since I was fascinated by the Underground. Then I used to get quite a thrill walking past the ivy-covered walls and the courts which had only a few weeks previously been graced by John Newcombe and Roy Emmerson. We did not play on the grass courts as juniors as we did not really benefit from the 'big serve-volley game'. Back in the dressing-rooms there was still the same old card-playing atmosphere, but the facilities were so much more spacious than those we used during the rest of the year that there was plenty of room to get away from it all. The baths were marvellous. I remember soaking for hours after particularly long matches. Towards the end of the week, there were fewer and fewer of us and we were like kings in those huge rooms.

I had no real trouble getting to the semi-final, and there I came up against an unseeded player and won the match 6–2, 6–0. Looking back at the programmes now, I recognize the names of many people I still meet playing at club or county level. Often I know I have played them somewhere before but it isn't until I dig out the souvenirs that I realize where and when it was. One occasion which gave me lots of pleasure was seeing Roger Cawley again, another of the hopefuls who had played along with me in 1966 and now Evonne Goolagong's husband.

This was much later on, in 1972, when I went along to Wimbledon as a spectator; I had failed to get through the qualifying rounds. I felt very uneasy there after such a lapse from the game and I cast glances up at the gallery above the centre court, where all the players were chatting, drinking and enjoying being feted as stars by the adulating crowd. I think I felt a twinge of envy – mainly embarrassment in case anyone recognized me. It was worse because I had tried to get back into it all . . . and failed.

I walked under the gallery, trying to make myself as inconspicuous as possible, when someone shouted down in an unmistakable Australian drawl . . . 'Hey, John – don't say you've forgotten us all, now that you're so famous.' It was Evonne Goolagong. I could have kissed her. She had won Wimbledon the year before but had no pretensions whatsoever. She is a complete natural both on and off the court and no amount of Wimbledon titles would ever change her.

But that was several years later. In 1966, Roger and I were both in the same boat at Junior Wimbledon and Evonne had not yet been brought over to England by Vic Edwards. The weather was fine all that week and everything was going fairly smoothly for me. I remember very little of the actual finals day except that when my father visited me in the dressing-room before my match with David Lloyd, I was sitting there calmly reading the *Beano*. I was in a much better position than David Lloyd as I had nothing to lose except perhaps my pride. Lloyd was expected to do great things and show everyone just how much he had improved in his year as a Barrett Boy. He was to be a playing advertisement for the set-up.

As underdog I went out on to the court and broke his service twice to win 6–4, 6–4. It was all over so quickly. I didn't really believe I had won at the end of the match, and I remember being far more worried that I wouldn't be able to jump the net than whether or not I would be able to serve properly at match point. Even when I was presented with the huge cup afterwards I still didn't really believe that I had finally made it after trying so many times before. It was not until I saw the reports in the papers on Sunday morning and I saw my name in print that it began to sink in.

Following that win, I had been offered a scholarship at Millfield on the strength of my tennis and rugby combined, and I had two weeks to decide whether to accept. It meant that my parents would have to pay a considerable amount, since it was not a full scholarship, but they were willing to help me all they could. It was a difficult decision since I was all prepared to move up to the upper sixth at Bridgend Grammar School and to become a prefect. I would have to leave all my friends and would probably not have much time in one year to make many new ones at Millfield, although I did know a few people there through tennis. In the end I decided to take up the offer, bearing in mind all the accomplished sportsmen and women who had emerged from the school – people like Mary Bignall (Rand) and Mark Cox. It was the chance of a lifetime and it was not as if I would have to leave home at too early an age.

Academically, it was a bad move – to transfer to a new school half-way through an 'A' level course is difficult; I had to get used to different methods of teaching and the extra distractions of all the sporting activities there. Also I had to adjust to living away from home. I had all the help I needed from the staff; the teacher/pupil ratio at Millfield is one to four which is unique in Britain. I mixed with all types of students, ranging from Iranian princes to extraordinarily gifted artists, and children whose IQ was so high that they were on a different wavelength from everyone else. After adjusting to this kind of life, the later adjustment to University life was comparatively easy. But I won my Welsh Secondary Schools rugby cap from Millfield, and that marked the climax of a really great year for me.

I had plenty of opportunity to play against my old rivals from the tennis circuit, Weatherly and Mendoza, but on reflection I think it meant that I lost the former edge I might have had over them: that of being an unknown quantity. Previously I had needed that little bit of extra aggression and pride, to convince myself that I was as good as them really, in spite of all their coaching and the circumstances of their birth. Now here I was, part of their set-up and mixing with them day in, day out. I was getting to know their strengths and weaknesses but, to my detriment, I was letting them get to know mine. The writing was on the wall. I lost to Mendoza in the Queens Covered Court Championships in January 1967, so my period of supremacy had been very short-lived.

For the rest of 1967 I had to concentrate on academic work and rugby, although I did play for the tennis team at Millfield. We were very strong indeed, fielding the six best juniors in the country as our first three pairs. We could beat most of the full county teams and on the strength of that we had a very good fixture list. But I had been accepted by St Mary's that year – a conditional offer, which depended on my getting a minimum of three E's at 'A' level. Unfortunately, for most of the summer when I should have been studying, I was out on the courts, and this was reflected in my 'A' level results.

I took the exams in July, then I was off to Canada, representing Great Britain in the Canadian Centennial Junior Open Tournament. This was quite an experience. I travelled over with Corrine Molesworth, who had won the girls' junior title the previous September when I had won mine. Neither of us knew a single soul there, but when we arrived in Ottawa, we were hosted by tennis-loving families.

I reached the final in what must have been my best form up to then and, sadly, my best ever since. I was competing against representatives from most of the tennis-playing countries, but by far the bulk of the players were from Canada and the States. I beat Dick Stockton and Alex (Sandy) Meyer to get a place in the final. At the time, their names meant very little to me and I was just pleased to get through to the next round. Now they are playing top class tennis and doing well in the big tournaments; it's very strange for me to see them on television playing at Wimbledon. I console myself that I beat them once and often ask myself whether I could have been in their position now, had I continued to play professionally. It's probably best that I never found out because I fear the answer would have been 'no'. I might have become a Davis Cup player, but I could not have held my own amongst the real 'world greats'. Not many of the British players do (at least in the men's competitions – the British ladies are more successful) and there was no reason to believe that I would have been any better than the average British Davis Cup player. I wasn't aggressive enough on court! A strange irony, since aggression is one of the hallmarks of my game in rugby. Anyway, at least I can retain that small moment of glory.

I came up against Ian Russell, an Australian, in the final. The weather was very hot and humid, as it tends to be in the eastern states of North America in July. My father had warned me about the dangers of losing too much salt in the form of sweat, so I had been taking salt tablets. I think this contributed a great deal to my ability to stand the pace in such heat; it was a five set match. I was losing by one set to two by the end of the third, but I sensed that Russell was getting tired. I started lobbying him and making him run. He got cramp in his left thigh early on in the fourth set, so I was able to take that, and then the fifth 6–3, 6–0. In the very last game, just as he was serving to save the match, he developed another bout of cramp so bad that it was all he could do to pick up his racquet and serve two double faults to end his agony. Whether it was my victory or that of the salt tablets I shall never know, but I do know that I did not have a single twinge of cramp during the whole game. I have never underestimated their value in hot, humid conditions.

I felt on top of the world that summer. Although I had failed one of my 'A' levels (physics) I was able to go up to St Mary's in the autumn and spend the year as a first MB (Bachelor of Medicine) student; I took physics at the end of the year to enable me to start the second MB course a year later. But I still had two months of solid tennis in front of me and I took advantage of it, though I ended up playing too much; either that or I was becoming too confident. I lost my Junior title to Mendoza in the September in a surprisingly easy final.

The hints that my best days of tennis could be over were confirmed; since there was no excuse for losing, as I had been playing regularly. It seemed that I played much better when I was the underdog. I think that had I won the title again that year, I might have been a little more inclined to try and make more time for tennis and for regular competition. It would have been expected of me at St Mary's since I would then be known as a tennis player instead of a rugby player.

As it was, tennis at St Mary's was played mainly for pleasure. As a hospital, St Mary's was always fairly strong at tennis and squash, but I could see that I would have to go elsewhere if I was to get enough regular play. So I went along to the London University trials at Motspur Park. The facilities there were tremendous – which was not surprising, considering the number of colleges and students that needed them. The grass courts were always kept in supreme condition whilst I was playing there. London University fielded a very good team; many of my old friends from the junior tournaments were amongst those playing for London University when I first settled in London. We played most of the stronger counties and better club teams and often came off the winners.

My first match for London University was up in Oxford. The weather was shocking and the match abandoned, but we had a marvellous day . . . in the pub! There was great spirit between us all, especially recalling all the escapades we had got up to in our youth. That day in Oxford set the seal of what has now become the 'Old Purples', named after the London colours. The pace is just right: two or three matches a year, plus the occasional tour to places of interest like Paris, or Birmingham.

Despite our leaving London, getting married and generally being ten years wiser, the 'OP's' live on, under the self-elected Life President, who keeps us all amused by his annual news letters and his second serve.

I played a few tournaments in the summer of 1968, but many coincided with activities at St Mary's, and I preferred the latter. The first year had been a bit of a joy ride. There were a small core of half a dozen of us who were all taking one or more subjects at first MB. We spent that year finding our feet at St Mary's and enjoying ourselves. By the time the freshers appeared on the scene in October, we were quite *blasé*.

I did take part in the under-21 championships at Didsbury during that summer vacation but the day when there would be a clash of important events in the tennis and rugby world had to come sooner or later and it came that week at Didsbury. I was seeded six which should have meant a place in the quarter finals. They were scheduled for the Thursday. That same Thursday I was also meant to be in Bridgend at the first training session for the Welsh rugby squad who had been picked to tour the Argentine. But I still wasn't going to make a decision. The training session wasn't until 6 p.m. and I reckoned that if I played my tennis match early that morning, I could still be in Bridgend by the evening. I planned a dramatic road and air dash to get round the dilemma. To that end I asked Captain Mike Gibson, the tournament referee, if I could be first on the courts in the morning. He was very co-operative, as he was a rugby fan himself, like his namesake, but we still had to compete with the elements. I knew that if play was delayed and it came to the crunch, I would have to scratch from the singles; I couldn't possibly miss that first training session; it was the chance of a lifetime to tour with Wales at the age of nineteen. Still the doubles events posed quite a problem; I had a responsibility to my partner and would probably have to play a doubles game out, if need be, get to Bridgend, then dash back to Manchester next morning.

The crunch did come. I was 5-7, 5-4 in the quarter final against Mendoza and rain stopped play. There was no telling when play would resume and I knew it was going to be a tough, long game when it did. I just had to retire. My father had driven up the M6 to collect me since there wasn't a suitable flight, and he just turned around and set off back down the motorway. I arrived at Bridgend with five minutes to spare.

The next day, I went back up to Manchester and met up again with Mendoza – this time on the same side of the net, in the doubles. It was obvious that this hectic two-timing could not last and I devoted the rest of that summer to the oval ball. Four weeks were spent in Argentina* getting a taste of senior rugby.

After my return from Argentina, I was plunged into a tough medical school curriculum which was to last two years until I took second MB. The first year was a holiday in comparison with all the work we had to get through before examinations. We also had to compete with all the bright chaps (and even brighter girls) who had sailed through their 'A' levels first time and gone straight into the second MB year. It was all very well being the casual group who 'knew it all' but it was a different matter when the exams came along. So there was very little time for anything except work and rugby – I played for the full Welsh team that winter, and had to ration my study hours to get everything done before the weekend of an international. The following summer I toured New Zealand† with Wales and had to get special permission from the Dean to delay the exams which I would miss on the six week tour. The tour was not successful. From being Triple Crown winners in April, we were well and truly put in our places in New Zealand.

After I arrived home, I was honoured to represent Glamorgan as one of the young escorts to Prince Charles during his Investiture as Prince of Wales. I remember being very impressed by his mastery of the Welsh language; I could read and understand a little but could not speak Welsh properly. From Caernarvon, I raced down to Devon to some of my most enjoyable tennis.

Every year St Mary's went on a tennis tour to South Devon where the men's team rented a cottage at Dittisham on the River Dart, next to a cottage rented the same week by the

---

* This tour is described in detail in Chapter 6.
† Also described in Chapter 6.

St Mary's ladies' team. It was a very good arrangement. The girls organized the food, the men organized the drink. Some tennis was played.

Dittisham was in the heart of the land of 'scrumpy' (rough cider) and we were not exempt from its after-effects. The setting was ideal. There were a row of seven or eight cottages right on the edge of the river, with the pub on the corner. The village shop was half-way up a steep, winding hill but that didn't concern the men. We went there after the end of term, after all the examinations and before we all went our separate ways for the summer vacation. The idea was to play fixtures against the local teams, like Torquay and Dartmouth, and to spend the rest of the time on or in the river or in the pub. We did spend a little time in the cottages, playing ridiculously lewd versions of 'buzz-buzz' . . . and watching Wimbledon, which was always in its second week when we were there. That summer Scilla who was one of the students at St Mary's and who became my wife four years later was down with the ladies, so we had a chance to catch up on my six week absence in New Zealand before she went off to the States to work in a hospital for three months. I could not convince her that in all the travelling I had done in the southern hemisphere, I hadn't found anything as beautiful as the British countryside. She would ply me with questions about Fiji and Australia and all the exotic customs. She was disappointed when I said I had seen nothing to compare with the view of the River Dart from the top of the hill.

After Dittisham, I had to concentrate on the task of catching up on six weeks of lost studies and to get through the whole of the year's work for the exams which awaited me at the beginning of term. I decided to ration myself to one week of studying and one week of tennis, and alternate in this way all through the summer. Luckily, Scilla had copied the notes from the lectures I had missed. She had written short comments among the notes; the day after a particular match it would be: 'congratulations on your try against Taranaki' at the top of a lecture on the Embden–Meyerhoff pathway. As I read, I could imagine the stuffy atmosphere in the biochemistry lab, and the students whispering about the report in the *Daily Telegraph*. And so it went on . . . Snippets like, 'Hard luck in the Test.' . . . 'The picture of Jeff Young's jaw is awful' . . . or whatever was topical at that particular lecture. It all made amusing reading three months later, and it certainly relieved the boredom going over the notes on my own.

I suppose it wasn't such a bad summer after all. I did get around a bit. I played at Galway in a tennis international between Wales and Ireland, and up and down the country in various tournaments. We are always fairly well matched against Ireland and Scotland and play triangular matches against them every year. Against England, it is quite a different matter. They have so much strength in depth that they can field their third or junior team against Wales, and win.

I tried the under-21 championships again, and still got no further than the quarter finals. I lost to John Paish 13–11 in the final set, after losing three match points. Losing match points was becoming a habit. This is one of the knacks you lose when you are not playing regularly. I think it is a bit like scoring goals if you are a striker.

For me, the highlight of 1970 as far as tennis was concerned was my match with Roger Taylor on the centre court at Newport, during the Welsh Open. He had just lost to Bungert in the semi-finals at Wimbledon and was a real crowd favourite. It was quite a billing, as I was bound to get the support of much of the Welsh crowd because of my rugby connections. It was a good match. I didn't feel too disgraced going down 6–4, 6–4 and I really enjoyed having a few drinks with him in the bar afterwards. Neither of us would have believed that evening that we would be meeting in vastly different circumstances, seven years later when we both received the MBE from the Queen at Buckingham Palace for services to sport – his to tennis and mine to rugby.

There was no tennis in 1971 as I was on tour with the British

Lions in New Zealand. The only other sport I played in New Zealand was squash. It was the first time I had tried the game, and it was an instant love-affair; it seemed the ideal game for me. If I did not have enough time for all the tennis I wanted, surely I would be able to spare an hour or so a week keeping fit, playing squash. We had excellent courts at St Mary's, just round the corner from the hospital – I couldn't understand why it had taken me so long to discover the game.

After missing a whole year of tennis and ruining my strokes from too much squash, it was very difficult to get back into the swing again. I did try a tournament in Surbiton, but it was a big ordeal. I remember playing a young lad about seven years my junior and feeling very sorry for him with all the photographers clicking away around the court, hoping for a spectacular shot from me. I did not feel so sorry for Chris Welles when I played him again four years later, in '76 during an England v Wales Tennis International. Then he beat me 7–5 in the third set. Again I had let match points slip away: the way he had improved and the way I had stagnated over those years was well demonstrated.

The tour with the Lions to South Africa in 1974* had a very different outcome. When the rest of the side got on the plane back to London, I boarded one to Durban to join Scilla who was working there as an intern for six months. I had planned to do various 'locums' in the hospitals around, as one can do in the UK. Unfortunately the system in South Africa is rather different, and no one can work as a locum in hospital or general practice unless he is fully registered; I had six months of medical internship left to do. So I turned my hand to tennis coaching. It turned out to be a very enjoyable and lucrative way of earning a temporary living, as can be seen later on in the book when I describe my time in South Africa as a whole.

Back home from South Africa, tennis unfortunately slipped back into fourth place behind medicine, rugby and squash,

---

* This tour is described in detail in Chapter 9.

though not always in that order. Only once have I ever really considered taking it up seriously again and that was after one of the Superstars competitions. I opted for the tennis, before they took it out of the competition, and beat Jonah Barrington in the final. David Hemery was very impressed with my game and had quite a chat with me, telling me that I was foolish not to be following it up and making a bit of money out of it. He gave me lots of offers to think about, since he was in sports promotion himself. I did consider it for a few weeks, and even started thinking about taking a year off medicine to go to the States. It was very tempting. But it would have been tough, for tennis is very demanding mentally. It's not the sort of thing you can just pick up and put down. I believe there are only differences in temperament and attitude separating the top players and the rest – otherwise what is it which makes the top players win time after time? After all, at that level, they all have the same strokes, so it's not just a matter of technique, it is that imperative 'killer instinct' which makes Connors and Borg win again and again; and that requires total dedication.

I think I respond better to the team spirit and much as I may seem to 'burst my breeches' to win something – even if it's only marbles – I would still prefer to play for fifteen men and the whole of Cardiff Arms Park, than to push the old ego and pick up £10,000.

I think I made the right decision.

4

Blue and White Fleur-de-lys

I started up at St Mary's on a blustery October day in 1967, wearing an old suede jacket and an air of apprehension. In spite of my experience at Millfield I was still nervous about embarking upon an entirely new part of my life. Being naturally shy, I knew that it would take some time to get to know people and settle down. Still, I had played against the United (London) Hospitals' side, and had been fortunate to meet the St Mary's first team captain, Murray McEwen. That was the best possible meeting from my point of view since his position was probably one of the most prestigious in the medical school. He sought me out on my first day and showed me around the place, giving me all sorts of useful tips, such as how to get into the Nurses Home after midnight. He may have regretted giving me one of those tips – the following year I was to ask his girlfriend out, something which was considered audacious at the time. That girl was Scilla, who later became my wife.

Being Welsh was a help. Those who were, needed no introduction to each other – our accents stood out a mile next to some of the plummier ones of our English public schoolboy friends, and as exiles we always stuck together.

Term always started on a Thursday for the freshers so that we could be shown around and 'experience' the freshers' lecture on the Friday before starting work seriously on the following Monday. 'Experience' is the key word: it's not easy to capture the atmosphere of that particular lecture unless you have actually taken part. It is held in the largest lecture theatre in the medical school in the Microbiology Department named after Sir Alexander Fleming. At 2 p.m. all students including the seniors amble along and take their place in hierarchical seating arrangements, the freshers being herded towards the front. Since it's a small college it's quite easy to pick out the new faces. The freshers, of course, don't realize anything is going on since they don't know all the other faces sitting next to them at the front. They assume they are taking part in their first clinical lecture and feel very excited about getting to the real nitty-gritty of medicine. In fact it's planned by the seniors to fool the freshers. There is usually a long book list read out and the juniors rush into taking notes of all the titles – that is until some of them realize that they are writing ridiculous titles like VENEREAL DISEASE TREATMENT FOR MEDICAL STUDENTS and THE FINER POINTS OF THE NURSE'S ANATOMY . . .!

Then one of the front row is invited to take part in a clinical demonstration. I remember when one poor soul was shown how to take off a leg plaster with an electric saw – the demonstration plaster was of normal thickness and was whisked off in a minute, but a pint of blood in a transfusion bag had been neatly hidden inside. Blood spurted out when the saw reached half-way and the 'patient' howled suitably. The fresher almost fainted – he really thought he had hit flesh and there seemed no way to stop the bleeding with the rest of the leg encased in plaster. Next a couple of girls were invited down to demonstrate varicose veins in a patient – only to find that they were required to take off their own tights in front of an audience of three or four hundred in order to demonstrate how normal veins appear! Two of the most timid-looking freshers were then asked to conduct an interview with a young couple about a problem that commonly presents itself to GPs. 'Just ask the relevant questions,' were the instructions . . . dead silence. Then lots of blushing and stammering of questions like 'Are your periods normal?', 'Does your husband wear Y-fronts?'

67

'How often . . .' 'Go on, ask them if they're doing it right,' came the heckling from the back. It was the perfect introduction to life at St Mary's.

After that ordeal we had the weekend to let our blushes wear off before normal lectures started on the Monday. As I was only doing physics for first MB I did not have many to attend and these were over with by Tuesday, leaving Wednesday morning for practical sessions. The rest of the week I was meant to be doing research into biochemistry. We were allotted various projects to work on in pairs with other PhD students. My partner in that first term was Ralph Gingell, who hailed from Cross Keys in Monmouthshire. Our research went very well – into the Lions selected for the Triple Crown matches and the favourites for the Hospitals' Cup! When we did get down to biochemistry we were concerned with the protein binding of drugs. It was quite interesting, dealing as it did with all aspects of drug metabolism and availability in the body – why, for example, some drugs act differently when taken with alcohol. Ralph and I got along very well together as we were both quiet types and I was very sorry when he left later to complete his research in the States. I bumped into him entirely by chance nine years later playing rugby in Chicago when I was touring North America with London Welsh.

I soon got into the rugby world at St Mary's – it was un-avoidable. The first game I watched was St Mary's Ist's playing against Cambridge, usually one of the toughest fixtures of the season. St Mary's were a good team that year, having won the Hospitals' Cup the year before, and they beat the Light Blues 3–0. Paul Eddington was the Ist's full-back and a very good one too. I could see that I would be playing for the second team, the A XV for quite some time. Young aspiring players often have to wait until older students qualify before they are ele-vated to the Ist's, and older players are often determined to show them that senior rugby is a far cry from the schoolboy stuff. Any airs and graces displayed by the youngsters who have been used to being tops at school are soon rubbed off. I took

68

part in the trials and after a couple of weeks managed to get in a few games for the Ist's when players were injured; as full-back or occasionally outside-half. It was quite an experience being in the company of the older players, some of whom were seven or eight years older than me and seemed real men of the world. The pride they had in the Hospital was reflected by the way they would take us under their wing and mould us into good 'Mary's men'. There is not the same age gap between students at other universities as the courses are not so long and they perhaps do not achieve quite the same cameraderie.

The legends which have built up around various past St Mary's students are legion and it was part of the moulding process to hear them all. Most of the incidents supposedly occurred during the annual Cornish Easter tour which still takes place, but there are now a limited number of hotels who are willing to risk accommodating the team! Other legends grew up around Rag Week. On one occasion, so they say, the lamp markings for a major road works were removed in the middle of the night to another spot half a mile down the road . . . so the road was dug up in the wrong place the following day. London University Rag Week eventually became so dangerous for the Inner London Council that it had to be banned in the 1960s.

All the London teaching hospitals possess sports grounds away from the medical school, usually on the outskirts of London. It is a good policy to be able to leave the hospital and get away from the centre of London. This is especially true in the early years when meeting so many ill patients on the wards and watching operations in theatre can be upsetting. St Mary's sports ground is in Teddington, Middlesex – about a mile from Twickenham. This beautiful ground was obtained for the College by Lord Moran in the 1930s, who used remarkable powers of persuasion to convince various monied gentlemen that its acquisition was necessary for the well-being of the students and hence the doctors of the next generation. He was the Dean of the medical school for many years and his contribution to the establishment was immense. He also had a great deal of foresight into the needs of the medical school and the difficulty that there would be in years to come in purchasing such large areas of land. It is without doubt one of the best rugby pitches in London, and used to be the venue for the Middlesex county matches. The club-house bar is full of trophies – not the silver variety (those being locked away in the medical school where no one can see them) but the more treasured souvenirs of tours, and booty obtained from raiding rival medical schools prior to the Hospitals' Cup final. There are traffic lights, the inevitable road signs and of course the Bart's Bear (the hospital mascot), which are locked away as each cup final approaches. The groundsman and his wife have to put up with a lot from the students who let off most of their steam down at Teddington. Most of the time I was at St Mary's it was Mr and Mrs Doug Chesson who had this unenviable task but fortunately they really entered into the spirit of the medical school. The sausages produced on a Saturday night to soak up the beer were renowned and the chicken curries which Mrs C. produced after the cup finals attracted far more people back to Teddington than just the team and reserves.

When I was getting lifts out to Teddington in the first year I never imagined that I would be living just round the corner five years later and using the ground for my own training sessions. Before Doug and Mrs C. took over it was the tradition to go back to the hall of residence, Wilson House, to complete the Saturday night drinking. This was named after John Wilson later to become Lord Moran and physician to the Queen. Wilson House is at the end of Sussex Gardens just round the corner from the Edgware Road. This part of London is very well known to the Welsh since it is full of bed-and-breakfast institutions and small hotels which seem to accommodate the whole Welsh nation when Wales plays England up at Twickenham. The bar steward at Wilson House in those days used to serve hot meals to all the lads who had played that afternoon. We thought it was great value since no money ever changed hands. It was fairly naïve of us – the chap was sacked about six months after I arrived for fiddling the bar accounts. We never had a steward after that – it was run by the students themselves, but things never seemed quite the same in Wilson House on a Saturday night after his dismissal.

Accommodation in London is a great headache for a student and there are no signs of change. There are various alternatives. There are London University Halls of Residence which are in great demand but which are not mixed and are very expensive; these were all full when I applied. There are digs where one lives with a family or in isolation in a bed-sit; flats are usually out of the question in the first year unless you have organized people to share with, people who have done all the flat-hunting before you start term. Finally there is Wilson House for the St Mary's students, but this is mainly reserved for clinical students – those who have passed the most important exam of the whole course – the second MB. It always seems a bit of a paradox, since the very time students need stability and a room to work in is during those first two years when the academic going is very tough and not during the last three years when there is plenty of time to organize accommodation and not so much exam pressure.

I found digs finally in Kilburn with a delightful Welsh couple who had moved from Wales just a few years previously. I think they had specially asked for Welsh students – my room-mate, Phil Evans, came from Pontardawe, near Swansea – and it certainly turned out to be a very good arrangement; it seemed just like home. Bill Maddocks had been a pillar of Maesteg schoolboy rugby and had been awarded the MBE for his service to youth clubs. His wife was a very motherly person who cooked us huge meals and generally treated us like sons, turning a blind eye to food being pinched from the fridge late on a Saturday night after a binge. We considered ourselves very fortunate, particularly by comparison with some of our friends. Phil was a year ahead of me and consequently a great help when it came to revising for exams. He qualified a year

71

before I did and is now practising as a GP in Gowerton near Swansea.

The night I heard I had been picked to play for Wales in 1969 at Murrayfield with my first full cap there was a real celebration in the local bowls' club. Bill Maddocks was the secretary and spent most of his spare time there; as a retired schoolmaster with a very active mind he made a good job of it. All my friends came to this unlikely venue and we celebrated till the early hours of the morning. I think it was the only time our behaviour prompted Mrs Maddocks to show any disapproval. I soon learned I had been forgiven, however, when I arrived back after that first International at Murrayfield and heard how she had shown me off to all her friends who had been invited round to see the match on television. I stayed with the Maddockses for well over two years until I was given a room in Wilson House.

I continued to play for the hospital until the Christmas of my first year, but was becoming increasingly disillusioned. Many of the first team players were losing interest as they came up to qualifying and their places were not being taken as enthusiastically as they ought to have been. We still had a fairly good fixture list but it was an embarrassment to be losing by such large margins to sides who the St Mary's team of four or five years previously could easily have beaten. The days when famous names like Nim Hall and Tommy Kemp appeared on the selection board downstairs in the medical school were gone. I decided that after the vac I would try to play a few weekend games for Bridgend. I had played one or two before going up to London but had not pursued the idea, since it seemed ridiculous to be travelling back and forth on Saturdays and missing most of the social life at St Mary's. In addition I knew I couldn't expect just to walk into the side as they already had a good full-back in David Griffiths, who was also vice-captain of the club.

By the time I had spent a few weeks at home over Christmas and played in a few hard games I realized that if my rugby was going to improve at all I would need to play in more top class games and sacrifice my social life for a while. So I started travelling down by train on Saturday mornings for matches in the afternoon. It was a tight schedule and St Mary's weren't too happy about it.

Bridgend weren't either, particularly if I arrived late. Once, I remember, the train halted about half a mile from Bridgend Station while workmen on the line made the inevitable weekend repairs and eventually I decided to get out and walk. Unfortunately the sides of the track were a bit steep to climb up with all my kit so I had to walk along the track itself. My mother, who was meeting me at the other end to make sure I reached the Brewery Field in time, was horrified when she saw me and the train, which by that time was not far behind.

After Easter my plan started to pay off. I had received enough recognition by playing in Wales before Welsh selectors to be named in the squad to tour Argentina that summer. Even my critics knew that I would not have been picked had I continued to play for St Mary's. My studies had not suffered too much in the process and I rounded off my initial year by passing first MB. Equally important, I had made a lot of good friends, with whom I was to go on to face the next hurdle, the second MB.

It was an exciting prospect – not just to be touring as part of the Welsh squad, but to be visiting a country I would never have the chance to visit otherwise.

Rugby is second to soccer as the national sport in Argentina* but that did not reduce either the enthusiasm or the capacity of the crowds we played to. In fact, the games were almost too well attended as the crowds were positively dangerous at times. We had thought the French crowd at the Stades Colombes a little mad with their brass bands dotted around, their cockerels flying and their firecrackers, and the South Africans, too, throwing naartjies (tangerines) on to the pitch; but the

---

* I discuss this tour in more detail in Chapter 6.

Latin temperament of the Argentinians far exceeded either. They threw anything that they could lay their hands on – coins, bottles, rockets, stones. Apart from the danger involved the rowdiness was very distracting and must be close to that often experienced in first division soccer. The referees were dishonest. After one particularly bad display of partiality I was moved to talk to the referee as we were running off the field at the end of the match. He agreed that he had not always interpreted the law equally fairly on both sides and added, 'I can't afford to lose my job.' And he wasn't talking about his refereeing job . . .

Argentinian society is divided into extremes. The rich are very rich but there are far more very poor to be seen begging in the streets.

Equally diverse were the geographical conditions: we saw dry flat plains in the north and lush green valleys in the south. Patagonia, further south still, was mountainous – the Welsh-speakers amongst us were invited down to spend a few days with the exiled Welsh community there.

Similarly, contrast was found between the noisiness of the matches in the city and the quiet life we led for four weeks in a hotel twenty miles outside Buenos Aires – we felt we were almost imprisoned. There was little to do except train . . . and drink, and since there was no beer our choice was limited to gin or rum. 'Cuba Libra' became our stock phrase, meaning rum and coke. John ('Syd') Dawes was captain then and rumour had it that he had never drunk spirits before the tour. Later rumour said that his eighteen-year-old full-back had taught him the rudiments. Suffice it to say that he sent a telegram to Scilla and me on our wedding day (he was on tour in South Africa at the time) saying, 'Best wishes from Syd and his GT boys.' (GT, for the uninitiated, is gin and tonic.)

It was not a very successful tour for various reasons. The squad was not strong as we were missing all the Welsh players who had been to South Africa with the Lions earlier that summer – players like Gareth Edwards and Barry John. It

74

had been planned as a testing ground for some of the younger players and we certainly were tested. We lost most of the games and not just to the referee. Argentina has always been under-estimated as a rugby force and regarded somewhat as a joke, but they do possess a very strong side, something which was well demonstrated when they almost beat Wales at the beginning of the 1976–7 season. It should be only a matter of time before they put their house in order and make use of neutral referees to achieve international panel status.

After touring with so many older players that summer, it was a bit of an anti-climax to spend the rest of the vacation with my brothers and playing tennis at a junior level. Even if I was playing second class tennis I made sure that I wouldn't be playing second class rugby the following season. I had talked at length with John Dawes during the Argentine tour and it was he who persuaded me to join London Welsh. It seemed such a good idea I couldn't understand why I hadn't thought of it before – that way I could play against many of the Welsh sides without having to make all those journeys back to Bridgend. So in the autumn of 1968 I started my career with a club whose style of play was to set the rugby world alight for many years. They really were going through a purple patch, often running in spectacular last-minute tries to snatch a win in injury time. I was very fortunate to be playing when there were so many brilliant members in the team. It is an impressive record to have sent seven players from one club on a Lions tour and played five of those in the Test team (as they did three years later in 1971). I know that the positive approach we adopted had a great influence on the attacking side of my play.

I still played for St Mary's in the Hospitals' Cup and the Cambridge game, and in some of the midweek games because London Welsh only played on Saturdays. In fact the Cambridge game developed into a tradition. In later years we always played up in Cambridge, at Grange Road, and afterwards went on to the famous Hawkes club. When Phil, my next brother, went up to Cambridge in 1969 we used to take ourselves off to his bar at Christ's College. The danger spot was round the corner from there – the Elm Tree. The landlord encouraged us since he was practised in the art of drinking himself – he was reputed to drink a bottle of vodka for breakfast. I think it was mainly through trying to keep up with him that we very nearly landed ourselves in trouble. Also we were away from home and much more likely to get up to mischief. Whatever it was, our antics after visiting the Elm Tree bordered on the criminal and seemed to get worse each year.

On one occasion a couple of bicycles standing unlocked outside proved too much of a temptation and before we knew it we were bowling along on a sight-seeing tour of the ancient colleges. Fortunately we managed to get back and replace the bikes having eluded the police after turning over a hamburger stall and making off with a couple of dozen hamburgers.

We had managed to scrounge a room from John de Mendoza, my old tennis rival, in Downing College. The following morning the hamburger man was waiting outside, kicking up an appalling fuss and demanding that we return the goods. Luckily we hadn't been able to eat them as they were frozen, but we had hoped to leave them as a gift for Mendoza. They weren't very frozen when we eventually handed them back and they certainly looked the worse for wear. We were horrified to think that he was actually going to heat them up and sell them to poor unsuspecting students. We looked for the man the following year but we never saw him selling his wares outside the Elm Tree again.

Autumn 1968 saw the start of our second year at St Mary's and we were looking forward to the freshers' lecture now that it was no longer us who were the source of ridicule. It was just as good that year. Sex changes had been topical that summer, I think, because of April Ashley. Slides were shown of a lovely girl on her wedding day and then an obviously male specimen complete with beard was shown into the theatre dressed up as a female, handbag and all. We needed one of the girl freshers to go down and prove that 'she' was still a female. There was an obvious choice: a shy-looking girl with long blonde hair tied back with a pink bow sitting second from the left in the second row. She thought she would be able to get away with trying to pretend she wasn't new. She had no hope: we all knew we hadn't seen her before. In the end, she performed the necessary examination perfectly, blushing to the roots of her hair amidst calls of 'Phone number, please' and wolf whistles from the back.

Meanwhile our studies kept us busy – two or three hours a day were spent in the lecture theatre and the rest of the time in the various 'practical' rooms. Physiology practical took place on a Monday morning, when we performed all kinds of experiments on the 'normal' human body. The 'normal' would be one out of each group of six and we needed volunteers each week. Sometimes for example we all took part in finding out our own blood group, or walking around the medical school with tubes passed into our stomachs through our nose. Sometimes it was less exacting being the subject than running around taking measurements. I remember once reclining in a deck chair on Monday morning after a particularly strenuous Sunday night party, with one arm immersed in ice and the other in hot water with electrodes all over my body, while the rest of the group frenziedly took temperatures and blood pressure readings every two minutes.

Writing up the practical sessions was tedious – there were so many measurements and graphs it could take four or five hours each week. The trouble was that we all knew what the results should have been and ours were never anywhere near, so we spent much longer trying to fiddle the measurements in order to end up with the right answer. Since the experiments did not change from year to year the best solution was to get hold of physiology practical books belonging to the third- or fourth-year students; everyone did it year in, year out.

Dissection was another major subject. We were split up into groups of four per body of which we were meant to dissect every muscle, nerve and vessel. It was impossible to maintain interest in this week after week. We grew quite attached to our 'companions' and used to try and guess something about their lives. Ours was a little old lady who hardly possessed a single muscle. How we were supposed to find them all bewildered us. She did have a marvellous pair of lungs though – we could tell she'd never let a cigarette pass her lips during her long life-time. The body next to us was completely different. He was a fine specimen of a young man with marvellously developed muscles, but lungs black as the coal tips back home. How he ever got there was a source of great speculation. Thus dissection often turned out to be a – reverent – general gossip session.

I never really got anything out of dissection until 1975. I returned as an anatomy demonstrator to the same room on the fourth floor, to experience the same smell of formalin stinging the back of my throat. Then it was altogether different because I was studying for the Primary FRCS exam and it really was important to site all the nerves and muscles in order to know the basic facts necessary for a surgical career.

The only good thing about the dissection sessions in those days before second MB was that the blonde fresher – Scilla – was at the next table. That didn't mean that we were on chatting terms – far from it. I was so shy that I hadn't plucked up courage to speak to her. She seemed very occupied with her work and anyway she was going out with Murray McEwen, captain of the 1st's. It wasn't until February that the ice was finally broken. One of the other lads on my table, a certain Neil Reginald Poulter from Doncaster, decided to help things along. He had been one of the first MB set and was a great practical joker. He knew I liked Scilla so he rigged up a Valentine's Day joke: he faked our signatures and sent a card from me to her with the predictable strong man on it tearing up the telephone directory. There was also a card to me from her – supposedly. I was very taken aback and thought for half a minute that she might have sent it – but the idea was too ridiculous. Then when I arrived at St Mary's and saw the expectant look on Neil's face, I guessed he'd sent it – and then he told me about the card to Scilla. The problem was how to put things straight with Scilla without scaring her off altogether.

We bumped into each other the next day outside the library. She was obviously embarrassed because she thought my card was serious. Until then she did not know that I had received one from her. I explained the joke, and an awkward silence followed. It seemed as if that was the end of the story but all the same I asked if 'Perhaps we could go for a drink some time?' She nodded, rather half-heartedly. 'I'm afraid it will have to be in a fortnight or so,' I continued, 'because I'm playing in an International next week and there's squad training down in Wales this weekend.' To someone who had never even seen a rugby ball till she came down to St Mary's from Derbyshire it cut no ice at all. I could hardly have made a very good impression – and when we did eventually meet for that first drink it was a disaster.

I wanted to change that first impression and was going to take her to the City Barge, a pub on the River Thames with a garden overlooking the river. Again it was Neil's idea. Unfortunately we never reached the City Barge. Instead we drove round and round in circles taking dead-end roads to warehouses and boathouses and ending in the George and Devonshire at Hogarth Roundabout. There we looked out, not to the gentle waves of the Thames, but to the incessant streams of traffic making their way to the M4. It was so noisy that we couldn't hear ourselves speak – which was just as well because I couldn't think of anything to say.

We would probably not have got any further than that were it not for the fact that out of the sparse conversation we did discover we had one thing in common – our birthdays were on the same day, 2 March. It seemed a great excuse for a party. She would be nineteen and I would be twenty. We planned to hold it in a flat in Castellain Road which housed a whole group of St Mary's friends including Neil – it was the least we could do considering we were his 'brainchild'. We decided to invite the whole year, about ninety altogether. It was a Sunday and unfortunately I had already agreed to take part in a sponsored walk with London Welsh that day. I left Neil and the others rigging up the acoustics and beer and Scilla organizing the food and set off on my twenty-mile walk, hardly the best preparation for a party which was going to last all night. As it was though it turned out tremendously. Nearly everybody showed up and we were still in high spirits when we strolled into the anatomy lecture theatre on the Monday morning, straight from the party. I still have part of a record token which the rest of the year had signed and given to us. Scilla still has the other part! The remainder of that term seemed to be divided between frantically trying to catch up on my studies after spending too many evenings with Scilla and preparing for Internationals and the Triple Crown. We were due to play England during the Easter vac and I had arranged for Scilla to come and watch.

We had a good weekend especially as some friends from Mary's came down for the match. I was due to play for London Welsh in the Sevenoaks VIIs that Sunday, so we all piled into my old Ford Cortina and drove straight to Sevenoaks. We stopped just once – outside Farnborough – for the nicest ham and eggs any of us had ever tasted. It had been a very eventful few hours and we were all starving. And that afternoon we won the VIIs on only three hours' sleep!

The summer term of 1969 had hardly started before I was off to New Zealand. I had a splendid stag party with Neil and all the lads at the flat in Castellain Road to get me in shape for the tour. They were all very envious of my going over there when all they would be doing was swotting and sitting exams. As I mentioned before, the tour was not a great success in spite of our winning all the provincial games. As in 1977 it was painfully clear that winning the Tests was the only thing which really mattered. I think it was the humiliation of losing those two Tests in 1969 which made the Welsh members of the Lions tour in 1971 so determined to avenge themselves.

It was my first taste of New Zealand rugby* and I was not altogether sure that I liked the after-taste. There were certainly some disgraceful incidents: Jeff Young for instance was 'felled' by Colin 'Pinetree' Meads in front of the line-out for all to see, an incident which left him with a broken jaw. We were intensely criticized both on and off the field for what seemed to us very trivial matters. For example, we were branded as being the scruffiest side ever to tour down under because one or two of the players grew moustaches during the five weeks.

Of those five weeks, only three were actually spent in New Zealand, it was far too short a time for a serious tour involving two Test matches. On the other hand a four month tour is definitely too long for amateur players to be away from their jobs and families. For a serious tour, nine or ten weeks ought to be enough to cover the stronger provincial sides and to include at least three Test matches.

Many of us in the team were just beginning to carve out our careers but we had the experience of the older, established players to fall back on. Keith Jarrett in particular had a brilliant tour and looked like having a tremendous future with Wales. Unfortunately he decided to sign up with a club in the North of England as a league player. His future with rugby league, however, was also curtailed when, like Mervyn Davies later, he suffered a serious brain haemorrhage and was put in the sad position of not being able to realize his full potential in either game. It was a salutary lesson to all players who were being tempted by offers to go North (i.e. turn professional). Your job depends entirely on being physically fit and even then injuries can be so unpredictable.

Returning from New Zealand we stopped over in Fiji and played a match there. The heat was overwhelming – we couldn't believe that we were actually going to play at temperatures of well over ninety. All the same we did, and won, enjoying afterwards the taste of replacing all the fluid lost. I dropped a

---

* Again, this tour is described in detail in Chapter 6.

goal in that match – one of two in my career. We were still wearing the Fijian flowered skirts when we landed at Heathrow and only had to see the expression on the faces of the wives and girlfriends meeting us to realize we had not looked in a mirror since leaving the island. The big men in the party raised the most laughs – people like Delme Thomas and Denzil Williams looking particularly fetching with their socks and shoes sticking out beneath their 'dresses'.

Apart from the Investiture of the Prince of Wales and the tennis tour down to Dittisham the summer vac dragged on as I sat at my desk at home poring over lecture notes trying to make some academic headway. The following term started badly. Scilla had returned from a holiday in the States much less interested in me. I had known it couldn't last anyway. Also I did badly in the exams and began to worry over my work. If this was the result of swotting all summer I began to wonder how I was going to cope with second MB, the big tester, the following spring. Second MB really is a hurdle because you need to pass it before you are allowed to start clinical work. You were given two chances: if you failed a second time you were kicked out. So for the next two terms, I devoted myself pretty single-mindedly to the task of passing second MB, merely playing enough rugby to keep my mind fresh. I'm sure I got through more work because I set myself a time limit, using my training time down at Old Deer Park as a reward when I had studied solidly for ten hours beforehand.

I'm a great believer in Parkinson's law which states that 'Work expands to fill the time available' – it is very easy to spend more time sitting at a desk and end up doing less. I'm also a great believer in the importance of having a diversion since that way one can end up doing two things well instead of one badly.

My method of working paid off. Although I had not done well in any of the exams leading up to second MB I made sure I passed the one that mattered by pacing myself, and ended up doing very much better than I (or my lecturers) thought possible, coming eighth out of a class of ninety.

I was able to wind down and relax a little when the exams were all over by going to Canada for three weeks with Middlesex County Rugby team. It couldn't have come at a better time and many of my friends from London Welsh were also on tour.

After Easter I was in the proud position of exchanging the long white coat I had worn in the labs for the short white one which is the trademark of a medical student on the wards. It was an important status symbol, like the brand new stethoscope dangling round one's neck.

The first few months on the wards were shattering. When confronted with real live patients the time spent learning biochemistry and anatomy seemed pointless. There was so much still to learn – it seemed an impossible feat. The housemen (interns) dashed around the wards exuding knowledge – the same people I had played with in the Ist's, only three years senior to me. It seemed inconceivable that I would be doing just the same in another three years (in the eyes of those who knew no better, at least!).

We were called junior 'dressers' when we first arrived on the wards – the equivalent of 'tea boy' in office jargon. We had a lot to learn, and started where we hoped to finish, with the most important object of our studies – the patient. We were allotted to 'firms' or teams headed by a consultant, followed in order by the senior registrar, registrar and houseman. It was our duty to 'clerk' (interview) patients, help the houseman and prepare presentations for ward rounds. We were also the resident vampires, taking all the blood necessary for the multitude of tests performed. This was part of our training for techniques we would need later on, such as putting up drips and giving drugs intravenously. The poor patients in a teaching hospital get bombarded with a barrage of questions – most of which seem entirely irrelevant to their complaint. For example, a gentleman being admitted for a hernia repair is likely to be asked his whole family history; what his father died of, how many pints he drinks a night and if he had whooping cough as a child – and all these usually three times over. No wonder such patients need a pre-med before going to the theatre. Just what you made of your time on the wards was entirely up to you. You might spend hours clerking patients and learn less than if you were to spend a quiet half-hour looking up a certain condition. On the other hand, you would learn more about multiple sclerosis by remembering a young person your own age, crippled with the disease, with whom you had talked on the wards; and Graves disease (hyperthyroidism) would stick in your mind for ever once you have seen a patient suffering from it. That is the beauty of a medical training: you have to decide for yourself just how much time you think you need on the wards and how much you need in the evenings reading up about what you've seen. The lectures are few and far between during those clinical years and you learn most on a ward with the consultant.

At the end of three months medicine and three months surgery there was an introductory course exam. Neil and I managed to come across a set of past papers and had learned by heart the multiple choice questions and answers without understanding half of them. Seventy per cent of those questions came up in our exam and, not surprisingly, Neil and I came an embarrassing first and second. It made a mockery of the exam system – some parts of medicine cannot be tested by multiple choice questions alone. Since there were no serious exams between the end of the introductory course and Part I MB (pathology) two years later, we were split up for the pathology course into groups according to our previous exam results. Neil and I had a lot to live up to – we were in the top group allotted to the professor and we certainly were not the whizz kids our results suggested.

After the introductory course we were allowed to take a more active part in patient management and got rather more than some of us had bargained for: suddenly we found ourselves delivering babies. Each student needed twenty deliveries under his belt. We did two stints of six weeks at different hospitals connected with the St Mary's group. Mine happened to be the teaching hospital – the old Paddington General, now St Mary's W9, on the Harrow Road. The first birth we witnessed was bad enough but one's own first delivery was terrifying. True it was breathtaking and miraculous that there could be a little living creature as the outcome of it all – but it was so bloody. We hadn't expected that, nor the mixture of feelings we experienced – mainly a cross between awe and repulsion. Once you had got over the initial shock, however, it wasn't too bad. Many of our patients at Harrow Road were immigrants and the response of the different ethnic groups to childbirth was very varied. We came to know that Greeks and Southern Europeans would have a low threshold of pain and would be screaming ('Mama Mia') throughout the ward if they did not receive heavy analgesia. The West Indians and the Irish were marvellous – they were naturals. We knew that we wouldn't have any trouble with the Africans, but there were various taboos to observe. One of the Nigerian tribes is strictly against Caesarean sections and we had a lot of difficulty persuading one lady's husband and brother that it was absolutely necessary to operate if the baby was to live. We felt very sorry for what she would have to put up with when she left hospital – she would probably be ostracized by other members of her family.

One of the night midwives was a formidable character, weighing in at around eighteen stone and with one blind eye. The story goes that Sister C. was blinded when clamping the cord of a patient with secondary syphilis when some blood spurted into her left eye . . . but there were always bound to be stories. She put the fear of God into us and we felt that she made some of the mothers deliver out of sheer fright. We got our own back one night after a session in Ward 12. There are only eleven wards up at Harrow, and Ward 12 was a euphemism for the 'Albert'. The labour ward was quiet and as there were no deliveries going on upstairs we decided to hold a ward round of our own on the ante-natal ward. All the patients were still awake. One of us pretended to be the consultant, Mr L., who taught us the rudiments of obstetrics in an austere, punishing fashion. Another mimicked our favourite Sister C. and we carried on all round the ward with the 'consultant' shouting abuse at the students who could not tell the difference between breech and ordinary presentation. The patients were in stitches – it was very life-like – until Sister C. stormed into the ward. She was furious; she knew she was being ridiculed on her own territory – it was just too much. She never forgot it and after that found all kinds of reasons for getting us up at night.

We were allowed one delivery in three sharing with the pupil midwives – that is, assuming all was straightforward. We also had to suture the episiotomies since the midwives weren't allowed to stitch them, although they were allowed to cut them: it seemed ironic and we used to feel that we were just there finishing up someone else's dirty work. It was our first taste of being on duty for twenty-four hours at a stretch or rather thirty-four hours by the time you were actually off-duty the following day. It used to make me mad when people said to me at night, 'Are you on the night shift then?' There was no such thing as a shift, except perhaps on Casualty. We always had to put in a full day's work the day after somehow, having been up all night.

The worst time to be called is about 4 a.m., since it will be light as you walk back to the residencies and you know you'll never get back to sleep – you just lie there listening to the traffic and the dawn chorus and wish you hadn't bothered to try. If you had stayed on the ward, someone would have made a cup of coffee and you could have got some reading done instead.

It was during my spell on obstetrics that I took part in the annual opera – that year it was 'HMS Pinafore', put on by a friend called Mike Hampton. For some reason he had faith in my singing and wouldn't allow me to stay in the ranks of the basses for the whole performance. I had to utter a few notes on my own as 'Bob Becket'. That hadn't been my plan at all. I had wanted to rehearse as little as was necessary in order to get into the production and do all the beer drinking that was necessary to keep the show moving. When I saw the costumes Mike produced for me and when he suggested tying my longer-than-average hair back in a pony tail, I knew that it was just a publicity stunt, and nothing to do with my voice at all – my pride was quite hurt. I just hoped that it wouldn't turn into a P. J. Proby act. In the end though, it produced a few laughs and that was all that mattered. The best night was always the Saturday night when we performed only for ourselves and the other students. The Dean brought his party on the Friday, so once that was over we could enjoy ourselves. The choruses on the Saturday were quite different from those sung during the week and everyone let rip. Practical jokes were played, things were thrown, lighting tampered with and words changed to describe topical incidents in the medical school in a way which is only possible with Gilbert and Sullivan. The orchestra too were allowed their own way. All through the week they had been improvising on various themes during the interval. Here was their chance to integrate 'Summertime' into 'Pinafore'. The orchestra comprised mainly students and staff and they did a marvellous job of balancing their efforts against the soloists whose talents varied each year.

By March 1971 the Lions team for the New Zealand tour* had been picked and it became obvious that I would have to start re-organizing my studies. I had less trouble arranging for time off than I had for the shorter tour with Wales, because I knew there would be no suggestion of my catching up on lost time. I would have had anyway to drop back six months since no one is allowed to sit MB finals without a full three years of clinical experience behind them. It was a small price to pay for the chance of a lifetime. I had decided to take advantage of being in New Zealand to stay on and do my elective over there. In St Mary's, there is an elective period during

* Described in detail in Chapter 7.

the fourth year when one can go anywhere in the world to do some form of medicine. It could be as varied as taking part in a flying doctor service in Australia, helping drug addicts in Soho, manning oil rigs in Alaska or coping with witch doctors in New Guinea. Most of the London Medical schools operate similar schemes, but many restrict the electives to the United Kingdom. I hear that the elective period has now been put forward at St Mary's until just before finals, which is unfortunate. That would surely defeat the object of allowing a little specialization and enterprise, since it is bound to be used as an extension of the revision period.

Anyway, in April 1971 I took part in my last ward round on British soil for six months, and said my goodbyes around the hospital.

I had arranged my elective at Auckland General Hospital to start immediately after the tour. As I stood at the airport watching the rest of the team board that 707 I was not too sure I had made the right decision. As I waved them off there were tears pouring down my face as I reflected on the tremendous four months we had spent together and on all our accomplishments. I knew there would be a tumultuous reception for them at Heathrow and I felt very envious. Deep down inside, I hoped that they wouldn't forget me in my absence and the small part I had played in the Test successes. I felt very sad and lost. For all that time we had been living on top of each other and having everything organized for us: for a moment I had no idea what to do. Then I decided that the only thing I could do was set off for the hospital, even though I knew not a soul there.

When I saw the modern building overlooking the harbour my spirits lifted a little; perhaps things weren't so bad after all. It was going to be a challenge and I usually thrive on challenges. I soon made friends, because everybody wanted to talk rugby with me, from theatre porters to lab technicians and consultants. They didn't want to talk about the brilliance of the Lions team, however, only to know why New Zealand had lost and what could be done about it. They were rather bitter in defeat, which I suppose is quite natural after you have been used to winning year after year. My greatest friend over there was my senior house officer, John Hawk. Just as well, because I had done little general medicine at the time and I really needed him around. Work apart we were very close during our time off. He was not quite the typical New Zealander and that was probably why we got on so well together.

After all that, being faced with ordinary lectures at St Mary's was a bit of an anti-climax. By Christmas, I was looking forward to playing again after a break of almost six months. I was also looking forward to seeing some patients again after a spell of pure pathology, even though they were all psychiatric cases.

I must have been a bit big for my boots for a while – not surprising, considering we had achieved the 'impossible' and had been treated like heroes. Luckily, it was all wasted on Neil and the lads. They immediately scotched any airs and graces I adopted and brought me down to size. I was pleased they did – I remembered when I had first been capped for Wales I was very conscious of trying to be just like the rest and used to get Phil Evans to tell me if he thought I was being big-headed.

Nothing had changed since I had been away – except that Phil had got married. He had had his stag party as tradition compelled in the bar of Wilson House. By all accounts it was a terrible night. By twelve they were all well away and after a brief rendering of 'Zulu Warrior', with appropriate clothes-shedding, they headed off round the corner into Edgware Road. There 'Evs' tried to hold up the traffic – all six lanes of it. Then they lifted up a car, which between them they were going to carry round to Wilson House as a wedding present. When Evs suddenly crashed at 2 a.m. he caused some concern – he had passed out on a bed and started breathing in a very irregular fashion; they were all terrified that he might stop breathing altogether. This sobered up Neil, who ran for a pharmacology book and started looking up 'Alcohol' in the back, as if there were an anti-dote. He stayed up all night with Evs, just the same, recording his respirations every ten minutes.

That season I broke my jaw during the Wales *v* Scotland match. I had been wearing a gum shield since the Lions tour and attributed to this the miraculous preservation of all my teeth. Much was made of the fact that I turned up at the after-match dinner, but once the fracture had been elevated and set by wiring to the upper teeth there was not really much pain. Since there was so much bruising there was swelling around most of the nerves and really there was more numbness than anything.

It was after that incident that I met Scilla for the first time in almost a year. She had left for Denver to spend three months elective just before I arrived back from New Zealand. Ever since the summer of '69, we had gone our separate ways.

'Hello, where have you been?' I asked.

'Fancy seeing you as I walk through the door – I've been in the Rockies, ski-ing. It wasn't too good – I broke my leg.'

'Funny you should say that – join the clan – I broke my jaw,' I replied and smiled to show the metal brace on my front teeth. Not a very pretty sight. Not a very good re-introduction.

By another quirk of circumstance, THE birthday was only a few days away. I couldn't resist the obvious temptation to suggest a few drinks together on 2 March, for old times' sakes. She agreed.

I had a narrow escape a few weeks later. Part of the psychiatry course involved a residential two weeks at psychiatric institutions. I was on my way to Basingstoke late one Sunday night, to start my course there, when I hit a crash barrier on the M4, taking a corner too fast. It looked as though I had written off my Spitfire which I had only had for six months.

The *Ark Royal* had been anchored in Auckland while I was there and one of the ship's doctors on board was John Isaacs, who had been at St Mary's a few years ahead of me. After a few gin and tonics in the ship's mess, it transpired that he had a car he didn't need any more . . . and that I was looking for one. I had managed to save quite a lot over there since all my entertainment was free and when I heard it was a Spitfire I bought it straight away trusting him completely. It had been a good car, I thought, as I got out after the crash, luckily unscathed, to survey the damage. I hitched a lift back into London and found myself outside Wilson House without a key. I had given up my room for the month to save paying rent and the keys had gone with it. There I was at 2.30 a.m., faced with the grim reality of having nearly lost my life and, to crown it all, the prospect of not being able to get into Wilson House. I threw stones up at windows and banged on doors. Luckily I hit on some unfortunate student swotting all night for an exam the next day. He came down and let me in and I slept on the sofa in the bar. It was a dreadful night.

I spent the next two weeks getting to and from Basingstoke by all manner of means. I remember on one occasion riding pillion on a friend, Geoff Dobb's motor-scooter, with an Adidas sweat-suit keeping out the elements, racing against the traffic in time to reach Old Deer Park before the kick-off against Coventry. We won the match but I needed a good few pints inside me before I could steel myself for the return journey.

It was well into the summer before I got my car back from the plastic surgeons and I was getting used to all the different gear boxes of the various cars I was borrowing from friends at St Mary's to get me around. One of them was an old Morris 1000 belonging to a friend who had temporarily lost his licence; this was on an occasion when I was on my way back from competing in a tennis tournament in Surbiton. It was a bit nerve-racking driving that particular car because the owner had let the tax expire whilst the car was out of use. Suddenly I saw a flashing light in the mirror. This is it, I thought. A young policeman beckoned me to get out:

'Your right back light is not working; did you know about it?' he asked.

'I'm afraid not, sir, since I don't usually take it out at night,' I replied.

It went down well – fitting exactly into the picture John Hopkins had painted of me in the *Sunday Times* only a few weeks before. He had made me out to be a real bore. According to the article, I studied all the time and certainly did not have the sports car image of the superstar with glamorous girl in tow. It was not quite the true picture, but instead of my Spitfire, this certainly was not a flashy car, and here I was making out that I didn't venture out at night either. There had been a photo accompanying the article and for one minute I thought I saw a shade of recognition cross his face then it was gone.

'Is this your car?' he asked.

'No, I borrowed it from a friend.'

'Do you possess a driving licence?' he went on.

I nodded and flipped through my wallet. I held my breath. I knew the question about the expired tax would come next. But no.

'Can you reproduce your signature for me here, please?' he asked, wanting proof that it really was my driving licence ... then it suddenly dawned on me – he was having me on. He had recognized me straight away and just wanted an excuse to stop me and get my autograph! I looked up and saw him break into a grin.

'Thanks very much, JPR.'

I walked round to the back of the car. The right back light was working perfectly well – but the tax had still expired.

That summer was pretty lax as far as my clinical work was concerned. I spent a few weeks touring – but these were very different affairs from the Lions tour. One was to Paris for the 'Old Purples' escapade, going straight down to Devon afterwards for the St Mary's tennis tour. Later that summer I was off to Sri Lanka for a rugby tour* with London Welsh.

About that time, I began to think seriously about getting myself qualified. Had I not gone to New Zealand with the

* Described in Chapter 8.

Lions I should have been taking finals with the rest of the lads in the spring, but I didn't have the required three years' clinical training. I was, however, able to take an external degree, the 'Conjoint' exam which takes place four times a year. This involves three sets of exams set by the Royal College of Surgeons and the Royal College of Physicians. One could take any of them at any time, and could space them out as one pleased. I decided that it would be good revision and would also be an insurance policy in case anything were to go wrong in the MB finals later in October 1973. I took the obstetrics paper first, after a week's revision back home in Bridgend. 'Read up and learn twenty side-effects of the pill,' my mother had suggested, and tested me at meal-times. Side-effects of the pill came up. I passed the exam and felt that I was a third of the way there. The next paper was medicine on 1 January – a silly date to hold an exam.

All the exams take place in Examining Hall, Queen's Square, in London and the exam days there became a ritual. I would always take the Tube to Euston Square and walk down Woburn Place, exactly the same way each day. There were lots of other routes I could have used, but I stuck to the one which was lucky for me. Scilla, for instance, always took the Tube to Holburn and walked up. The cloakroom was always crowded, full of overseas students, many of whom had flown over specially – and everyone would be making for the loo. Then we had to walk up three or four flights of stairs, *en masse*; it was just like a big pilgrimage. There was usually an hour or so between papers at lunchtime and there were two pubs to choose from, one at either end of Queen's Square. It was a matter of pride to sink at least one pint and it was sometimes a help to have a couple if there were vivas (orals) in the afternoon. I wore my Lions tie on viva days, mainly because I was proud of it and because it matched my three-piece suit, but I can't deny that I secretly hoped it might be a talking point. As it happened, during the medicine viva, the examiner latched on to it straight away and started asking me questions about

93

rugby and the tour.

At the end of the interview he took me over to the window. Here we go, I thought – the tree speech, just as I was beginning to think I had got off lightly. That speech was a euphemism for letting you know gently that you'd failed. 'See that tree over there?' the examiner would say. 'Well go away and learn something and come back when the leaves are turning brown.'

There I was at the window. 'See that tree over there?' he asked. 'Do you happen to know what it is called?' I had no idea – it was a laburnum, I was told. He smiled and said, 'I just wanted to know if you had any other interests and knew anything about trees.' A mean trick. Still, he hadn't wanted to know whether I knew anything about medicine – I must have done better in the paper than I thought.

The third and final exam was surgery, in March. Swotting during the rugby season hadn't been the best preparation and it was the most difficult of the lot. There are three vivas as well as the written paper and viva day is really exhausting. The anatomical vivas are held in the pathology museum in the Royal College itself and it is an extremely awe-inspiring place. The tie had not worked very well so far that day and the anatomy viva was no exception. The examiner grilled me with question upon question and showed me pot upon pot (specimen jars). The final pot was a spleen. As I walked out of the room, he called me back. 'Make sure *you* don't end up with a ruptured spleen with those tackles of yours.' He had known all along. I later found out that he would have loved to ask me about rugby, but I was in line for the Gold Medal so he just had to limit the questions to surgery or anatomy. I didn't get the Gold Medal, of course, but hearing that I was ever considered was enough for me to decide to go ahead with my ambition to become a surgeon.

The announcement of the exam results in Conjoint is barbaric. At the end of viva day, everyone gathers downstairs in the cramped cloakroom and waits whilst one of the secretaries from Examining Hall reads out the numbers of the successful candidates. Those who have failed have to walk up the stairs in full view of the rest and those who have passed can walk proudly out of the door. It is agony waiting and hoping you'll hear your number called. Inevitably there is a long gap just before it is called and it seems as though they are failing everybody. For the surgery exam it is totally different – those who have passed are invited up the stairs to be accepted formally into the Royal College, since we are still on the premises. It is a very grand occasion, taking part in a procession led by the elders of the College who are decked in crimson gowns. It really made the day special for me because there was something to commemorate my achievement of qualifying at last. I had finally replaced Mr with Dr after six years of studying. The irony is that I spent another five studying to be able to replace Dr with Mr and become a Fellow, instead of just a Member, of the Royal College of Surgeons.

5

Wales and the Grand Slams

1971

Having just missed out on the 'Grand Slam' in 1969 by drawing in France, we were determined to go one better two years later when we were in with a chance. John Dawes had at last become established as Welsh captain and furthermore we all had the incentive of a Lions tour to New Zealand that summer.

The home matches were against England and Ireland, and these were won fairly easily. The away games, however, were full of incident and remain much more of a memory to me. In the Scotland game we seemed to be in control until the Scots hit back with two quick tries, one from the front of a line-out and the other from a charged-down clearance kick from John Bevan, the winger now playing rugby league for Warrington. Chris Rea, now with the BBC, was on to it in a flash to score near the posts. The Scottish captain, Peter Brown, who had been kicking goals all day, unaccountably missed the conversion, which meant we were four points behind and not six. I remember thinking at the time that that would prove to be a costly miss. And I was right.

We came back with only five minutes to go and forced a line-out in the Scottish twenty-five. Delme Thomas leaped high (was there help from Denzil Williams?) and the ball was spun out quickly to the three-quarters. I came into the line and the ball was in Gerald Davies's hands. I could see that the Scottish

full-back, Ian Smith, was not far enough across and Gerald
had little difficulty in scoring far out to the right. So it all
depended on the conversion, and a difficult one it was, too.
JT (John Taylor), who kicked around the corner with his left
foot, strode up to take the kick, looking full of confidence.
However, even JT admitted afterwards that he was nervous.
There was a deathly hush as the ball sped on its way. Then the
touch judge flags were raised and you could almost hear Bill
McLaren's gasp of despair in the commentary box. No wonder
it was called the 'greatest conversion since St Paul'!

Again, on reflection, I can remember thinking confidently
that JT would put it over. Why I don't know, but perhaps that
summed up the great spirit and confidence that the players in
the team had in each other.

There was just France to go. This is where we had come
unstuck in 1969 and what a pressure game it turned out to be.
The French had most of the territorial advantage and were
pounding away on our line. I pulled off a tackle on their right
wing, Roger Bougarel and then there they came again. JT
was coming across and I could see he had Bougarel covered.
I suddenly decided that he was going to pass. I don't know what
made me do it but I went for the interception, something I
never do usually. Probably because of the previous tackle
Bougarel had decided not to take me on again. Anyway,
suddenly I was in possession, running towards the French line.
I had breached the first line of defence but could see the opposite
centre and wing coming across. Denzil Williams was up with me
somehow, but I was leaving him behind – after all he was
a prop. I realized I was running out of time as I was being
caught by the two French defenders. At the last minute I caught
a glimpse of Gareth Edwards out of the corner of my eye. How
he had got there I never will know. So, I jinked in-field to
check the two defenders and threw a big pass out to Gareth,
going at full speed for the corner. He just made it and we had
scored three points instead of having at least three scored against
us. It was interesting seeing the try on film, and observing just

how much Gareth was carrying his leg, for it was at this stage of his career that he was having so much trouble with his hamstring. This was especially so later that year in New Zealand, though he suffered less as the years went by. We all said it was 'rust' from him spending so much time in the water, fishing!

The rest of the match saw continual pressure from France, although we managed to get a further six points. They scored one converted try from Dauga and so the score was 9–5 when BJ (Barry John) felled Dauga with an amazing tackle in front of the posts. Barry was not renowned for his tackling, especially against big forwards, and he sustained a broken nose in the collision. Some of the lads teased him that his nose had got in the way and brought Dauga to the ground. There was one more tremendous tackle from John Bevan, again a last ditch affair and then the whistle went – we had won the 'Grand Slam'.

That evening Merv and I took over behind the bar in the Winston Churchill pub in Paris. The owner didn't seem to mind and we thoroughly enjoyed the hospitality into the early hours of the morning.

The strength of our side then was our workman-like pack with the very mobile back row of Dai Morris, Mervyn Davies and John Taylor. However, it was our backs who were the trumps and this was made possible by the best pair of half-backs I have played with – Gareth Edwards and Barry John. They were tremendous individually, but it was as a combination that they excelled. It was interesting that the previous season they had not played too well together, especially in Ireland. However, that twelve months in 1971 they were supreme, culminating in the winning of the Test series in New Zealand.

1976

We had to wait five years before our next 'Grand Slam'. This shows how elusive it is, because we had been doing well, but not able to win all four matches in the same season.

Mervyn Davies had taken over the captaincy and the side had developed into a very strong one. We had begun the previous season with our surprisingly easy win in France with six or seven new caps. Then came the tour to Hong Kong and Japan, followed by the visit to Australia in the November. Thus we had had very good preparation and quite a few matches together. Our first game at Twickenham was a bit of a triumph for me. We had made our usual hesitant start at HQ but settled down after about fifteen minutes. I managed to score two tries for the first time in an International and the media described it as 'my match'. But I did not look on it like this. I have never believed that the players actually scoring points are the heroes. It is a team game and every player is equally important. But, I must confess to a few tears on scoring the second try and making the game safe. They overplayed my supposed 'heroism' just because I had blood streaming down my face for the second try. I had received eight stitches the previous week over the right eye in a game for London Welsh against Bath and went on to receive another piece of embroidery under my left eye after this match. The annoying thing was that the second cut kept on oozing, right up to the dinner. Incredibly, I could find no one who had any tissues! The presence of the persistent blood seemed to convince everyone except me that I was a 'war hero'!

The last game of the season was against France at Cardiff and there was a shock at the beginning when Mervyn Davies sustained a burst blood vessel in his calf. It was a really tough match and we were rather lucky to hold out in the end. I managed to pull off a tackle on Gourdon to prevent him scoring and then the final whistle went – the 'Grand Slam' had been won again.

1978

It was our turn to lose in the Wales–France game in 1977 and although completely outplayed we lost fairly narrowly to a side containing the mighty Bastiat and that magnificent pair of flankers – Jean-Claude Skrela and Jean-Paul Rives. A few of us teamed up afterwards with these jubilant French players in a 'night-club crawl' where we drank Moet-et-Chandon champagne all night on their success. I have never had such a good head the morning after: a reflection on the quality of the drink.

The following year we had a new captain in Phil Bennett, following Mervyn's tragic accident.

Again we played England and Ireland away and Scotland and France at home. We started at Twickenham in atrocious conditions and sneaked home 9–6. Gareth had a great game and really 'killed' the English forwards with his kicking.

Scotland at home was a funny game. We were well ahead and seemed to relax, whereupon the Scots came back and made the score quite close in the end. It was interesting how much better Scotland played when they became more adventurous. This has been one of the criticisms of the Scottish team and they certainly showed what they could do when they moved the ball.

Another amazing thing happened that weekend. It had snowed a few days before the match but South Wales as usual had got off lightly. The day of the match it was bitterly cold and everyone said it was too cold to snow. But we were in for a shock. It started to snow immediately the match ended and we all watched it coming down at the dinner in the evening. We were sure it would be gone the following morning. We were wrong. South Wales was hit by a freak blizzard – all traffic was at a standstill and though some of the players made an attempt to get home we were advised to stay put. After the initial shock we settled down to enjoy ourselves – it was just like being on tour again, only this time in Cardiff. The players who tried to get out of Cardiff were unsuccessful and so they returned and we were all marooned in the Angel Hotel.

It could have been much worse. At least, we had all organized family baby-sitters, since we knew we would be staying one night – and we were in the best hotel in Cardiff. But soon the wives started to worry about their children and the phone calls home were getting more and more frequent. Worse was to follow for us, as we lived out in the country and the snow had drifted up against the tall hedgerows so that there were solid banks of snow up to ten foot across the lanes. The farmers near us were in a terrible plight since they could not dispatch their milk to the dairies and were having to pour churns of it away. At least Lauren, our daughter, was not short of fresh farm milk those few days! Luckily I was able to get to work, but we couldn't get back to see Lauren who was being looked after by Scilla's mother. Scilla eventually got home on the Tuesday and I managed to return on the Wednesday. Even so, we had to hike the last two miles over fields as the lanes were cut off. Eventually, the snow plough got through to us at 6 p.m. on Wednesday evening, but it was an experience I will never forget. The irony of the weekend was that the Scottish players had managed to get back to Scotland the next day by heading off east down the M4 which had very little snow, but the Welsh players could not manage even ten or twenty miles.

We travelled to Dublin in 1978 with a chance of the Triple Crown – a unique achievement. I have never known the Irish so 'uptight' before a game and we suffered much abuse from the press and public over there. The game had been going our way when suddenly the Irish really came back at us and they looked like scoring.

I later obstructed Mike Gibson marginally and the whole stadium erupted. I thought I was going to be lynched on the spot. I have never been so abused during a game and it was probably contributory to a horrendous mistake I made when I mis-kicked on my line to allow Ireland to score and draw level at 13–13. Luckily for me and the Welsh team JJ scored a winning try, albeit with a hint of obstruction in mid-field.

I have never felt so upset after a game, with the exception of the Tommy Bedford incident in Natal (see chapter 9). I immediately apologized to Mike afterwards and we sorted it out amongst ourselves in a friendly way. However, the insults were still being thrown and I'm afraid I let myself become involved in the furore by saying some rash and stupid things in the heat of the moment after the game and these were widely quoted by the media.

The tackle was late, but was completely unintentional – a reflex action. In no way would I deliberately obstruct a player as people claimed I did. I am only sorry it happened between myself and a great player and good friend of mine. There is no such thing as a 'professional foul' in rugby – but there are very few players who do not realize that whilst defending, a stoppage of play can result in three points whereas an un-interrupted run to the line can result in six.

So, in the last game against France we again had a chance of a complete sweep. France went into the lead – not unusual against us, but we fought back to win 16–7, in a game which I thought was a bit of an anti-climax. Once we got ahead the French seemed to lose heart and there was never really any chance that we would lose then. As often, when a game is billed as the battle of the giants and everyone has great anticipation of a tight contest, it never quite turns out as expected.

The Welsh crowd, in spite of their 'will to win', enjoyed a close contest and they seemed almost disappointed that we had won by a good margin. But I also feel that during the recent successes over the past decade they have become a bit quieter – almost taking victory for granted. A win was not good enough, it either had to be a close win or had to be by thirty points. This sums up the competitiveness of the Welsh and, I believe, the reason why Gareth, Gerald, Mervyn and I were able to maintain our standard. If you had a bad game you knew the public would be calling for you to be dropped – whoever you were. This carries the saying 'you're only as good as your last game' to the extreme. However, it was not only the matches during the 'Grand Slam' seasons that gave me great enjoyment and satisfaction. There were many other games which stand out in my memory – mostly because of incidents involving me in particular.

No one ever forgets his first cap, and I am no exception.

I was treated like royalty by the lads at St Mary's for the first few days after the news of my selection, and fortunately, I was out of reach of the media down in Wales. It is perhaps as well that I did not see some of the reactions of the Welsh sports writers to my selection, because there was a fair amount of scepticism!

'Dangers caused by his lack of positional sense . . .'

'Wales will live dangerously with Williams behind them.'

'Faulty with line-kicking . . .'

'Williams could win matches for Wales, but he could well also lose them too.'

As it was I did not read some of these criticisms until many years later, but on the big day I was able to play a more orthodox full-back game anyway, because our forwards surprised the Scots by more than matching them and with plenty of possession we were able to score three tries to win by 17–3. Merv had played an exceptionally good game, also his first for Wales, and we both had plenty to celebrate that Saturday night, despite our 'premature selections'. It was ironic that we both had a meteoric rise to fame under the guidance and influence of John Dawes, during those first few months playing for London Welsh, but that 'Syd' (John Dawes) himself had not been selected for that Murrayfield game, and was to wait till later in the season to re-find favour with the Welsh selectors.

My first experience of playing at the 'old' Cardiff Arms Park came when I maintained my place for the Wales–Ireland game. I could not believe the atmosphere down there on the pitch. Although I had attended matches there with my father, when I was younger, for some reason I thought that only the crowd would hear all the noise and the singing. It was unfortunate that I did not see the pitch at its best as the new stadium was being built, and there were patches of bare earth, with bits of straw floating around on top. There were also a couple of unsavoury punch-ups amongst the forwards to mar the game, but none of these things really spoilt my day – when I fulfilled a childhood dream, and played for Wales at the Arms Park.

To top it all, the team to fly to Paris was announced the following day and I was included again: it really looked as if I was quietening those critics after all. We did remarkably well in Paris that year and held the French to an 8–8 draw. And we could have won, had Keith Jarrett had a happier day with his goal-kicking. Altogether he missed seven kicks at goal, including one in the last minutes of the game when Gerald Davies had been double tackled and had dislocated his elbow. The replacement on the right wing was none other than Phil Bennett, who ran on for his first senior cap.

Anyway, we were still in line for the Triple Crown, albeit not the 'Grand Slam', and the match at the Arms Park, with a decisive 30–9 win over England, really clinched it. It was almost too good to be true – four caps for Wales, finishing with the Triple Crown, all in my first season – and even the possibility of a trip to New Zealand.

We really came down to earth with a bump in New Zealand, but were still contending for the Triple Crown in 1970. It was Scotland and France at home, but it was those tough matches, England and Ireland away, which we knew we would have trouble with. Just before the England game I injured my right knee and there was doubt over my fitness for the match. Incredibly, the player asked to stand by, in case I did not make it, was Grahame Hodgson, who had been teaching in Bridgend, and giving me invaluable help, whilst I was still at the under-15 stage. He had not played for Wales for six years and must have been a little surprised, if not a little non-plussed, to have to act as reserve to little John Williams.

Fortunately for me, his services were not required and I was able to make my first appearance at HQ since those under-15 days. By half-time, the score was 13–3 and we looked like losing by quite a margin. Then England seemed to relax their hold a little, and Barry John was able to sneak an easy try which I failed to convert. I had been kicking a fair amount for London Welsh and was trying to fill the goal-kicking gap which Keith Jarrett had left in the Welsh team on his decision to play rugby league. After all it was traditionally the role of full-back to kick goals, if nothing else. Now, that role seems to be taken over, or shared at least with the fly-half, or anyone in the side with an accurate boot. It seems a much better arrangement.

But in 1970, for some reason, Barry John was not taking kicks, although he went on to break goal-kicking records the following year in New Zealand!

Anyway, I had a chance to make amends later on in the match, when I scored my very first try for Wales, after a cheeky pass from Chico Hopkins down the blind side. Chico had come on in place of Gareth Edwards, just beforehand, and was making the most of his first cap by playing the match of his life. Just before the final whistle, he levelled the score with a magically quick try from a line-out. Everything depended upon the conversion. Gareth (captain that day) and I had shared the kicks up till his injury, and between us, we had missed three penalties and three conversions: a stark contrast to the accurate kicking of Bob Hiller for England. So it was left to me to take the conversion – what a relief to see it sail through the posts, and what a roar from the Welsh contingent in the crowd!

I was not to know then that BJ was to drop a magnificent goal from forty yards only minutes later to put the final nail in England's coffin, so that conversion had shown a great triumph of nerve, rather than skill on my part. I was celebrating my tenth cap for Wales that day, and my twenty-first birthday on the following Monday, so I had plenty to celebrate that weekend.

After all that euphoria, I had a taste of failure and controversy in 1970 in that fateful match over in Ireland, where the whole Welsh team played badly to lose both the match to Ireland, and the chance of a successive Triple Crown. And I was to become involved in controversy for the first time. Wales were well beaten by Ireland in Dublin and Gareth Edwards, then captain, and I were reported to have had a big argument. I have since learned that any Welsh defeat is always accompanied by incredible stories made up by Welsh fans, sometimes journalists, in an attempt to find a reason for the defeat. Since I was still goal-kicking in those days I was supposed to have been upset with Gareth for not giving me the kicks at goal. We even had a supposed punch-up in the dressing-room after the game and later were supposed to steal each other's girlfriends! This was rather disturbing to us both at the time as nothing of the kind had occurred. Also nothing like it had happened to us before and we were annoyed that such lies could be circulated.

After having no attempts at goal that day, it was rather a surprise to find myself in the Arms Park later that season kicking over two penalty goals and one conversion, to contribute to an 11–6 win over the French. Much of the success must be attributed to John Dawes, who had by then returned to the side, and had taken over the captaincy in the same decisive manner as he had shown as captain up at London Welsh. His confidence in my ability to kick must have had a lot to do with my success that day.

But my goal-kicking days were numbered, as Barry John rose to prominence the following year, and continued thereafter as the goal-kicker *par excellence*. I was more relieved than upset to lose that role, since I felt it took a great deal of pressure (and criticism) off me, and enabled me to concentrate on developing my own particular style of full-back play.

That season we also played South Africa for the last time at the 'old' Cardiff Arms Park. This was the only occasion that I have witnessed the infamous mud. The players were soon unrecognizable and Gareth rescued us with a try near the end for a 6–6 draw. What was amazing was that Phil Bennett played on the wing that day with his opposite number almost twice his size.

Wales *v* England 1971 was memorable as I sustained a depressed fracture of my right cheekbone when running into Gareth Edwards's head – not a clever thing to do. I managed to play the rest of the game out and then went back to London on the Sunday to have it operated on the following week.

The Scotland game in Cardiff the following year was one of my saddest days. I had been involved in an unpleasant incident early in the game with Peter Brown, the Scottish captain. The next time Scotland won the ball they put up a towering up and under. I could see the whole Scottish pack descending on me as I caught the ball: I was knocked out, but unwisely carried on. Some minutes later, Billy Steele was put clear on the right wing with only me to beat. I anticipated his 'jink' but unfortunately mistimed my tackle and his knees hit me on the face. I am a great believer that the *timing* is the crucial part of a good tackle, but I'm sure my previous concussions caused me to misjudge my movements. As it was, I didn't know what had happened except that I had saved a certain try. The reaction of my team mates said it all when I opened my eyes – they all looked grey. My upper jaw had caved in and there was no alternative – to go off the field. I was carried off on a stretcher in a state of shock and taken to Cardiff Royal Infirmary. The crowd could not believe it – they had never seen me really injured before. Apparently, my foot moved as the stretcher was almost clear of the pitch and people started saying: 'He's ok – he'll be back on in a few minutes . . .'!

The Infirmary was deserted – very unusual for a Saturday afternoon but not unusual in view of the fact that Wales were playing at home. I had some X-rays taken and listened to the rest of the game on the wireless. Gareth scored a great try that day and 'Benny' (Phil Bennett) moved to full-back when I went off. Just after the end of the game the facio-maxillary specialist Mr Russell Hopkins arrived – straight from the Arms Park. He looked at the X-rays and my jaw and gave me a choice: he could either reduce the fracture under full general anaesthetic or have a go under local (anaesthetic). I knew the former would mean staying in hospital overnight, so I chose the latter. My jaw already felt numb anyway. Mr Hopkins pulled my jaw straight and then put a metal brace on to keep it in place. Then came the good news – he told me I had to take some alcohol to relieve the pain. This was the first time I had ever been prescribed alcohol medicinally. Afterwards I returned to the Angel Hotel to join in the after-match festivities. While I had no trouble with the alcohol, I found the steak a little difficult to manage!

Luckily for me, the next International was not two weeks away, as it so often is, but a full five weeks, by which time I had had the brace removed and had regained confidence in the strength of the jaw. That year, the match in Ireland was cancelled because of the troubles there, and so we only played three matches, winning all of them, but forfeiting the Triple Crown, with that unplayed Irish game.

The Home Championship in 1973 was the year when the home side won on every occasion and thus there was a four-way split: a very unusual occurrence. 1974 was Wales's worst season for ages with only one win against Scotland at home, two draws against Ireland away and France at home and a rare loss against England. This was the season preceding the Lions tour to South Africa and so it was perhaps surprising that so many Welsh players were selected.

Ireland won the Championship and thus it was only appropriate that Syd Millar and Willie-John McBride were invited to manage the highly successful Lions tour.

1975 saw the emergence of a new Welsh side, beginning with the surprise win in Paris using six new caps. Wales had been struggling for several years to find a settled pack of forwards. Good scrummagers were at a premium and so we were fortunate to have the 'Pontypool Front Row'. Charlie Faulkner was almost unheard of, even in Wales at this time, but soon made a name for himself even though already in the 'twilight' of his rugby career. Bobby Windsor was at his peak, while Graham Price was the youngster with everything in front of him. He has since established himself in many eyes as the best tight-head-prop in the world today, with sufficient mobility to enable him to score tries like the one in his début for Wales in Paris.

Allan Martin and Geoff Wheel complemented each other ideally in the power house and between them in the scrum was the incomparable Mervyn Davies. He took over the captaincy and lead by example. The flankers were Terry Cobner and Trevor Evans with Tommy David being the automatic replacement on one or two occasions.

While our pack from 1976–8 was superb, we tended to be rather stereotyped behind, and because of this I feel that 1976 was our greater year from the point of view of entertaining rugby. I think the 1978 pack were supreme, but our rugby in 1976 was far more exciting and this was reflected in the number of points that were scored.

It is a shame that this Welsh side never had a chance to play New Zealand as it was at its peak between the two visits in 1974 and 1978.

I have been so lucky to have played with so many outstanding Welsh players in my time that it is very difficult to compare individuals. However, for choice I would pick the 1976 pack with the 1971 three-quarters as my ideal Welsh team.

6

Touring with Wales

in Australia and other
far away places

Argentina 1968

Having played twelve or so games for Bridgend in the 1967–8 season, I was delighted, though slightly surprised, to find myself picked to tour Argentina with the Welsh side. This was not the full Welsh team because a large number of players had just returned from the 1968 Lions tour of South Africa. Very few teams had had any experience of playing against the Argentinians and I can remember being amazed by their high standard of play. I'm sure the Welsh selectors were also amazed and may well have regretted sending only a second string team! Nowadays, they are certainly making their presence felt and have since impressed greatly on their overseas tours.

The captain of the touring party in 1968 was (Sydney) John Dawes, who up until that time I had not met. I had no idea then of the enormous influence he was later to have on my playing career. He seemed such an important person to me as captain, whilst I was only barely out of school, that I could not envisage the idea of developing a lasting friendship with one so distant. My big mate from tennis, Gareth James, was playing well for London Welsh at the time and I was a shock selection, with him named as stand-by reserve.

The tour was a difficult one for many reasons and our results were disastrous. The refereeing left much to be desired, but it is always difficult to make any positive changes as a result of such refereeing. The fact remains that it is difficult to substantiate any complaints; these are always deemed 'sour grapes'. Those who watched the World Cup in 1978 may also have had their suspicions about the impartiality of the referees when Argentina were playing.

The first problem was that we stayed about twenty miles out of Buenos Aires for most of the tour, in a country club. This was well equipped and situated in very pleasant surroundings, but four weeks of isolation there proved a little too much for such experienced 'tourists' as Billy Mainwaring and Max Wiltshire. As far as I was concerned just to be on tour was a thrill so it didn't matter whether I was in the North Pole or the desert. Looking back, with the experience of other tours behind me, I can see that most of the players were bored to tears. There was a good golf course at the club – but even fanatics cannot play golf all day, every day!

An amusing incident occurred on one of the few nights when we were allowed into Buenos Aires – I suppose it was after one of the matches. One of our large forwards let off a stink bomb in the middle of a noisy night-club; this caused such a commotion that everyone was banished from the club. The following morning a serious team meeting was called. The manager of the tour asked the culprit to own up. The sight of this particular forward standing up to his enormous height, going pink and admitting it was *his* doing was so funny that everyone, including the manager, collapsed with laughter. It was rather a childish incident but I think it emphasized how short we were of things to occupy our minds those four weeks.

Our second problem was that of coping with the crowd at the games. The Argentinians, as everyone knows, are very volatile and their Latin American temperaments were very much on display at the grounds. I have never been so frightened on a rugby field in all my life and probably never will be again. Bottles, beer cans, coins, programmes, even fireworks, came hurtling on to the pitch, and it was a miracle that no one got badly injured. Not only were we trying to side-step the opposition, we were also dodging the missiles. We had heard that a referee had been shot a couple of months before we arrived and seeing the crowd's behaviour it seemed quite a plausible occurrence. Then when Manchester United played Estudiantes in a brutal match, I began to wonder just what sort of a place Argentina was. We were fortunate to meet some of the Manchester United players before their match and it was quite a thrill at that age to come face to face with household names such as Bobby Charlton and George Best.

The local fans started calling me 'Canasta'. I assumed this was some derogatory term – perhaps describing my inexperience and youth. I was flattered to learn later that it meant 'basket' so it appeared I was at least performing adequately in their eyes. Our supporters (Welsh) on that tour have never forgotten that nickname and some of them remind me of it today when they see me from time to time.

We lost the Test series 1–0 with one drawn and I remember the effect on our morale when the English referee, Ken John who had been given one game to control, pulled a muscle when we were leading 9–0 and had to leave the field. Our fortunes in that first Test suddenly took a downward trend, following his departure.

Although many people were quick to point out that we were only a second team our return to Wales was an unhappy event. That didn't help our morale either, as many of us were hoping to gain full caps. In spite of the poor results, it was excellent experience for me. In fact, *because* of the poor results, it went without saying that I was under pressure the whole time I played and my defensive game must have improved considerably.

At that stage I had been playing for Bridgend whilst studying in London and playing only a few games for St Mary's. This

was obviously not a very satisfactory position to be in especially
as the other full-back (David Griffiths) at Bridgend was playing
well and was also vice-captain of the club. It was fortuitous
that I should become friendly with John Dawes on the tour.
I had discussed my position with him, when he challenged me
about my future club rugby plans, but I was in no position to
make any definite decisions.

John was firmly established as captain of the highly successful
London Welsh Club. In playing at least six sides every Saturday
they were certainly not short of players. Anyway, they already
had a good full-back in Gar James. To make matters worse,
since he was a close friend, though a little older, from my tennis
days, I was very reluctant to set up in direct opposition to him.
I had almost decided at the back of my mind to carry on playing for Bridgend and St Mary's until perhaps Gareth James
decided to retire – when fate stepped in.

The Saturday after our return from Argentina, I was due to
play for St Mary's *v* Old Cranleians, while London Welsh were
due to play at Richmond. On the Friday night, Gareth dropped
out with a shoulder injury. Club policy was that the second
team (Dragons) full-back should automatically step in. There
was an emergency meeting and John Dawes insisted I should
play – not for the sixth team as it should have been, but for
his side. Obviously, I was delighted to have been asked so
unexpectedly, but it was a difficult situation, not only from the
point of view of the London Welsh. Having promised to play
for St Mary's I had a certain loyalty to them – I knew I would
(hopefully) be there for five–six years, and that had I not been
a Welsh Schoolboy International, I might never have been
offered a place there. I spent a long time on the phone that
Friday night, explaining the position to the captain, secretary
and president (Dr Tommy Kemp, the ex-England International
fly-half) of the rugby club at St Mary's. They were not at all
happy at my playing for London Welsh and I did not sleep
much that night, worrying whether I had made the right
decision.

Anyway, the game went well and I was never to regret that decision, since I went on to play for London Welsh for eight glorious seasons. But I was always aware that if Gareth had not been injured for that particular game, so soon after the tour, I might never have had my chance with London Welsh.

The 1968–9 season was important as I still had not won a full cap. I eventually achieved this at Murrayfield in February 1969. The newly adopted Welsh squad system had enabled me to train with and gain experience from the established Welsh players and this helped greatly in making my first full game for Wales a marvellous occasion. After the initial worry that I might let everyone down I was not at all nervous once the game started and in fact I ran the ball the first time I touched it.

That season was successful and we set off for New Zealand in high spirits and with great hopes.

New Zealand, Australia and Fiji 1969

This was a really exciting tour. I had needed to make special arrangements with the Dean of St Mary's to obtain permission to miss the last six weeks of term, including the first year exams. It was arranged that I would take the exams at the beginning of the new term along with the 'Re-sits'. This meant giving up most of the summer vacation to study – but it was worth it. To tour New Zealand at that early stage in my rugby career was a marvellous chance.

My first impression of the New Zealanders was that they were even more fanatical than the Welsh about rugby. I just couldn't believe it. We received a fantastic reception after travelling thirteen thousand miles without a stop-over, but were soon to discover that their hospitality did not extend to the rugby pitch.

We drew our first game against Taranaki 9–9, having picked only half the side which had won the Triple Crown in April. It wasn't a very good gamble, since we badly needed a win to start with. I remember misjudging some of my touch kicks and feeling miserable about my performance. Even the fact that I had scored a try did not cheer me too much. We all knew we could do better. The pessimism which we carried with us to the first Test at Canterbury was justified. We took a hiding, 19–0 from one of the most efficient All Blacks sides I may ever see. Their huge forwards, including Ken Gray, Ian Kirkpatrick, Colin Meads and Brian Lochore, won ruck after ruck and steamrolled their way down the field, with Sid Going playing brilliantly behind them. To make matters worse Gareth Edwards was playing under the threat of a hamstring injury. We just didn't have a chance. I had plenty to do all afternoon and felt I had earned my place on the tour, but it seemed an awful long way to come for such a hiding. That day taught me more about the technique of turning my back against the on-coming forwards after fielding the ball than all my rugby years up until then.

We were all dreadfully depressed that night and I remember most of us phoned home, a practice common on later tours, but at that time a phone call to the other side of the world seemed extortionate.

I phoned Scilla at her parents' home in Buxton – she had been taking lecture notes for me during my absence – only to find myself talking to her sister. Melanie had been waiting by the phone all day to hear from her boyfriend a few miles away and she was furious to find that it was not he, but a chap phoning all the way from New Zealand for Scilla.

Somehow the morale in the side picked up after that first Test defeat, although the tour was never the same for Jeff Young who had his jaw broken by Colin Meads and also had to put up with being penalized for it at the same time. For the match which followed against Otago we had a desperate 'do or die' attitude. Defeat was unthinkable, if we were to restore some of our pride and self-respect – we had left Wales as European Champions and had not really struggled during the previous season.

Well, we did save the tour, with a 27–9 win, including three brilliant tries by Maurice Richards and some beautiful kicks by Keith Jarrett. But it was the pack, with a much improved performance, which heartened us all. Mervyn Davies was splendid, having got to grips with the line-out tactics used in New Zealand, and Delme Thomas proved that he was challenging for a Test place. The happiest man of all was Clive Rowlands (Welsh coach) who had spent a nightmarish afternoon in bed with 'flu, having to listen to the match on the radio. Just before the first of Maurice Richards's tries, the commentary was broken by the news and he had to listen to each news item before he heard that Maurice had scored.

We then went on to play even better against Wellington who were easily the best provincial side we had met – talented, full of initiative and determination. The score was 14–6, with Wales scoring the only tries.

Perhaps we were over-confident in our approach to the second Test. Certainly we were showing that our backs, given a smattering of possession, were scoring more easily than the New Zealanders with a good deal more ball to use.

But on the day we lost the second Test 32–12, in a game which we could have won. We kept up with the All Blacks in scoring try for try, but we were heavily penalized, to the delight of Fergie McCormick, who set a world Test record with a total of twenty-four points. The sight of Pat Murphy, the referee, jumping in the air following a dropped goal by McCormick, will live with me for the rest of my life.

So, we had lost the Test series 2–0 and thus we had failed. But it was the turning point for our backs, many of whom were to return two years later with the Lions. We were beginning to find a way around the forward domination we had come to expect (and admire, I might add) from the men in black.

From Auckland we flew to Sydney for a Test match against Australia on the Sydney cricket ground. Relieved to be playing against ordinary mortals once more we came back from 11–0 down to win 19–16 in the pouring rain and felt we had restored a little more Welsh faith down under. We then wrapped up the tour with a flourish at Buckhurst Park, Fiji and made the most of our short stop-over in this beautiful island. It was a superb game, played under the scorching sun, in front of some ten thousand spectators, many of whom were hanging from trees. The local drink was made of coconut oil and tasted like mud, but we had to drink it as part of a ceremony – to refuse would have been an insult.

After the game, we showered and with towels round our waists went straight to the beer area – open air, of course. It was late in the evening before we had stopped sweating from the game and could get dressed, but many of us ended up wearing the Fijian *sarongs* instead of our tour kit. Some of these found their way on to the plane. It was a funny sight at Heathrow, seeing the lads with their red and white flowered skirts, Welsh blazers and black shoes!

My memories of the game itself are two: that of Dennis Hughes playing at lock scoring three tries, and of my dropping a rare fifty-yard goal. It was an ideal finish to the tour which had been so tough up until then. To play two Test matches against New Zealand in a tour shorter than six weeks will hopefully never be attempted again. Considering the odds our tour record was reasonable, with four wins and one draw, but it was the enormity of our Test defeats which marred what could have been a proud record.

Canada 1973

This was a far more relaxed tour than my previous two with Wales. I had visited Canada before – once in 1967 when I had won the Canadian Open Junior Tennis Tournament and again in 1970 after passing second MB when I toured with the Middlesex side – so I had very pleasant memories of Canadian hospitality.

I was again fortunate in being at a stage in my medical training when I was in a position to have some time off. I had qualified as a doctor on the London Conjoint examination, but had to wait till the following November to take the St Mary's final examination: MBBS. This was as a result of missing three months on the Lions tour – but it did mean that I was reasonably free to come and go as I pleased. In fact, I spent most of those six months working as a locum doctor in various hospitals around London.

We played sides in both the British and French parts of Canada and found that much the stiffest opposition came from British Columbia in our first game. There were so many British ex-patriots there it was hardly surprising that they were mad keen about rugby, even though the unions were all relatively new. We won all our games including the Test against Canada, but I'm not so sure whether Welsh sides in ten years' time will make such light work of Canadian rugby because, as in America, the game is increasing in popularity every year.

It was the first tour, for a British side, which included it's own physiotherapist and that proved an excellent addition. Mr Gerry Lewis had been physio to the Welsh team for many years, following in his father's footsteps, but he had never before travelled with the team. We had always had to make do with the local physiotherapists in the area we were playing and thus there was no continuity. We suffered many soft tissue injuries on the hard grounds in Canada and I really don't know what we would have done without him. His superb diagnostic and manipulative skill was far superior to that which any of the 'rub-a-dub' trainers could have provided and we all had (still have) great confidence in him. Back home in Wales (before, say, an International) players are prepared to travel eighty miles a day to receive treatment for a week, if Gerry says it is necessary. He was also a great help to me, as I was the 'unofficial doctor' on that tour. When a player needed a cut stitching, Gerry would sterilize all the instruments and assist at my 'operations'. It was a real pleasure to work with one so knowledgeable and dedicated. The presence of a trained physiotherapist also meant that we did not have to send for replacements, which I'm sure would have been necessary otherwise. Since then Gerry has been with us to Hong Kong and Japan in 1975 and Australia in 1978.

Our flight home was a little irregular: we were scheduled to land at Gatwick, and would have arrived there had the airport not closed for the night. So we were redirected to Heathrow and looked as if we were not going to be allowed to land there either until our referee on the tour, a prominent RAF figure, managed to convince the air traffic controllers to let us through. Even so we were well over fourteen hours late. Jeff Young's wife, Pat and their two small boys were with Scilla at the airport, having driven up and down from Gatwick all day, trying to entertain the little ones and still keep them clean to meet their daddy off the plane. Poor little Stephen and Robin were so tired, still up well after midnight, that there was no question of them going back to Aylesbury. So they all came back with us to our tiny flat in Wembley and took over the bedroom whilst we, married only four weeks, three of which I had spent in Canada, slept the night on the sofa!

Many people had been amazed that I went on that tour as we had only got married about ten days beforehand and arrived back from our honeymoon in Rumania just in time for me to meet up with the tour party. It wasn't even due to bad planning, because the wedding was fixed for the first Saturday after the rugby season ended, so that we could invite all my rugby friends up to Derbyshire for the occasion. The idea of taking about ten London Welsh players out of the first side was just not on.

What made it worse was that Scilla was due to take her psychiatric residency at that time. Part of the final year studies includes six weeks of psychiatry when we had to spend two weeks in an old-fashioned 'nut house', two weeks on a modern psychiatric unit involving work with drug addicts and two weeks in the psychiatric unit at St Mary's.

As I was sending off my postcards to Mrs J. P. R. Williams, Park Prewett Psychiatric Hospital, Basingstoke, UK, one of the lads saw the address, and, knowing that I'd only just got married thought the strain of that early separation had sent Scilla round the bend! As it was she was bearing up, although a little worried that there were no locks on the doors to the staff quarters. It was yet another occasion when I had to thank Scilla for her understanding. Even talking about it now there is no resentment – she always assumed I would be going on the tour, so there was really no question of arguing about it. In fact we had a second honeymoon after my return – on the premises of Park Prewitt. It was not as ridiculous as it sounds, since the grounds surrounding the hospital were beautiful, with grass tennis courts to play on, a miniature golf course and the five star treatment in the dining-room.

Hong Kong and Japan 1975

Many rugby people were greatly surprised at the Welsh Rugby Union's decision to accept the invitation tour to Japan. It seemed that the difference in standard between us would be too great to make any of the games worthwhile, but the Japanese were anxious to repay Welsh hospitality after their 1973 tour and we were anxious to get a chance to mould our new side – so it turned out well for both parties concerned.

The tour was pre-season (August) so everyone had to work on their own fitness before we left, since nobody had had the benefit of playing matches just beforehand. I remember our squad preparation for that tour being particularly tough.

This was the beginning of our great side which went on to win three Triple Crowns in a row and the Japanese experience obviously helped to develop our style of play.

The previous season had seen multiple changes in the Welsh team and the win in Paris with seven new caps was an admirable taste of what was to come, given the right directives.

We were very aware of the keen attitude of the Japanese and also how much we had to lose if we were not successful.

I had again been fortunate with the timing of the tour, because I was in fact unemployed at the time, with no problems about getting time off work. I had finished my second house-job at Hillingdon Hospital at the end of June and was filling in time with locum appointments until the academic term started when I would be taking up a lecturer's post in anatomy at St Mary's. I knew then that all my medical work would be directed towards surgery and gaining my Primary FRCS examination.

Mervyn Davies was our captain and he led by example. The amount of work this man got through was incredible. I had played with him in his first game for London Welsh and for Wales and it was amazing how much his game improved over the years. In fact one became so used to his presence that we only really appreciated him when he was no longer there, following his tragic accident in 1976. Merv was a quiet chap, but really a great character. He had an enormous amount of stamina and he never knew when he was beaten – which of course was not often. A great man to have on your side. It is interesting that Colin Meads was so impressed by Merv's play at the back of the line-out and in the loose in the 1971 tour that he felt he was one of the two players who had contributed most to the All Blacks' defeat. The other was Mike Gibson – and from Meads, that is praise indeed.

Even though our scores against the Japanese were high, we still had to work very hard especially in the first half of every game. We also felt we played well to earn those scores and that they were not just the result of poor opposition, which was how our critics saw it. All I can say is that *they* were not on the pitch butting against the Japanese. In the first 'Test' in Osaka we only got out of our own half four times, but managed to score on all four occasions. In the first half, they put us under so much pressure we would have been in real trouble had we not been able to counter-attack. In the end we wore them down and dispirited them and managed to play attacking rugby for the last twenty minutes. It is interesting that for most of those Triple Crown games which followed this was the pattern of our play.

The Japanese are so small that they have an obvious problem with their lines-out. However, they have all sorts of ingenious ploys to overcome this and here they were able to teach us a thing or two. Their scrummaging was also impressive for such small men because they packed tight and low. But the thing which impressed me most (and terrified me on occasions) was their tackling. They take off about ten yards away and hit you like a bullet.

In spite of all their obvious improvements since their Welsh tour, I was very disappointed in their attitude after the first Test. Shiggy Kono, their manager, sent them all home in disgrace and this I think reflects the difference between the philosophy of the East and West. They had let their country down and as such needed 'punishment'. Japan is so westernized today that this attitude really does seem anachronistic.

While in Tokyo, Gareth Edwards and I played a tennis match against the champions of one of the clubs there. We were down 5-1 and 40-15 and about to lose the first set. I remember appealing to Gareth's 'big match temperament' and saying we *must* win. We managed to take that set! The second set was identical and again he came back to win 7-5, 7-5. Gareth is such a natural athlete and ball player that I'm sure he could have been a top class soccer or tennis player as well as the most complete rugby player I believe I have ever seen.

Although we were invited to many receptions and offered splendid hospitality, we found the language and culture difference difficult to cope with. So as a tour party we spent a lot of time amongst ourselves, making our own entertainment. We were not short of performers, although our two best stars were the two most unlikely – our locks, Geoff Wheel and Allan Martin. Geoff plays the ukelele and accordion, both well, and Panth (Allan Martin's nickname after we had seen the Pink Panther films) accompanied all our sing-songs with his guitar.

So, the idea that the forwards were just a pack of 'donkeys' was quickly dispelled on that tour, especially after we'd visited a Sony factory and discovered that Graham Price had studied 'A' level physics and knew more about electronics than anyone on the tour.

But when Charlie Faulkner phoned home from Japan, I'm afraid he put all the forwards back in the 'donkey' class: he couldn't understand how his bill was so enormous; it was easily explained by his room-mate – he'd fallen asleep whilst on the phone!

Japan is an unusual country – so much of it is developed for factory use that there is no land left for agriculture. Most of the food is imported except the fish, which is caught locally. In fact a steak cost us about ten pounds a head. The over-development of their small island was well illustrated when we used the high speed train from Tokyo to Osaka. This travelled at almost two hundred miles an hour and during the whole journey (about eighty minutes), I don't think we moved out of built up areas. I didn't see any fields. When you think of travelling two hundred miles from Euston to Newcastle and all the countryside you pass, it makes the comparison between the two countries all the greater.

Australia 1978

It was only just before this tour that I realized that my first tour with Wales had been ten years previously. When the media started talking of me as 'old' I began to realize that I *had* been around for a long time. But I was still only twenty-nine, even though a lot of people thought I must be well into my thirties.

The tour to Australia came at the end of a very long period of pressure for many of the Welsh players. Half the party had been to New Zealand with the 1977 Lions and had undergone two heavy seasons of domestic rugby where we were playing under pressure not to lose the Triple Crown and Grand Slam prestige we had won the season before. Therefore I think many of the players were rather jaded by the time we left for Perth in May 1978.

I was in the middle of a six-month neurosurgery appointment as part of my surgical rotation and had been worried about my availability for the tour as a result of this. Fortunately, I was able to make up the five weeks' touring as part of my annual holiday plus a few weeks as part of the study leave allotted to Registrars.

I had been invited to give a lecture at North Shore Hospital, Sydney on sports medicine and to attend a number of their important ward rounds there. I know many people raised eyebrows when they heard I was taking part of the tour as study leave, so I was delighted to discover that one of the most senior orthopaedic surgeons at Cardiff was in Australia on a supporters tour. He was also able to support me on the ward rounds and report back that I was not *just* playing rugby over there.

The grounds were very hard and we sustained a lot of injuries as a result of this. Possibly the tiredness of the players also had something to do with it. We had a good welcome in Australia, and there was great interest from the public, but in certain areas where the game of 'Australian Rules' was the main attraction, our matches had to be played on Sundays to allow the crowds to attend both games.

The fact that Phil Bennett and Gareth Edwards were unable to make the tour made it certain that Wales would cap at least two new half-backs.

The first setback was our loss to Sydney on a very hot day when either side could have won. The match was lost, yet again, by a failed touch kick. It is amazing how often this has happened in big matches recently and was also responsible for the Lions losing the series in New Zealand. We recovered well from this defeat and had good wins against New South Wales and Queensland. However, there was a controversy when we were offered only one referee for the first Test in Brisbane. Burnett was the man offered and we were not at all happy that the customary panel of three or four referees were not offered. In fact International Board Regulations demanded this. To crown it all, we were suspicious of Burnett since the Queensland match when he had refereed whilst openly wearing Queensland socks. We threatened not to play unless we were given a panel, but made the mistake of giving in to the home union. I feel that this was a grave error as the financial position of the Australian Rugby Union would not have allowed us to fly home without playing the Test. As it was we played 'under protest'.

I have never heard a referee admit he is biased before or since and I was amazed at what I heard on that occasion. He said at one scrum '*our* put in, *not yours*' and took great pleasure in smiling at us whenever he penalized us, which was fairly often. I am not saying that we were completely exonerated, for we were rather undisciplined, but I don't believe that the penalty count in any International can be such a wide margin in favour of any side. Had we not been so tired we might have overcome the odds, but as it was it became painfully obvious that there was no way we would win the series. Even their manager, whom I had always believed to be a good rugby man when on tour in Britain, said he believed in 'winning at all costs'. My philosophy of the game was greatly changed following this experience for I believe that the *game* is the thing that counts in the long run.

So, we were 1–0 down and naturally a lot of the younger players did not know what was going on. On top of this we arrived at the second Test in Sydney with very few fit players. In the end, I had to play as a flanker (which I enjoyed greatly), and *five* new caps were awarded. It was an amazing gamble to take, since there were many points in favour of keeping me at full-back and putting someone else at flanker. We might have been able to do that in this country, but in countries with hard fast grounds, flankers can win or lose games. We weren't even in a position to switch the pack around because Terry Cobner, Jeff Squire and Derek Quinnell were all injured and we had three new caps in their positions anyway. Since we had a few more backs available to play, putting me on the flank was about the only course open to us. I had in fact 'covered' as flanker out there on a couple of occasions, when one of the back row was injured during a match and Alan Donovan came on as substitute for me at full-back.

All the lads knew how delighted I was to be amongst the forwards and, later, when they saw me wearing French FFR cufflinks, I was nicknamed 'Jean-Pierre' after Jean-Pierre Rive who had given them to me.

Needless to say, nothing was going to make me part with my No. 7 Welsh jersey and it now takes pride of place in my jersey collection.

Anyway, that selection shows the desperate plight we were in. Without Gerry Lewis, we would probably have had to call the whole game off.

Up until half-time things were going really well and we had put Paul McLean, their outside half, under pressure for the first time on tour. This, I believe, was because our small makeshift back row were quick around the field and able to get in amongst the Australians. Unfortunately, fate struck in the second half – Alan Donovan (full-back) had a nasty knee injury, Gareth Evans had a depressed fracture of the cheekbone and J. J. Williams a pulled hamstring. As Graham Price had departed in the first five minutes with a broken jaw, we could only use another substitute and so played with thirteen fit players for the remainder of the game. I can't remember any other game in which Wales ran out of substitutes. What made it worse was the way the injuries had been sustained – they were not all accidents.

The Graham Price incident was appalling. Finnane, his

opposite number, had obviously decided that Price was too good for him in the set pieces and decided to get rid of him. This happened thirty yards from the ball and the fact that Finnane's hand was strapped as a boxer's left no one in doubt as to his intentions.

Paul McLean's dropped goal was awarded though it was obviously three or four yards wide of the post. This was confirmed immediately after the game by apologetic Australian photographers who had it on film. The game was lost 19–17, but I felt really proud of our team that day: we played our hearts out against the odds. The reaction of the record Australian crowd made it obvious that we had been the better team in spite of all the problems. Immediately after the game I met an Australian surgeon with whom I had been friendly, at the North Middlesex Hospital just after I had qualified. He had tears of shame in his eyes to be associated with the disgraceful events he had watched that day. It was a small consolation because when I had seen him before the game he was really routing for the Wallabies.

We had lost the series 2–0, but what was worse the *game* was the true loser. Australia saw it as their chance for a return to world status, which in itself was not unreasonable. But the way they went about it certainly was. The Welsh players were not blameless either, but I feel this was mainly as a reaction to the tactics adopted by the opposition. I only hope that this is never repeated, as it can only do the game a lot of harm.

We were dreading our return home, expecting a poor reception. But the spirit of the team was incredible and we were singing on our arrival in Cardiff. The Welsh people were magnificent and we were allowed to settle back at home quickly. In fact I was back at work the following day in an attempt to erase the memories of a very bitter experience. I had thought that the Argentina tour had provided us with problems, but what I was to come up against ten years later in Australia was far worse. It seemed that the game of rugby was taking steps backwards, not forwards.

After the tour I seriously considered whether it was worth still playing rugby, if that was what I would have to put up with.

Fortunately, my next game was a VIIs match for Bridgend – that put it all back in perspective.

Five of the six doctors in the Williams family – my mother with Philip, Chris, Mike and myself in the foreground – with the sixth doctor, my father, behind the camera.

An admiring look at my first coach – my father – during the Junior Tennis Championships at Penarth in 1965.

The British Junior team for the Davis Cup, again in 1965. Dan Maskell is standing, extreme left, with Bob Weaver on the extreme right and David Lloyd seated second from the right.

A tricky backhand on the way to winning the Junior Wimbledon title, 1966.

The Centre Court at Newport after Gerald Battrick and I beat Paish and Weatherby in a Wales/England encounter in July 1967.

My first cap, against
Scotland in 1969, came
when I was still at
St Mary's. Celebrations
took place in the
traditional way.

My nerves came later – as
can be seen from this
photograph as I ran on to
the Murrayfield pitch,
closely followed by my
namesake, Denzil Williams.

Out walking with Scilla
just before finals at
St Mary's, 1973.

The wedding day itself, 1973.
J. Taylor (Basil Brush) was
my best man and had to
hire a morning suit for the
occasion. Unfortunately
they did not stock braces.

On the rampage in New Zealand in 1971.

Opposite above Home internationals – my first try against England was in 1970 when we took on the old enemy at Twickenham. The final score had us winners by 17 – 13.

Opposite below The tackle that ensured our grand slam of 1976. With time running out and Wales only six points up France's right wing, Jean Pierre Gourdon, was inches from the corner flag when I bounced him in to touch with a perfectly legitimate forearm to the Frenchman's body. The photographer's face behind us tells his story: almost in the right place for the perfect photograph, but he must have missed it all.

In 1969 the Welsh team made a tour of New Zealand. Here we are in full voice with Barry John and I trying to hit the right notes.

With the Lions in South Africa, 1974. Early on in the tour Alan Old broke his leg but with Ian McClauchlan giving a practised right shoulder transport proved no difficulty.

Opposite Violence on tour, 1974. Surprisingly enough, Tony Roux never touched me as I took this ball during the first Test against South Africa at Newlands.

END THIS THUGGERY!

IT WAS a magnificent victory for the British Lions — but Natal was not shamed. Perhaps it was the very fact that the score was so close 30 minutes into the second half — nine points to six in favour of a Lions side determined to retain an unbeaten record — which precipitated the disgusting punch-ups and the unedifying spectacle of a section of the crowd hurling oranges, cans and other debris at the visitors.

The tragedy was that it was all so unnecessary. The Lions were clearly going to win, as they did so handsomely without need of the vicious assault on Tommy Bedford by J. P. R. Williams, a player who should have been sent off immediately. Possibly the same could have

been said of others in the match but until players are made acutely aware that they will be kicked off for dirty play — no matter who starts it — rugby lovers will continue to be sickened by this sort of crude violence which has no place on any sportsfield.

No one will deny that referees have a difficult time of it and that there is a natural reluctance to act when there is doubt about the real instigator. But there will be no remedy until every player knows that punches, or foul tactics of any description, have only one consequence.

Saturday's crowd behaviour should be evidence enough that unless there is a crackdown on the field, spectators too will become more unruly.

Let's have an end to this thuggery in sport!

The Tommy Bedford incident. The South African press had a field day over this thirty-second flare-up and for the rest of the tour I carried the reputation of the Lions' 'tough guy'.

If an injury seems serious or life-threatening I step in; but to decide whether a key player in the opposition should leave the field is asking too much of my impartiality.

An attempted break during the closing minutes of the fourth Test against South Africa, where we could only draw 13 – 13.

That Test also had its skirmishes. Here Fergus Slattery, mouth bloody, holds up a restraining hand.

Dr. Williams on duty at Cardiff General Hospital. I was posing for a picture when my bleeper went off – so the photographer was delighted.

Not a pleasant sight for the schoolboy spectators – Bridgend v New Zealand, December 1978.

7

Victory at Last

The New Zealand Tour, 1971

The 1971 Lions tour to New Zealand was a boyhood dream come true.

Wales had won the Grand Slam conclusively earlier that year, and so it was obvious that there would be many Welsh players short-listed for selection by the four Home Unions Committees. The selection of captain and coach from Wales was in fact thought by some to be more of a liability than an asset, as there had already been arguments brewing that there would be too many Taffs on the plane. This was understandable from the competitive viewpoint of the other Home Unions, but there was also a firm basis for their fears. In the past the Welsh had been notoriously bad travellers; no matter how talented a Welsh side was, or how many Triple Crowns it had won, the players always seemed below par on their trips to the southern hemisphere, only to get more homesick and to find the formalities of the tour more distracting than their Scottish, Irish or English counterparts. Consequently they would become clannish on Lions tours, which would undermine the spirit of a touring party.

The extent to which this was recognized was illustrated in 1966, when Alun Pask was firm favourite for the captaincy of the Lions tour to New Zealand. At the last minute, Mike Campbell-Lamerton was given the job of leading the team, in the belief that he could perform the job better than any Welsh-man.

Until the selection of John Dawes in 1971, there had never been a Welsh captain of a Lions tour. And so the few days before the selections were announced, were full of excitement and speculation in rugby circles. I had my own little list drawn up of players I thought likely to go . . . but would they ever choose all those Welshmen? Would they even choose me? Had I enough experience?

When the letter arrived, reading it was as much of a thrill as getting notification of my first cap for Wales; hearing the announcement on the one o'clock news made it even more special. I felt as if we were going on an MCC tour, and not only were the British public interested but it seemed this time as if they were hoping for something different. The tour selection paid tremendous tribute to London Welsh, the club I had been playing with for three seasons, by selecting six of its members out of the thirty players chosen. We were then easily the best club side in the country, due to the commitment of our captain, John Dawes, to attacking rugby. Surely we would benefit from our club experience together, by keeping some form of continuity in the side? The only real selection surprise I remember was the omission of Jeff Young as hooker and Denzil Williams as loose-head prop, but since there were already two experienced props in Sandy Carmichael and Ray McLoughlin, it was felt that this wouldn't cause any problems. Frank Laidlaw and Ian McLauchlan were chosen and they certainly made up for the top-heavy selection of Welsh in the backs.

For the next six weeks our first concern was to maintain the fitness we had achieved the previous season and to avoid injury. We were not allowed to play in any games from four weeks before departure. I even held the banister every time I climbed upstairs. In 1971 that four-week rule really only affected the VIIs tournaments, since there were no English or Welsh Cup Finals in that period. As Cup Finals are held now at the end of April it is much more difficult for a player to put his country before his club even though he may be captain of it. For two weeks before we joined the party, John Dawes, John Taylor and I spent our mornings training at Old Deer Park, finishing off with ten or twelve games of squash. In those days I had not yet learned the finer points of squash, so it was really a question of racing around the court, hitting the ball as hard as possible. This training schedule meant that my attendance at the paediatrics course I was on at the time dropped considerably. I was reminded of this recently, when my youngest brother Mike approached the paediatric secretary with a view to having some time off from the same course. 'I can't really see how I can refuse you, when your brother spent most of this course preparing for the Lions tour,' came the answer.

After the tour party assembled in London and trained briefly at the Richmond ground we were herded off to Eastbourne for a week. This was the traditional start to a Lions tour, but by 1971, it was already outliving its usefulness. True, we had a chance of getting to know the players from different countries, so that everyone could put up a solid front on foreign soil, but the actual benefit gained was outweighed by the common fear that we might get ourselves injured during training and never make the tour.

Well, we did all make it – but we didn't all finish it, thanks to our friends in Canterbury, New Zealand. But of that more later.

The tour was planned to include a stop-over in Hong Kong, during the long flight, with the intention of providing us with a night's rest. This did not quite turn out according to plan – Hong Kong really is the last place to stop off for a quiet night! Most of us found the place irresistible having been let loose after all the pre-tour tensions at Eastbourne. I remember that night particularly as my first experience of the tremendous character of Sean Lynch. We were sharing a room and had both been equally late. The next morning I was horrified to find that I had woken five minutes after the bus had left for the training ground. I was really upset and started panicking, because I had wanted to start the tour well and give a good impression. Sean, however, was quite unperturbed. He proceeded to order a full breakfast, with egg, bacon, sausages and so forth and took his time enjoying every mouthful. Meanwhile I was getting more and more anxious, and embarrassed by the calm of this gentleman. In due course we ordered a taxi and rolled up at training a good half hour late. Sean's attitude had been infectious and I was beginning to wonder if I had not been a bit schoolboyish in my wish to do everything just right. I soon changed that idea after my first encounter with the wrath of Dr Doug Smith the manager. He gave me the biggest 'talking to' I have ever received during my rugby life – in front of all the other players. I was trembling at the finish, and the other players, sensing how shaken I was, stayed quiet. Luckily, I was to have no repeat of that wrath, but it served to remind us all that we were on a serious mission and that we had at least to be disciplined as far as the rugby went. The game of rugby was the purpose of the tour, after all. I have never been late for a training session since; even when I had to travel down to Wales for squad training on Sunday mornings, I would arrive earlier than players who only lived ten minutes away.

We arrived in Brisbane, greeted by a beautiful blue sky, and we made the most of the weather, relaxing by the pool and sunbathing. We were all very tired, and some of us went to sleep in the afternoon. This, of course, was the worst thing we could have done, and sure enough, many of the lads were wandering the hotel in the middle of the night, bright pink and unable to sleep.

The game against Queensland was only two days away. We were soon to find out about 'Circadian dysrhythmia', as our medical manager called it. The match started brilliantly for us, with a try straight from the kick-off, but in spite of the fact that Queensland did not score a try we went down 15–11, as our jet-lag caught up with us. This is not an uncommon occurrence in Australia, as I was to discover during the tour with Wales in 1978. But instead of demoralizing the team, the defeat seemed to pull us together and make us all the more determined to achieve our potential when we reached New Zealand, if not sooner. To the Welsh players in the side, the humiliation suffered at the hands of the All Blacks in 1969 was still fresh in our memories and our resolve to settle the score became infectious. The fact that a British side had never won a series there did not dim our ambitions. For some reason we were confident of victory from the start. The enthusiasm of Doug Smith and the quiet confidence in us of Carwyn James were worth a good few points on the board. The very fact that right at the start of the tour Doug Smith predicted a 2–1 win to the Lions, with one Test drawn in the series, was proof of his feelings about the outcome. However, nobody in New Zealand (or in Britain) really believed we could win the series.

But we were hardly going to convince people if we could not even win our matches in Australia. Our next game was in Sydney, which did not have at all the holiday atmosphere of Brisbane. The weather helped; it rained solidly for the forty-eight hours up to the match and that suited us rather than the Australians. It was a grim match, in appalling conditions, but we held on to win by the narrow margin of 14–12.

As John Dawes said of our winning after the match, 'We had to.' And he was right – we all knew that. In fact pep talks throughout the tour here were very few: we all knew already just what we had to do.

With our first win under our belts we felt a lot better, and even happier when we heard that New South Wales had beaten Queensland a week later. I am convinced that we played our first game too soon after arriving in Australia, and could see from the side-line how jaded some of the players looked. People who have never travelled from one side of the world to the other have no idea what a toll it takes especially when one is unused to covering such distances, and playing a demanding sport.

The New Zealand tour began with a match against Thames

Valley Counties combined side and resulted in a competent 25-3 win by us. I remember the score, but that is about all I do remember from that match. Our forwards more than held their own, which gave them a great psychological lift. Although it was impossible to say much on the basis of one game, Terry Maclean, the world-renowned rugby critic, wrote that perhaps this Lions team was not going to be a push-over after all. There had been great sides from Britain over there in the past, but no matter how brilliant their backs were the tourists even in the 1959 side had difficulty finding enough ball to supply them. In the King County game the following Wednesday we came out victors 22-9, and this against a side containing the immortal Colin Meads, a man whom we proved could after all be reduced to a mere mortal. So that night we duly celebrated. We soon came to respect this great man as he led the New Zealanders in the Tests. For his part he was one of the first to praise our efforts and even admitted after that King County game that his side were 'bloody lucky to get nine' (points).

For all of us the following Thursday morning training session was a struggle. This is the hardest session of the week anyway on tour, not only because it follows on straight after the mid-week game (and party) but because it is also the last full session before a tough Saturday game. At least after the weekend game there is a day of rest, or of travelling on the Sunday. But Carwyn really pushed us hard that Thursday. He was not going to lay down the law about our socializing, but he was certainly not going to make any concessions to us either. That evening we had a players' meeting and decided to make Saturday night our official party night and cut out the heavy mid-week celebrations. By then everyone had played once and there was no telling whether one would be required for a mid-week or weekend game, so we stuck to our resolution for a good few weeks until we were splitting up into roughly two teams who knew when they could relax or not during the week. Still, it was a serious decision and one which underlined our collective attitude to the task in hand.

The Wellington game was our next important hurdle before the first Test. By then I was appreciating Barry John more and more, not only for his play but for enabling *me* to play with him. He was producing better rugby than I had ever seen and in addition his goal-kicking had been immaculate. Bob Hiller was also a splendid points collector with his goal-kicking, but BJ's success was making even Bob look like a hit-or-miss man. That meant that Barry was likely to be number one kicker on tour, which in turn strengthened my chance of being picked as full-back for the Test side. I knew I couldn't compete against Bob Hiller as full-back if he were also needed as a kicker. Up to then the forwards had been playing superbly, but the backs had not quite got it together. It was not for want of practice, nor because 'flair' was being stifled – far from it. Too often backs have their own individual flair coached out of them but Carwyn James is one man who sets great store by it. The most natural move can often be the most unexpected and therefore the most effective one. No, I think it was just a question of waiting until we clicked into form and it would not be boasting to say that we 'clicked' that Saturday against Wellington. We scored nine tries to nil to win 47–9 and it was probably the best display of running rugby any British side has ever performed. It is true that it is easy to play that type of rugby against a much weaker side, but Wellington was an extremely powerful team. It was in the Wellington game that John Bevan scored four of his seventeen tries on tour. He was undoubtedly the strongest wing I have ever seen. He even had the vote of confidence from Ray McLoughlin, who reckoned that 'Bev' was stronger than half the forwards! He did not need fancy side-steps or kicks ahead because he could hand off defenders or run straight through them to power his way over the line. Once he got the ball (despite not always being the most reliable handler) that was it. It seems amazing that he didn't get seriously injured during the tour, but I suppose that reinforces my belief that the harder you go into a tackle the less likely you are to get hurt. It was no real surprise to hear later that he had decided to 'go north' since he was ideally suited to the league game. It certainly gave me an interest in watching rugby league on television if I knew he was playing and I have enjoyed following his success.

Several facts were emerging at this stage of the tour (almost a month old): Ray McLoughlin was coaching the forwards under Carwyn James's directorship and his experience and personality were paying great dividends. Mike Gibson was playing extremely well in the centre, although he had been picked as a fly-half. This meant that with the long pass of Gareth Edwards and the clever tactical play of Barry John, the wings were seeing a lot of the ball, and being used by John Dawes (in his calling of the moves) to their best advantage. Doug Smith was proving a popular manager, not only with his players but with the New Zealand officials, press and public. He was careful, in selecting the invitations to functions we were to accept, to upset as few people as possible. He was also sensitive to our needs, however small. One of these was negotiating for us to have a reasonable choice from menus at hotels and to include BW (bottles of wine, preferably F-French) with our meals. It was not much to ask, but we had been treated rather shabbily at one of our first stops and felt that if we were to survive fifteen weeks in hotels things had better improve. Choice was important, since many places assumed that all we wanted to eat was steak. That may seem a marvellous idea, but if you have eaten steak after steak then you long for something like beans on toast, or bubble and squeak! Not that we were ever served either of those, but we stressed the point and got our way, thanks to Doug.

After Wellington the game at Timaru was a bit of an anticlimax. However we managed to win 25–6 against the combined side, and were able to show off the skills of Gerald Davies with two good tries. Gerald had arrived two weeks late on the scene

because of exams, and had hitherto not been seen playing on
that tour. Many of us were depressed that evening, despite
winning, and began to wonder if the Wellington game had been
a bit of a freak. The match against Otago the following
Saturday gave us a lift for many reasons, not least that it had
made Doug Smith happy to gain revenge for a terrible hiding
he had received from Otago as a member of the 1970 Lions.
Two things stand out in that game – for me at least. One was
scoring one of only two tries on the tour, and only my second
at International level by that time. The other was the refereeing
of John Pring. It was the first time he had controlled one of
our matches and he did an admirable job. The fact that he
was not mentioned in the match write-ups reflects the quiet
and quick way he went about his duties. We were to find
good referees hard to come by and ended up by choosing him
to referee all four Test matches.

We had at this point won eight games in succession and the
New Zealand people were beginning to take notice. They were
aware of our try-scoring potential but seemed confident that
this would be squashed by the 'harder' men in the South
Island. In this respect, the Canterbury (New Zealand) players,
in particular, had a lot to live up to. But the match against
Canterbury on 19 June (1971) turned out not to be just a
'hard' match, but a bloodbath. We must have read the writing
on the wall, because Barry John was withdrawn from the side
at the last minute to avoid possible injury. Mike Gibson took
his place at fly-half – whilst strong Arthur Lewis took over from
Mike Gibson in the centre. It was a most astute decision by the
management, since Barry would almost certainly have been
heavily marked and probably injured. For this decision, the
match remained all the more firmly in my mind as I had to
share the kicking with Mike Gibson. The 'Battle of Canterbury'
started in the first ten minutes, when the position of the ball
on the field seemed to bear little relation to the groups of
players brawling. Canterbury had been the leading provincial
side the previous year, by winning the Ranburly Shield, the

New Zealand Provincial knock-out competition, and they seemed to think it was their duty to prove that we could be beaten. Not only that, they seemed to take it upon themselves to make sure that we *would* not, or rather *could* not, feature in the Tests. They certainly made sure of marking Sandy Carmichael, whose only crime was to have propped so well throughout the tour. He was the main target and had already received such bad facial injuries during the first twelve minutes that he had to receive medical attention. But Sandy was not easily put down by such intimidation and unfortunately he returned to the field. At the end of the day he had received five fractures of the left cheekbone; his opposition prop was Hopkinson. All in all, nine of our players received medical attention. Our dressing-room was, in Carwyn's words, 'A casualty clearing station'. Having seen a good few of the latter I agreed with him – except that our dressing-room seemed even worse.

In spite of the fact that Canterbury were barely penalized for their part in the battle, while any retaliation by us was soon followed by a penalty, we limped off winners by 14–3. This was far more impressive than our previous score of 49–6 at Greymouth, against West Coast/Buller and the fact that it included two tries in the face of such thuggery was a great tribute to the side. Had we not retaliated at all we would never have won, nor would we have done so well later in the Tests, because it would then have become clear to the All Blacks that their recipe for success was simple: intimidation. It was ironic that it was through retaliation that Ray ended up with a broken thumb, never to play again on the tour. Altogether we lost Sandy, Ray and Mick Hipwell, who had a torn knee ligament, from the side which would have played the New Zealand team the following week; it was a heavy price to pay.

To make matters worse, Doc Stewart, the coach of the Canterbury forwards, declared after the match that Canterbury would have beaten any of the New Zealand provincial sides, the way they had played that day. It was unfortunate phrasing, because I am sure he referred to the seventy per cent possession they won, rather than their other tactics. But we were rather sensitive, and when the All Blacks' coach, Ivan Vodanovich, suggested that the first Test would be a second 'Passchendaele' because we were asking for trouble by lying on the ball, we were incensed. We appreciated that our rucking was not as good technically as the New Zealanders' and that there were sometimes occasions when we were guilty through inexperience of not making the ball available, but none of the incidents that Saturday had occurred during the rucks.

Amidst all this furore the first Test came upon us. Fortunately the Passchendaele reference cut little ice with us after one of the Irish members of the tour started asking: 'What's sex in some hollow got to do with the first Test. What's all this about a passion dale?' Although he protested that he couldn't read properly, let alone read New Zealand newspapers, it was a good joke and better left as such.

The only consolation for the three players knocked out of the Test was that the rest of the team were given an extra incentive to win. It also meant that our chances had been reduced to less than even, which was healthy in a way as we would have found ourselves in trouble had we gone in as firm favourites.

On the morning of the Test we received a splendid telegram from two jokers of the 1959 Lions team . . . VICTORY WILL MAKE US AS RELEVANT AS DINOSAURS STOP WILL PRESS FOR WELSH AS UNIVERSAL LANGUAGE IN COMMON MARKET STOP . . . and so it went on, full of Cymru am Byth's, or rather CYMRU AM BLOODY BYTH! Obviously from Andy Mulligan and Tony O'Reilly. We remembered just how close they had come in 1959, so not only did the cable relieve a little tension, but it also made us aware of the narrow difference between success and failure.

It was just as well. The first Test at Dunedin turned out rather one-sided. New Zealand had all the ball, and played all the rugby, but couldn't score. The Lions defence was magnificent: at times we were just holding on till Barry John could find some way to kick the ball out of danger. Time after time the All Blacks were within inches of our goal line, but somehow we managed to find their forwards in disarray. Ian McLauchlan went over for a try – and the first points of the match were to us. Perhaps it seemed lucky but we had not thought ourselves very lucky to have lost those key players. To cap it all, Gareth Edwards went off after only six minutes with recurrence of a hamstring injury. Even Barry John did not have his best goal-kicking day: he missed three penalties, a conversion and a dropped goal. But his defensive kicking was immaculate, and he kicked the two goals which gave us victory 9–3. Fergie McCormick was even unluckier with his penalty attempt, missing one right under the posts. So in the end Ivan Vodanovich's remark backfired a little, and it turned out to be our Waterloo, rather than their Passchendaele. They were committed to playing fifteen-man rugby, whilst we had to content ourselves with a defensive ten-man game. As it happened, the three replacements – 'Mighty Mouse' McLauchlan, Sean Lynch and Peter Dixon – more than lived up to their predecessors. In spite of the fact that they conceded about seven stone to the All Black pack they held their own in the scrums. It was in the loose ball and the lines-out that the All Blacks had the advantage. But New Zealanders could no longer tease Ian about being 'Mouse' McLauchlan – he proved he was mighty enough by coping with Jazz Muller, who was over three stone heavier.

We were ecstatic in the dressing-room afterwards, not just because we had won, but because we were aware that we had been lucky in doing so.

Colin Meads was the first into our dressing-room to congratulate us. As captain of an All Blacks side which had won seventy per cent of the ball, yet had failed to take scoring chances, he was noble in defeat. 'I thought the Lions were a fine side from the start, and I still think they are,' he admitted during the speeches later.

There were only three matches between the first and second Tests, and none of these was a particularly good performance. The match against Taranaki was especially close. It marked a particularly low spot in the tour. We had had further trouble with injuries, causing problems at half-back. With Mike Gibson firmly established in the centre we were posed with problems of selection: obviously Barry John was playing such a vital role that he needed rest mid-week, but so did Mike Gibson. At one point we thought that John Dawes himself would have to play at fly-half; but he needed rest too. In the end Mike Gibson played – quite brilliantly – but we were lucky to win by five points, 14–9.

We were beginning to tire a little of the tour formalities, and it seemed that having won the first Test we were under greater scrutiny. We would have preferred the first Test to be much earlier, perhaps around the time of the Wellington match. And so the feeling for the second Test was never quite right. I remember that our last training session ended up a very scrappy affair, and there was not the feeling of confidence we had had for the first Test. That was an irony, for theoretically we should have been more confident since we were yet to lose a match. Perhaps we were flushed with our success. Anyway, we lost that one.

New Zealand had changed their side and now included Laurie Mains, the goal-kicking full-back from Otago. We were worried by this because Fergie McCormick whom Mains had replaced had played poorly in the first Test and had missed match-winning penalties. Whether he was the 'weak link' constantly referred to by the Lions' manager may always remain a mystery . . . The press made a big thing of his 'weak link' quotes but we were convinced that Doug Smith was just conning everyone in an attempt to 'psych' various All Blacks.

The match was a good one and for much of the game we played well. However, too many early points were given away, and New Zealand won deservedly, 22–12. They scored four tries and one penalty try, and I felt that our tackling was as poor in that Test as it had been good in the first. The All Blacks were thus able to capitalize on their possession and got the tries they were unlucky not to make in the previous Test. Although they did not dominate the line-out so drastically as they had done before and our scrummaging again held its own, they were still far superior in the loose, especially the rucks. Sid Going more than flourished with his pack supplying plenty of possession and he was able to set off fly-half Bob Burgess to his best advantage. We backs in the Lions had much admiration for Bob Burgess, both as an instinctive player and as a person off the field. In fact, Barry John struck up quite a friendship with him which has continued over the years.

Mid-way through the first half I found myself struggling at the bottom of a ruck feeling rather peculiar. I could not remember what I was doing there, what had happened, what day it was – anything at all. But there was no time to think about stupid things like that: somehow an automatic pilot took over in my brain and told me to get back and cover the box. Sid Going had seen I was stuck and had aimed a beautiful kick to where I should have been. Fortunately I just managed to cover it and then I did another automatic thing – one which I would not have attempted had I remembered that we were struggling in the important Test match – I ran the ball! I sold a dummy, then passed to Mike Gibson, who then set up Gerald Davies. Gerald had quite a run to make – but that did not seem to stop me following him as if mesmerized and just after he had dotted down for a try I collapsed over the line, half-conscious. I had obviously been concussed and should have received attention before Sid Going ever made his kick. I know now that I should have been sent off the field and replaced. As it was, we scored the try and that seemed, to me, to justify my staying on. It was a difficult decision because no one, referee, trainer or captain had suggested that I should go off, when it was plainer to them than to me that I was not quite right. Since then there has been more medical evidence that concussion should not be treated lightly, and the idea of a replacement is now acceptable, so there is really no excuse for anyone staying on the field if they cannot remember which day it is.

Whether that decision jeopardized the Lions chances that day I will never know, but I suspect that the break-up of our defence must have had a lot to do with it. I felt that I had made a contribution to both our tries, in running from defence in the first and coming into the line for the second – but was that at the expense of five tries to the All Blacks? Had we in fact concentrated too much on running rugby? After all we had beaten them before by our kicking. We were worried that the second Test could mark a turning point in the tour. We had won all our matches till then, but the All Blacks had achieved a better win in the second Test than we had in the first, and we all knew it. Nothing had gone right in Christchurch – first the Canterbury game, then the second Test – 'like a cemetery', said John Taylor.

After two training sessions, including Carwyn's 'psychology' classes, we were given the following day off to relax together, getting back the spirit of the tour. It was a marvellous tonic – we rode, fished, hunted, did anything but play rugby, or commiserate over our losses.

For the next match the management came up trumps once again. Bob Hiller was selected to captain the team at Masterton against Wairarapa-Bush. If anyone was still feeling gloomy after the Saturday massacre, Doug Smith and Carwyn knew that it wouldn't last for long with Bob in charge. Bob was one of the great characters of the tour. He really kept us above water with his remarkable humour. It is perhaps true to say that without the 'stars' amongst the 'Ts and Ws' we would never have been so successful in New Zealand. The 'Ts and Ws' were the mid-week side (Tuesday and Wednesday). Originally we had not wanted to make any differentiation between the weekend and the mid-week teams and Carwyn wanted to integrate as much as possible. But as the Test series became more and more competitive, it was inevitable that there would be some division. If Carwyn had been worried about this, then he underestimated the mid-week boys. They not only kept our morale up but they took their role seriously in maintaining our unbeaten record against the provincial sides. Although not always reaching the limelight, they played consistently week after week and gave us great encouragement for the weekend games by their attitude and their loyalty. John Spencer and Ray 'Chico' Hopkins were of the same mould as Bob, though they were from different parts of the UK with different backgrounds. That illustrated the way in which all the players integrated as a group. There were no cliques on the 1971 tour. Welsh players had not been allowed to share rooms with fellow Welshmen and this was a big step towards avoiding the Welsh tendency for home-sickness. I am not sure in fact whether that would even have happened anyway, because many of us were away from home most of the time anyway, living in London: we were also mostly young and unmarried, which helped on a long tour.

Hawkes Bay was the next team to try to intimidate the Lions physically. Luckily Gerald Davies showed his brilliant class with four great tries and this overshadowed some of the unsavoury incidents in the game. But they were still numerous enough for one of our side to ask, tongue in cheek, 'When are Hawkes Bay playing Canterbury?' Many of the players were beginning to look jaded and it was interesting that Gerald was the one who really showed his form, having joined the party later. It was just as well he did, because he was able to inject a little new life into us. 'Stack' Stevens and Geoff Evans had also joined the tour as replacements for Sandy Carmichael and Ray McLoughlin. Sandy could not have played again that tour with his facial injuries but the decision to send Ray home as well was a little surprising. A fractured thumb can mend within six weeks and it's not as if a thumb is the most important asset to a prop! Ray had been so influential in coaching the forwards that when he said his goodbyes after the first Test there was an air of disbelief amongst us. For a moment, we didn't think we would survive without him. It is a tribute to Willie-John McBride that we did, since he stepped into Ray's shoes as coach and was the perfect successor.

Personally, I was happy to see Geoff Evans arrive as a utility pack player, since he was a club mate from London Welsh. The idea had been to move Mike Roberts in to the front row, so that Geoff, his predecessor in the Welsh team, would fill his own place at lock. But this did not really work, mainly because of their different sizes which altered the structure of the front row and the other three props spent the last weeks of the tour playing in two out of three games.

The Auckland game was the last before the third Test, and it had been so close that we were relieved to have no mid-week game in between. We were able to spend that week in North Auckland, at the Bay of Islands – a lovely spot, quiet and beautiful. We were away from press scrutiny and, to cap it all, the weather was good. It was ideal for picking ourselves up and preparing for what was certain to be the most important game any of us had played in.

Then came a great morale booster. The All Blacks had selected Brian Lochore, the former number eight and captain, to play alongside Colin Meads in the second row. We couldn't believe it. Meads had a suspect ankle, and Whiting had dropped out with a back injury. We had played against Lochore previously on tour and were amazed that he had agreed to play in the Test. Although once a fine player and leader, he had lost his old fervour and would also be playing out of position. Were the All Blacks getting desperate? Bryan Williams also withdrew injured the night before the game – he had caused us many problems in the second Test, with his speed and strength.

We, in the meantime, had also made several changes. Gordon Brown played at lock instead of Delme Thomas, for his first Test cap, and David Duckham had replaced John Bevan from the first Test, because of his greater all round ball distribution. Derek Quinnell was picked at blind side wing-forward with a view to containing Sid Going, and Fergus Slattery was selected instead of John Taylor. However 'Bas' (John Taylor) played in the end when Slattery went down with tonsillitis. John Taylor was nicknamed 'Basil Brush' because of his shock of unruly hair – an apt description. The selection of Quinnell was vital, for he played Sid Going out of the game. We had the best possible start. Perhaps there was the underlying feeling that as we had done so well in Wellington earlier in the tour, playing the third Test there was a good omen. Three minutes into the game Barry John had scored three points with a dropped goal. By nine minutes we had added a try by Gerald Davies, which was converted by BJ. Before twenty minutes had passed, Barry had again shown his brilliance by scoring another five points with a try between the posts, which he duly converted.

It looked as if we were going to score fifty points. The All Blacks had yet to score and I certainly had not been pushed for defence near our lines.

The crowd were silent. They couldn't believe it after the last Test. Just as Sid Going and Bob Burgess had controlled things in the second Test, Gareth Edwards and Barry John were the controllers in the third. As we changed ends we wondered if our lead was big enough, for there was a terrific wind which could easily have turned the tables on us, had the All Blacks' tactics improved. But we needn't have worried; the match was really over at half-time, except for a try near the end by Laurie Mains, the newcomer to the All Blacks.

I ought perhaps to mention an injury I had received during the early stages of this match. Only minutes after Barry John had coolly dropped his goal, one of the All Blacks, probably Sid Going, had hoisted a particularly dangerous kick towards him, with the All Blacks pack descending. I knew we couldn't let Barry take the kick. He was already showing that he was on his best form that day and we were going to need him. The All Blacks knew it as well. So I called for the ball, ran up, and virtually pushed BJ out of the way. I think he was a bit cross, for a moment, but when he heard the thud of the All Blacks on me as I turned with the ball – he realized. I felt knees going into both buttocks as I curled with the ball to keep it safe, but for the rest of the match I only felt numbness. It was afterwards that I began to suffer – I couldn't sit down for three days! But somehow it was easy to stand pain in victory, it would have been a different matter had we lost.

In fact, I do not feel particularly heroic about my action. If you were to ask any member of our team they would probably say they would have done the same. We knew we had to shield our 'star'. He was a good few stone lighter than many of us and was not renowned for the physical side of his game – he didn't need to be.

Another little incident occurred which I was to recollect when I later became involved with injuries on the field. Towards the end of the game Bob Burgess had been double tackled, with one Lions player taking the top part of his body, and another the lower part. It was perfectly legitimate. For a moment we feared he may have broken his neck as he lay unconscious on the ground before someone, I think Barry John, called for a stretcher. Eventually one arrived, but for an age, it seemed, there were St John ambulance men, the referee and the trainer all standing around looking at him. I looked across and suddenly realized that not only was he still unconscious but that he was going blue as well. So I rushed over and felt inside his mouth. Sure enough, his tongue had slipped back, cutting off his air passage. Once his tongue was held forward, his colour picked up. I was furious at the time, because it seemed such a basic error on the part of the first aid team. Ideally, a person should also be turned on their side to make sure that there is no obstruction. I realize that no one wanted to do that as they were still not sure if there was anything broken, but he should not have been allowed to turn blue: the brain only needs its oxygen supply cut off for three minutes before irreparable damage is done. As it happened he turned out to have severe concussion but no actual injury. I just felt grateful that I had completed my casualty stint before going on tour.

It was a nice gesture that prompted Barry John and Carwyn James to visit Bob in hospital, the following day. Unfortunately, though, he could not play rugby again for many weeks after that.

But really, there was little else to think about after the match except the result. There it was up on the scoreboard: 13–3. It seemed like a dream. If we had had doubts about the first Test, then we need not have had any about the third. Everything seemed to go according to Carwyn's plan. All the new players justified their selection, Gordon Brown especially. He came into his own during the tour, having lived in the shadow of his brother Peter for so long. Where a jumper was needed who could also cope with the clever line-out tactics – then he was the one. The policy of marking Sid Going, almost to the exclusion of following other back-row play, had also been successful, and had changed the course of the game. So, if we were the winners, we felt it was only due to Carwyn's intelligent planning – he had even phoned the Met Office to get a better idea of the wind forecast.

The British press on the party were jubilant, and bought us champagne to celebrate. We had enjoyed a very good relationship with the press, both our own and the New Zealanders, and it seemed fitting to be celebrating with them in this way. They were more aware than we, at the time, of the immense significance of our win. We all knew that history had been made, in that no other British Lions touring team had ever won two Test matches in New Zealand, and that the least we could do was to draw the series. But history means very little when it is only a few hours old, and we celebrated that night as if only that one match – the third Test – mattered.

We were able to get things in better perspective the following day when we arrived in Palmerston North. Our reception there was quite remarkable. We couldn't believe that the New Zealanders would fête us in such a way. Every member of the party had a chauffeur-driven vintage car to drive him from the airport and around the streets to receive the accolades of the crowd. We found it amazing that they had time to organize it all in the space of the few hours after our win. Perhaps they had expected us to win after all. We got the impression that the New Zealand people were more concerned we should beat the Springboks in 1974 (as the All Blacks had failed yet again in South Africa in 1970) than that we should lose to the All Blacks in the final Test. They were already looking further ahead than we were and they seemed to think that defeat for them might allow the All Blacks to rise again like the phoenix. There was to be a lot of bitterness amongst the people down under as the tour came to a close because we had been so successful. But that weekend was ours.

After we had recovered from our reception, and had settled into our rooms, we congregated in the bar for one of our most memorable 'Sunday school' sessions. Up till that point in the tour, about half the players and some of the press party who enjoyed a quiet drink used to gather together on our only real day of rest and relaxation. The term 'Sunday school' was coined, I believe by Cliff Morgan – with his chapel background. He had even been out and bought ties which we could all sport on the appointed day. He also played the piano on these occasions, so it was not always such a quiet drink.

That Sunday, everybody joined in Sunday school, including all the members of the press party, and we had a marvellous time together without all the 'hangers-on' or the inevitable bevy of girls anxious to share in the glory. It was then that we really got down to the roots of the victory: that we could make history, for no other British side had ever done so well in New Zealand. Only the manager of the hotel found it hard going behind the bar, so he put Barry John in charge. We thought this was a great idea at the time, but the following morning at training we were not too sure. John Taylor and I swore that we caught the lift to bed at 4 a.m., but were unable to find any trace of a lift in the hotel the next day . . . it had been that kind of night!

We had another cause for celebration, the following Wednesday, but of a different sort. Willie-John McBride was chosen to captain the side in recognition of his services to the tour, and to rugby in general. His team contained five International captains in their own right: John Dawes, John Spencer, Mike Gibson, Bob Hiller, and Frank Laidlaw. The side honoured Willie-John by scoring eight tries, passing the five hundred point mark on tour, and finally by chairing him off the pitch. I am sure no one knew, least of all Willie-John, that he would be similarly chaired off from a Lions game, three years hence, when another mark was to be made in rugby history. Everyone assumed that he would retire after the New Zealand tour.

The North Auckland match which followed gave us a bit of a scare. We were holding on desperately to our unbeaten provincial record and were leading only 3–0 when one of the Going brothers, Brian, almost improved on our score. He sold a dummy, and was running straight for the line, near the posts, with only me to beat. Two yards from our line I tackled him, in what I remember as one of the most crucial, bone-shaking tackles in my rugby life hitherto. It gave me immense satisfaction, and I really had to control myself from shouting out about it.

There were three brothers Going on the field that day in the prominent positions of scrum-half, fly-half, and full-back. They produced some marvellous scissor moves together, and there were many times during the match when it looked as if the Going family would succeed where the rest of the clubs had failed. As well as my tackle on Brian, I also produced a handy one on Sid, and got past Ken Going for my second try of the tour, so that I felt I had done my bit in preventing the brothers from taking away our record. It was a memorable match, and a memorable stay in North Auckland. John Bevan also scored his seventeenth try of the tour, in the closing minutes of the match, which equalled Tony O'Reilly's record, still standing after fifteen years. We were all delighted for him, as we were not sure which of the two remaining matches he might be playing in. I must admit that the final pass to him was a bit contrived to make absolutely sure that all he had to do was fall over the line, but I didn't mind: I had already scored my try.

The last provincial game proved to be a bigger hurdle than we had anticipated, and we had to rely heavily on the goal-kicking of Bob Hiller, and of BJ. If we were shaken in North Auckland, then we were certainly tested by the Bay of Plenty at Tauranga, when they scored three tries to our two. Fortunately, they failed to convert two of them and failed two penalty attempts as well. Bob Hiller kicked three penalties and one conversion, which brought his tally to 102 points in only ten games. It was a remarkable achievement, since that was his second tour century, having scored 108 points on the previous Lions tour to South Africa. Barry John was to score even more, ending up with a total of 180. So there we were, facing the last Test in Auckland, having maintained our unbeaten record in the provincial games. Could we win the Test series as well?

The last Test of a long tour is always a difficult occasion. The players are looking forward to going home and some of them are even there mentally. Then there is always last-minute shopping to upset timetables. With these distractions, I felt that our preparation for that final Test was not good. Instead of being determined to 'drive the point home' by winning the fourth Test convincingly, we seemed prepared to go out on to the field and accept a draw. And that's just what happened.

We had been losing 8–0 after only eight minutes, and had to contain the All Blacks as best as we could if we were to avoid a reversal of the third Test. In the last minute of the first half we managed to equalize by adding a try by Gerald Davies, as well as a conversion to an earlier penalty by Barry John.

We felt then that at least we would not lose. Later we were still level, but the score had moved to eleven all. So when I found myself in the middle of the field, just inside their half and with virtually no support around me, I thought I might make a shot at the drop. Probably the idea would never have come into my head had I not for some reason said to the lads on our way to the match that I would drop a goal. This produced a great uproar because I never seemed to have dropped goals as part of my repertoire as had BJ or Gareth. So it was taken as a bit of a joke. I can't think for the life of me what prompted me to say such a thing. So when I saw it sailing over I was ecstatic. I waved up to the other lads in the stand. They couldn't believe it, but I was more surprised than anyone. For twenty minutes I really thought that we might have won, and that I had scored the winning points. But it was not to be. Later we missed two dropped goal attempts and one penalty. The luck of the opposition changed too and the one penalty they were given after my kick was successful. But in the end the score was 14–14 and I had had the satisfaction of that rare dropped goal from about forty-five yards. I feel that on that occasion we played better rugby than in any of the other Tests but we just weren't hungry for points. Maybe we believed that winning was asking too much of ourselves. Still, we had won the series.

As I stood at the airport, and waved off my companions of the last four months, I regretted my decision to stay on and work in Auckland for my elective.* I had to restrain my tears: we had gone through so much together; made sacrifices, shared success, and disappointments, and had really been one

* c.f. Chapter 4.

big happy family. I felt orphaned. I also envied the reception
they would get from the British people, and started thinking
about the excitement of the Welsh people at the result. They
would probably be having a national holiday to celebrate . . .
Then I thought of the likely reception I would get in Auckland.
There would be post-mortems, bitterness over the last Test,
repercussions. I really was not looking forward to it.

As it turned out, I spent an enjoyable three months of medical
studies there – once I could convince the staff at the hospital
that I was serious about medicine and not just there for an
extended holiday. I also took up squash, in an effort to keep
fit, for the tour had left its toll with all the training, eating, and
of course drinking. Altogether I had put on over twenty pounds
and increased my neck size by almost two inches. The Auckland
College Rifles club 'adopted' me (for the squash, not shooting)
and I was able to play squash seriously for the first time in my
life. I became an addict. It gave me the excuse to avoid playing
any rugby, despite the numerous invitations.

When I did eventually return to Britain the following
October, I received a pleasant surprise. I was met off the plane
by many of my London Welsh friends, my family and many
people who had travelled up from Wales specially. Then there
was John Dawes and many of the Lions team. I was over-
whelmed. John Dawes had arranged for some of the numerous
functions they had been invited to on their return, to be
postponed until I could join them. So, I had not been left out
at all. It was a great gesture by John, or Syd as we nicknamed
him (S. J. D.) and typical of the attitude of people on the tour.
We had been members of a highly successful party, in which
every member had contributed to the success. So, John Dawes
made sure that we all shared in the success. During those first
days back, amidst the social whirl of dinners and parties, and in
the days that followed, which included a civic reception in
Bridgend, I came to understand more fully the implications
of the tour's success and what it had meant to the British
people.

I reflected on the words of Colin Meads after the last Test: 'You have won the Test series and you have gone round our provinces unbeaten. This is a great achievement and it will probably never be equalled.'

I wonder if it will?

8

The Golden Days of London Welsh

My game for London Welsh *v* Richmond on returning from Argentina in 1968 was the beginning of a new way of life for me. I had been playing the occasional game for Bridgend and was not enjoying my rugby at St Mary's as the side found great difficulty competing against such strong opposition. So when the chance came to play for London Welsh I knew I had to take it with both hands.

London Welsh had already made a name for themselves with their exciting fifteen-man ball-handling game and it didn't take me long to find out why. When I trained with them, I was amazed at the overall fitness of the team. Even the forwards seemed to be mobile around the field and ready to contribute to handling. I was only just out of school and yet had great difficulty in keeping up with some of these 'old men'. The majority were school teachers and so spent most of their day out on the fields or in the gym with youngsters, participating in physical activity. In those days of the sixties and early seventies it was commonplace for Welsh lads to aim for PE Colleges in England, like Loughborough or St Luke's, Exeter and then move on to teach in the London area. When I started playing for the Welsh, our team seemed to consist solely of teachers or medics. Even the front row contained Brian Rees (then a junior doctor) and Jeff Young who taught at that time.

We adjusted our game to a lighter front row than was usual amongst the miners in the valleys. Those Tuesday and Thursday evenings were really tough. Tuesdays were fitness only, while Thursdays were the team practice night, with touch rugby playing a big part in the 'warming up' activity. This was important as our game was based on continual support and being able to give and take a pass.

Colin Gibbons, Dai Richards, George Patterson and Freddie Williams were playing when I started as well as the more famous names like John Dawes, John Taylor and Tony Gray. Mervyn Davies and I arrived the same year, although I think I had played about six games before he made his début against Moseley at Old Deer Park. In those days, the Old Clubhouse had just been taken down to make way for a new £100,000 complex. So, we used to change in the Richmond Baths next door and have our post-match meals and refreshments in the Bowls Club across the other end of the ground. Old Deer Park caters for many sports – rugby, hockey, cricket, squash, tennis, bowls and some others such as archery during the summer. The setting is beautiful as it lies just behind Kew Gardens near Richmond with the famous Pagoda overlooking the rugby posts at one end. There are two rugby pitches, one used by the second team and for training sessions and the other for the first or second team when playing at home.

The second pitch has training lights which are not quite strong enough for playing matches under, which, I think, is very lucky for the club. Every first-class side in Wales has good floodlights and so plays innumerable mid-week games under the lights. This makes for congested fixture lists and far too much rugby. I have noticed this since returning to Wales. While at London Welsh there was just one game to look forward to each week, the Welsh clubs often have only a few days to recover between two really hard matches. The whole 'set-up' is different as most Welsh clubs do not have even a second team and therefore need a squad of players – all of whom are worthy of first team rugby. London Welsh and most English clubs have six or seven sides and so everyone is getting regular rugby with a chance of promotion if they play well. I would like the Welsh clubs to have more sides within their club and thus ease the burden of the amount of rugby there is on the top players.

The next game after the Richmond one was against Llanelli (spelt Llanelly at this time). I drew the game 11–11 with a penalty goal from near the half-way and was immediately accepted by the highly critical Old Deer Park crowd. After that, I always seemed to play well against Llanelli, especially on the away matches, which took place annually on Boxing Day. The promise of a good game against a team who were also willing to run the ball gave me the incentive to keep off the inevitable Christmas drinks – but as the years passed by it became more and more difficult to keep up my standards.

Next came two incredible games which I will never forget: one against Cape Town Universities, who were on tour, and the other against Newport, who were the leading Welsh club at that time. Both matches were won by over thirty points and I think that this was some of the most remarkable rugby I have ever taken part in. The ball never seemed to stop moving and even as very fit players we were exhausted by the end of the match. What the opposition must have felt like I dread to think.

Of course one of the reasons that London Welsh played this type of game was because we simply did not have the size of forwards to be able to play a tight game. So our small mobile forwards had to be able to play like three-quarters. Set piece ball (scrums and lines-out) was a very rare privilege, but we very rarely failed to win it from loose situations. This resulted in a lot of tries and a lot of near misses: we were always vulnerable to problems like interception as I was always up in the line as an attacker. I remember this happening one Easter at Newport and one Christmas at Llanelli. We were attacking strongly at the time and both incidents eventually cost us the game.

Mervyn Davies had as dramatic a début for London Welsh

as I had and everyone was amazed when he was selected to play in the Moseley game at Old Deer Park as a virtually unknown player. He was a very unlikely-looking forward – tall and gangly and more like a basketball player (which he already was). At that time he was still very raw but he made a forceful impression in that first game and within a couple of weeks found himself in the Welsh Trial as a little-known player.

London Welsh were acquiring a bit of a reputation for this sort of thing – John Taylor was capped in 1967 after five first-class games.

That 1968–9 season was tremendously exciting, not only because it was my first full season with London Welsh, but also because of the trips down to Wales for the squad sessions with the Welsh team. Even though these became rather tiring year after year, we made the most of them at the start by turning them into good weekends. There were always a fair number of us from London Welsh at the time in the Welsh Squad so we made up quite a party. These sessions took place on Sundays at the Afan Lido, Aberavon (Port Talbot). We would play the match on the Saturday afternoon and leave early after the match for Wales. In those days there was no M4 motorway and we had a special route devised by John Dawes to take us down all the short cuts in Wiltshire and Berkshire. This was not so important on the downward journey, but was of vital importance on returning to London. We would all be very tired after the session on a Sunday and we used to make a bee-line for the Lamb and Flag at Kingston Bagpuize on the Farringdon–Abingdon road. This made a nice break in the journey and had the advantage of offering real ale from the wood and a magnificent selection of food such as game-pie, pheasant, duck and many other delicacies. We all looked forward to this stop and often ended up staying till closing time. I should think Mike Roberts probably enjoyed it the most as he has one of the biggest appetites I have ever come across.

The Saturday nights were usually spent in Bridgend at

Ashfield. Most of the London Welsh players stayed at my parents' house at some time. John Dawes, John Taylor, Mervyn Davies and Geoff Evans were regulars and Mike Roberts, Jim Shanklin and Gerald Davies all sampled the Williams hospitality at some time. We would depart for pints of 'BB' (best bitter) off the wood (of course) in the Ogmore Club, a men's drinking club in Bridgend, and return to continue our conversation well into the early hours. My mother seemed to cope with our huge appetites and irregular hours: I suppose she was used to it with a family of four boys.

We had many memorable arguments, one of which was as to who should be the full-back reserve to me. My father was all for David Griffiths, the Bridgend full-back at the time. In the end John Dawes said his choice would be John Taylor – a flanker. On reflection, I think there was a fair amount of sense in the suggestion. In fact John Taylor did move to full-back at London Welsh on a number of occasions and he played excellently in that position. I remember him moving back during the game against Bath in '75 after I had received the first of my facial cuts before the famous Wales *v* England game. The quality of his playing that day made people suggest that he could easily have played the following week in that position in the International. It should be added that I have also played in John Taylor's position as flanker on several occasions since, including a game on the flank for Wales.

Squad training was only just beginning in Wales in those days and in fact was frowned upon by the other countries. But they soon adopted the system when they saw how successful we were being with it. We had a couple of squad weekends – as opposed to just the Sunday sessions which were very intense, but not all that popular with the individual clubs. London Welsh were very lucky in having tremendous reserves who could step in and play so well that the established players weren't missed at all. This, of course, is the strength of a club; not just the first fifteen players, but the reserve strength as well. The same fifteen players are not always available for every match, especially during the International season. Since London Welsh was based in England with many English fixtures, there would frequently be a game for the Welsh International on a Saturday morning which automatically ruled out six to eight players from the first team. Welsh clubs do not have quite the same problem, as they often play on the Monday after the International instead and can sometimes use their Welsh team players.

While we were almost invincible at Old Deer Park during this period, we never achieved so much success away from home. At Old Deer Park, we would regularly draw four to five thousand supporters who encouraged us by their confidence in our ability to win. We would often be losing right up to the last few minutes, but the crowd never worried till that final whistle went because they knew we would probably run in a couple of dazzling last minute tries. In our hey-day there was almost an air of euphoria around the pitch, with the crowd getting more and more hungry for exciting rugby. But playing away to the Welsh clubs, many of whom had suffered at our hands in London and were determined for revenge on their own patch, was different altogether. One match I remember in particular, in which we were able to produce our London form away from home, was at Aberavon. I was, in fact, not playing in this game due to injury and so had a good view of everything from the stand. To make it worse from Aberavon's point of view, the match was televised. The London Welsh team really clicked and won by forty points or so. But, as I have mentioned, this was not often the case in these matches, which were usually during the Christmas and Easter holidays – Swansea and Llanelli (Christmas) and Aberavon, Newport and Pontypool (Easter).

John Dawes was an outstanding captain. He had received a first-class honours degree in chemistry before turning to teaching and showed that he could use that brain both on and off the field. Although quiet and modest he was instigator of many of our attacking methods. As mid-field general he kept the forwards and backs running, and to this day I have yet to play with someone who can give and take a pass as swiftly as SJD could. Although he didn't make his place in the Welsh side secure until 1971, he was then such a success as captain of Wales that he was a firm favourite for captaincy of the Lions tour to New Zealand. The club was obviously delighted, especially as five others of its members were also selected – John Taylor, Mike Roberts, Mervyn Davies, Gerald Davies and myself. Geoff Evans was to join us later in the tour as a replacement. It was a compliment to the players and the club that four of the seven selected were forwards, for the play was expected to be dominated by the forwards in New Zealand.

Naturally during this period of success, we had our critics, but we knew that this was mostly jealousy, especially as it came mainly from club sides down in Wales. We were accused of being airy-fairy and not tough enough to play proper rugby. It was also suggested that our weaker fixture list against some of the English clubs enabled us to run in the tries we scored game after game. This was partly true, but it does not explain the similar results we also obtained on occasions against the toughest Welsh sides.

When we all returned from New Zealand (I later than the others), we were not allowed to play until November. This was slightly frustrating at the time, but in retrospect was very sensible and was typical of the thoroughness of the club. It took a lot of control on their part as they obviously wanted us back playing. However, as mentioned previously, the reserves were playing so well we were not really missed. I feel that this policy should have applied to those 1977 Lions who started playing far too soon after the tour. As a result some of them were very tired towards the end of the 1978 season.

The year following the Lions tour Tony Gray was captain and we played very successfully to win the *Western Mail* unofficial Welsh Championship. This is an unsatisfactory league as all the teams play a different number of games and the figure is given in percentages rather than points. It will never be really recognized until a proper league can be instituted. The 'Merit Table' is far more representative, although Cardiff chose not to take part in it. Wales has introduced a 'Knock-Out Cup' which has been a great success although there is a need for fewer fixtures against more equal opposition. In recent years, clubs have been winning the championship while playing perhaps only half the number of strong fixtures that clubs below them in the table do.

In spite of all this success, London Welsh has never so far done well in the English Knock-Out Cup. This is, I suppose, because they just aren't a typical Cup side. Good Cup sides tend to be steady rather than spectacular, concentrating on not making mistakes rather than on taking chances.

London Welsh was one of the first sides to initiate the now popular club tours. These started as long weekend trips to areas within the United Kingdom where we would not normally have fixtures. They were at the beginning of the season and used to be used as preparation for the season to come.

In 1972 we embarked on our first overseas tour. This was to Ceylon (Sri Lanka as it now is). This may seem an odd place to travel to play rugby – and so it was. We did not know what to expect but luckily the rugby was very easy, mainly because of the small stature of the players. There were many Europeans working on the tea plantations and I think they must have had an influence on promoting the game in Sri Lanka. It was a very entertaining tour and one journey from Colombo to the tea plantations up-country was memorable. We had taken a fairly large selection of drinks on board as even though the journey was only seventy miles or so, we knew it was going to take a fair time to get there – it was up-hill all the way. What we didn't realize was that the driver of the train had been helping himself to our beer, and half-way up to the mountains the train ground to a halt. We rushed into the driver's cab to see what had happened – he had passed out and was unable to continue the journey. So we had no alternative; Mike Roberts and Jim Shanklin became instant train drivers and took us the rest of the way to Kandy!

Sri Lanka is a country with a sharp contrast between the rich and the poor and we were shocked on our journey up-country to see the tracks lined with children and adults begging. Till then, we had stayed with Europeans and had not experienced the other side of life there. There was virtually no industry apart from the tea plantations and all the money went to the people who owned them. While I was there, I managed to look around the hospital in Colombo and observed many diseases which I am unlikely to encounter ever again in my medical practice. Typhoid fever was as common as a cold and tetanus was also prevalent.

Our main hosts were a family called the Bostocks and my friendship with them has continued since. I cannot recommend Ceylon beer – nor for that matter their local gin which we were forced to sample. It bore no resemblance whatsoever to Gordons. It was even tinged dark yellow.

The local rugby supporters were a very curious crowd. Tries could be scored galore, but there would be only applause when fifty or a hundred points were scored. This must have been due to their love of cricket! Luckily, we were able to accommodate them on a few occasions, so it can be appreciated that our games were not too strenuous. But the temperatures were very high and we played one match at 90°F and 85% humidity.

We soon came down to earth on our return home when we were thrashed by Llanelli at Stradey Park three days after our return. It was easy to see why.

The previous year we had played a match in France against the French champions Beziers from the South of France. This was billed as the 'European Club Championship' and involved a very arduous schedule on our part. We played Neath away on the Saturday and travelled back to London to prepare for an early departure on the Sunday morning. The match was to be played in Paris, so we arrived in time for lunch and were amazed to see bottles of wine served before the match. This is not unusual for French teams, but we certainly didn't feel like drinking wine.

The game was a disgrace and typical of many French club games. We were kicked and punched all over the field. But we came away on top as we won the game 12–8. I remember the French wing showing our wing Terry Davies the outside gap. Terry was an international sprinter and one of the quickest players I have ever played with or against. The Frenchman expected to tackle him from the side, but the look on his face when Terry accelerated away and left him standing could only be described as disbelief. That try turned out to be very important for the final result, but the match made me disinclined to play against French club sides again.

After the retirement of John Dawes, the fortunes of London Welsh took a turn for the worse. The school teachers, who formed the nucleus of the club in the past, were no longer coming to London in such vast numbers and the standard of fitness unquestionably dropped. It is difficult to know why this happened, since there were still many medical people playing for the club as before. I think it coincided with the upsurgence of Welsh nationalism: there was more of a tendency for school-leavers to apply for Welsh colleges, especially if they were Welsh-speaking. They preferred this to moving to London. There was also more pride in Wales and what it had to offer: no longer did fathers who had spent a life-time down the pits do all they could to give their sons a proper education to get them away from the mines. No longer was it prestigious to be able to say 'My son is up at college in London', and so the potential London Welsh players all stayed in Wales and the club itself was relying more and more heavily on English-born players of some (sometimes dubious) Welsh parentage. The club spirit also seemed to diminish with this gradual change – after all we could not really be called exiles any more. But up to 1973, we were still winning most of our games at Old Deer Park. Then Mervyn Davies departed for Swansea, Gerald Davies left

for Cardiff and Tony Gray departed for his native North
Wales. So there was a transition period in the club, and the
golden days were over.

After these changes, the forwards continued to win more
possession, but the backs were not using it too well. It was
interesting that a similar thing was also happening in the
national Welsh side at the same time, and that the Triple Crown
in 1974 was won by Ireland with a forward-dominated team.
This was a frustrating period for me at London Welsh as the
team came to rely on me more and more to launch attacks,
instead of using my energies skilfully in the three-quarter line
as they had before. I was also disappointed by some of the
decisions of the selectors, which resulted in inconsistency in the
side playing from one week to the next.

In fact, I think there was also a certain amount of sheer
incompetence and lack of responsibility at one period in '75–6
and I was beginning to feel that I no longer wanted any part
in organizing the club . . . There had been some suggestion
that I might become captain that year, but apart from my
feelings about the direction the club was taking, I felt I would
not be able to lead by example. I was heavily involved at this
time in the 'primary' course for first part of the FRCS examination and would not be able to make training sessions every
week, even though I had no on-call commitments at the time.
This was, as it turned out, my last season with the club and it was
fortunate that I decided to make my last appearance for London
Welsh on their tour to USA.

We were due to visit the Mid-West and Colorado, areas which
had not previously been visited by many rugby sides. Rugby
was flourishing in Canada and also making an impact in
California and the more anglicized parts of the States. Our
aim was to introduce it to the people in between. Jim Shanklin
had been elected captain for the following year, but he was
injured after the first game. So Tony Gray and I took over on
the playing side and developed a good team spirit which augured
well for the future and countered my disillusion with the team.

Tony Gray had missed the London Welsh style of rugby so much up in North Wales that he had been making the long journey to and fro from Bangor at the weekends, for much of the season prior to the tour. I have never seen anyone with so much stamina. Not only was he one of those naturally (and perennially) fit people, but he would stay the pace till well after the early hours and then be up bright and early cooking breakfast for everybody.

We won our matches in Chicago, Colombus, Vail and Denver by convincing margins and with attractive running rugby, but had unfortunately lost our first game in Indianapolis, having been taken by surprise by the strength of American rugby. Once we took the games seriously and played to our strengths, we did ourselves more justice and paid tribute to the American sides by giving them the game they deserved. The hospitality was second to none and we did a number of coaching sessions in each area in an effort to promote the game further. But we were worried by the attitude of some Americans to the game. Many drop-outs from other sports seemed to take up rugby, being drawn by the rough play, and thought they could go on the field and give a display of brute strength (and ignorance). But on the whole the game was obviously flourishing and its rapid expansion is reflected in the emergence of the 'Eagles'. This is their national team, who recently toured Britain and played well against an England XV, and later managed to beat Northern Transvaal whilst touring South Africa – a side which the 1974 Lions had difficulty beating.

While we were in the clubhouse at Old Deer Park, having a welcome British pint of beer after a horrendous forty-eight-hour flight back from Denver, I phoned Teddington to find out if Scilla had returned from a visit to Canada to stay with some friends. I discovered that not only had she returned but that she was expecting the removal van two days earlier than arranged – it was arriving in a couple of hours. I just could not believe it. The removal people were friends of the family, and only made one journey a week so we had no choice but to knuckle under and start packing up. As I was carrying a heavy oak wardrobe down the narrow staircase I remarked: '. . . if you'd told me I would be doing this twenty-four hours ago, I would just have laughed.' As it was I felt more like crying, but was just too tired to do either, and certainly too tired to protest. The driver could see how tired we both were and suggested that we should drive our little Fiat 600 up the ramp of the van and sleep all the way down the M4 behind the furniture. It seemed a funny suggestion at the time, but after stopping at every service station on the way, for coffee to keep us awake, we didn't think it was so ridiculous.

We finally crossed the Severn Bridge into Wales, and my days at London Welsh were over. I will always look back on my days there as being the most formative in my process of learning to adapt my game to full-back play. This had become my trademark by this time. So my memories of both the club and people connected with it are fond and grateful ones. It was a tremendous thrill to return there in 1978 as captain of Bridgend RFC, in the centenary season and to receive such a wonderful welcome.

Before completing this chapter, I must say something of how I fitted in my medical studies with this concentrated rugby playing. When I qualified in 1973 I did not realize how difficult it would be combining 'working on the house' as a houseman and first-class rugby. I passed the MRCS LRCP (Conjoint) examination in London on the Wednesday prior to the World VIIs in Scotland, held as part of the Scottish Centenary Celebrations. Because of my rugby travels, I was not allowed to sit the London MBBS examination until October 1973. So for those summer months I worked as a locum house officer at various hospitals in London – North Middlesex, King Edward VII, Windsor and Hillingdon. This was to stand me in good stead for my first full-time job as a house surgeon at St Mary's. We were on duty every other night and so our leisure time was at a premium. Scilla also worked at St Mary's at this time and we had carefully applied for jobs which would allow us to be off duty on the same nights. But I spent many of these training at Old Deer Park. Also, I was only able to play for certain every other Saturday. The fact that Scilla worked at the same hospital was useful – especially as she was also a house surgeon: she was able to cover for me if we had a home game or a game against another London club. Our house was conveniently situated in Teddington – ten minutes from Old Deer Park and with easy access to the M4.

In spite of this, I was still not able to give as much time to rugby as I had in the past. I missed several squad training sessions with Wales and roughly one in three matches for London Welsh.

At St Mary's it was fortunate that, like other teaching hospitals, they specialized in 'cold' (planned) surgery – there were not too many emergencies and therefore not too much lost sleep. But I did have to assist at renal transplants and as these never got under way until midnight at least and lasted four to five hours, there was always an air of depression in the 'mess' when there was a possible donor kidney available for transplantation. Another lucky factor was that the surgical unit and not my unit were 'on call' for emergencies every Saturday. The Professor of Surgery had asked me at my interview if I was going to continue playing rugby. When I gave my answer in the affirmative, I knew I would not become part of his unit.

During this period, I was out of the game for several months with a knee injury. So I didn't need to ask colleagues to cover for me quite so much and I could get treatment on the spot, as I was in the hospital for one hundred and twenty hours a week.

Working a 'one in two' rota, as it is called, is a very strenuous existence especially as we had to get up early on our nights off to travel into London from Teddington to miss the rush hour. I never experienced this again as my second house job was at Hillingdon Hospital, where we had only one night in four on call. This was much easier and allowed me more time off. Again

I was helped greatly by my fellow housemen, and by my Registrar in particular. This job was arranged before I left for South Africa and I was lucky to have it to come back to after the tour.

Hillingdon and St Mary's were completely different; the former was a big provincial hospital and the other one of the old established London teaching hospitals. To work in both was very good experience and, although it was hard work, I enjoyed them equally.

I had decided that I wanted to become a surgeon and so I had to try the first part of the surgery degree (FRCS, Fellow of the Royal College of Surgeons). This has a very low pass rate. I reckoned the best way to re-learn my anatomy was to teach it. So I returned once again to St Mary's, this time as a lecturer in the anatomy department. It was quite an experience to put myself on the other side of the fence and to be for the first time the person who faced the difficult questions. At this time I also attended a special 'Primary' course in Kensington.

Unfortunately, I failed the exam the first time so I thought that I would be clever and go to Edinburgh to sit the exam. Up there the examination is entirely oral and for that reason is supposed to be easier, but that did not do the trick.

On my return from Edinburgh, I was rather depressed and was not at all sure what I would do for the next six months till I could resit the exam again. Just a few hours after getting off the train at Euston, I saw a casualty job advertised in the British Medical Journal. This was at Battle Hospital in Reading which had strong contacts with St Mary's. They were always short of casualty officers at Battle and so I got the job without too much difficulty. This was a step in the right direction – that is, down the M4 towards Wales. The experience at Battle was invaluable especially as the casualty department received many of the motorway (M4) accidents. I always felt the name of the hospital was very apt.

During this period, I could easily continue with my rugby – many of the London Welsh players lived in the Reading area and it is within easy reach of London. But by this time we were already thinking of coming home to Wales, though I knew that I had to pass the Primary exam first.

I did pass in June 1976 and this worked out well – the interviews for the job of Senior House Officer in General Surgery at Cardiff were the following week. Having passed the Primary exam the job was virtually assured.

9

The Lions Tour of South Africa, 1974

It was touch and go whether I would be fit for the Lions' tour of South Africa in 1974. An injury to my right knee the previous January in a match for London Welsh against London Scottish had meant that I had missed my only match for Wales when they played against England at Twickenham. It was a traumatic experience: I had to be completely honest with myself and admit that I wasn't able to run flat out, even though I had managed to play a few reasonably sound games after the injury, before realizing how serious it was. It was even worse, having to be honest with the Welsh selectors, because had I been selfish and allowed myself the benefit of the doubt, I'm sure I could have run out on to the field with that extra cap, only to be replaced at the first sign of trouble with the knee. As it was, Roger Blyth's name appeared first in the announcement of the Welsh team.

I remember getting a taste of that feeling of having fallen from grace – I could not even get a ticket for the game. Finally I swallowed my pride and asked Clive Rowlands if he could help. It was a black day all round for Welshmen, as England took the honours, but Roger Blyth emerged with great credit, playing an excellent first game for Wales. This was in spite of bearing the intense pressure of being billed as the understudy. My only consolation was that perhaps I could have anticipated Dave

Duckham's side-step for I knew he tended to go off his left foot, and could thus have stopped their winning try.

Anyway, my right cruciate knee ligaments were still damaged, and there were only about ten weeks to go before the South African tour. It was a terribly depressing time for me as I had never suffered an injury which had kept me out of the game for so long. I had to work on building up my thigh muscles (quadriceps mainly) to compensate for the weakened ligaments. It was fortunate to have the physiotherapy department at St Mary's at hand and I was able to receive intensive treatment. I knew, and the girls in the department knew, that without Pat Clifton and Miss Cowie I would never have made the tour. I even spent a week with my right leg in plaster to stabilize the knee, which almost drove me (and Scilla) round the bend. I played no rugby for three months and rested the knee completely. Then one month of gradual intensive running exercises made me confident of my ability to play again. Once more, I was lucky, because the St Mary's sports ground was just round the corner from our little house in Teddington, and I had the whole place to myself most of those spring evenings.

There was one doubt, however. Would I be picked for the Lions? I had kept the seriousness of my injury quite a secret, so while many people thought I would be an automatic choice, I had several phone calls from the Lions management about my fitness. After all I had been out of the game for over three months. I assured them that I *was* fit, and on the strength of that I was picked. It was a great credit to them that they took my word for it – I'm sure the fact that I was a doctor and was able to explain everything in detail helped convince them.

I can remember the feeling of excitement the day the team was announced. I was still at St Mary's, but by then, coming towards the end of my first house job (internship) and – for the first time in my life – working for a living. I was twenty-five at the time. Not only was it a tremendous relief to hear my name, after all those months getting fit again, but the prospect of playing rugby and training in the sun after being on call in the hospital every other night for the previous six months filled me with anticipation. On a long tour, players are 'professional' in their outlook, and I think that if one cannot play well on a long tour, then one will never really play well.

I had made my private choice of thirty players in advance, and there were very few surprises. But I had not expected John Pullin to be omitted. He was still playing well for England and had a wealth of experience. Having often shared a room with him in New Zealand, I knew him to be a very good tourist. I had not expected Dick Millicken and Stuart Mckinney to be included, as I had not come into much contact with them before the tour, but after spending three months with them, I could fully justify their selection. All the same, Jim Renwick of Scotland was unlucky, and might easily have qualified for the third or fourth centre spot.

The choice of Willie-John McBride as captain, with his compatriot, Syd Millar, as coach, was an inspired one, and seemed a good omen after the success of the Welsh duo of John Dawes and Carwyn James in 1971. Syd and Willie-John had been together at Ballymena, as well as being both involved in Irish international rugby, so there was no question of time being spent to get the captain and coach on the same wavelength. Alan Thomas was manager to the side: he had been a former Welsh selector who had resigned over the WRU's initial refusal to accept a proper coaching policy; so there was no doubt that he was also on their wavelength when it came to adopting a 'professional' attitude towards coaching. He returned to the Welsh 'Big Five' in 1978-9 after a ten-year absence, during which time he had seen considerable proof of the success of the official coaching policy.

We assembled at the Britannia Hotel, just round the corner from St Mary's. Our biggest problem was to avoid the demonstrators protesting at our touring a country with apartheid laws. We had been under intense pressure both as individuals and as a group to call off the tour. In fact, Dennis Howell, as Minister of Sport, had met with members of the Four Home

Unions Committee, in an attempt to stop the tour. It was no secret that the party, with the official name of British Isles Rugby Union Team, was an embarrassment to Labour Party policy – if we had been called the Monty Python Flying Rugby Team, no one would have objected to our presence in South Africa. Most of us had thought deeply about the issues involved, but as sportsmen felt that we were being used as pawns in a political game of chess. It was not pleasant to openly defy one's own government; I wonder whether South African players would have made the same sacrifice for their sport.

Personally, I felt that a sense of proportion had been lost over apartheid, and although I could not condone it, it seemed to me that there were other and often worse violations of human rights going on in the rest of the world – the Soviet Union and South America, for instance. At that time, 1974, there had been no large scale demonstrations against athletes or gymnasts visiting Russia as a national team, although with the 1980 Olympics due to be staged in Moscow it now seems likely that this will happen.

So there we were, billeted in the Britannia Hotel for three days, coming and going through the back entrance for training sessions. The secrecy and the deliberate misleading of the press about our movements gave us a tremendous tour spirit right from the start – we had all made a decision: we were there for a purpose and all had a common goal. It was amusing to read the morning papers and find that we had apparently sneaked out of Heathrow the previous night, to avoid confrontation or last minute pressure from the government. In fact we were sitting enjoying our bacon and eggs in the Britannia Hotel.

We had a tumultuous reception in Johannesburg when we finally arrived, on schedule. Many of the South Africans had been pessimistic and never really believed that the tour would take place. We moved straight to Stilfontein from Jo'burg, for the week's training which had traditionally taken place at Eastbourne, on previous tours. This was a much better arrangement; quite apart from our wish to get out of the country before any further interference, we were able to take advantage of training at altitude. That week at Stilfontein was just what we needed.

The altitude problem was immediately obvious to us and for several days we struggled to find our breath, felt light-headed and experienced pain at the back of the neck. Ken Kennedy, the Irish hooker, also a doctor, devised special breathing exercises aimed at getting more air into the lungs, and in fact we continued these to the end of the tour, and during all the games. At certain times in our training it was quite a relief to stop and do our breathing exercises. We probably looked like a group of pregnant women at their ante-natal classes doing their elementary breathing, or a group of transcendental meditators!

I also helped Ken Kennedy take blood samples from the players, before and after our training week, in an attempt to evaluate some of the changes which take place at altitude. Unfortunately, we were not able to prove as much as we would have liked, since many of the changes are biochemical and are better revealed on arterial blood, using specialized apparatus. We had no access to this in Stilfontein. What we did show, to everyone's amazement, was that a number of our players were quite anaemic and they were the players who could run around all day, it seemed, without getting tired. On the strength of that Tony Neary, Johnny Maloney and the other two 'anaemic' players were put on iron tablets and steaks.

We were about six thousand feet up in a small town with no distractions, and there we set about preparing for what was going to be an arduous tour. The weather was beautiful, which helped our task enormously. We knew we could win, and felt that there was a lot of pressure on us to do so. We had beaten New Zealand in 1971, but that proved nothing, unless we could hold our own against the Springboks. The All Blacks had not won a Test series in South Africa, and unless we could make some impact in the Tests, we had no way of showing that our win in 1971 was not just a freak result, or that the opposition had just been weak. If we lost to South Africa we knew that apartheid would continue unchanged – many of us thought that by winning the series we could perhaps help to change the system to some degree in that beautiful, unenlightened country. Certainly it would justify our tour if some change were to take place.

Syd and Willie-John started to develop the powerful forward play which was to be a feature of the side. They knew that even the mighty All Black pack, in the past, had suffered at the hands of the Springboks. They also knew that there was the possibility of our forwards challenging their forward domination, if the correct techniques and attitudes were stressed. The backs practised amongst themselves with the senior players given a free hand by Syd Millar.

By the end of our ten days, we were ready for our first match at Potchefstrom against Western Transvaal. They had a good record against touring sides but we won easily, getting the tour off to an impressive start with a win of 59–13.

South West Africa was our next visit and we very nearly came unstuck there. It is a very dry, dusty place and the team found the pace hard going. But we just scraped home.

Boland (representing the wine-making areas of the Cape) were accounted for comfortably, but then came our first taste of the physical confrontation to come, against Eastern Province at Port Elizabeth. This was a brutal game with much niggling off the ball. We heard later that the Eastern Province side had been sent out to soften us up in the way which had probably been used in the past against British sides. But we had many players who could give as much as they could take, and while I do not like this type of rugby, it was essential for the Lions to show early on in the tour that they were not going to be intimidated in the way sides had been in the past.

There was an uncomfortable display of anti-British feeling at this match. It was the first we had come up against, since up till then people just seemed relieved that we had made the tour possible. One small boy supporting the Lions (because of British ancestry) was slapped in the face by a schoolmaster because he was apparently supporting the wrong side. Another lad had obtained a ticket from Gordon Brown, as one of the many relatives of the 'Broons' of Troon, and was ostracized at the match for shouting for the Lions. We heard all this after the match, and it made the Eastern Province game all the more unpleasant in our memories.

At this stage of the tour Mervyn Davies had not been playing as well as everyone knew he could and the press were convinced that Andy Ripley ('Rippers') would be the Test No. 8. They were probably fooled by some of Rippers's comments, including the message splashed across one of his less orthodox T-shirts: 'I'm so perfect, it scares me.' Andy was a tremendous tourist. He took charge of the music department and carried his tape recorder with him everywhere. His long hair and sandals were often frowned upon but he proved to be a second Francis of Assissi, showing remarkable kindness to animals. During our first week in Stilfontein he befriended a stray kitten and nursed it back to health in his hotel room, carrying up saucers of milk from the restaurant.

But those of us who knew Merv knew what the man was made of and there was little doubt that he would be up to top form for the first Test. The rest of the party were also sorting themselves out, but Syd Millar was able to make a gamble on the Western Province game, the week before that first Test. The Western Province game was billed as a fifth Test by many people, and the South African selectors had expected Syd to pick a 'shadow' Test team. Since we had been winning our games fairly convincingly up till then Sid deliberately included strong contenders for the Western Province game, like Sandy Carmichael, Roy Bergires, Stuart McKinney, Clive Rees and Andy Ripley – none of whom actually played in the first Test. Western Province played entertainingly, and ran the ball at us the whole time, making our eventual win a very close one (17–8 – well, close for us!). So it appeared to the

Springbok selectors that they had found a way round our formidable pack of forwards, and they included a hard core of the Western Province players in their Test side. At the end of all this planning came one unplanned factor, which was to prove our trump card – the rain. It rained solidly for a week in Cape Town, and Newlands, the ground was in a terribly waterlogged state. To make matters worse the traditional curtain-raiser game was played, which ruined the pitch for the actual Test. So the Western Province players could not possibly play their hard ground attacking rugby – and neither could we. It was ten-man stuff all the way – or rather nine-man, since the mud suited our forwards and Gareth Edwards ideally, and between them they controlled the game. Although we only won 12–3, there was only really one team unit. After the Springbok pack had been pushed back yards in the mud, Gareth would kick the ball fifty yards downfield to rub it in – I almost felt sorry for their forwards.

Still, we were delighted with our first Test win – it is such a psychological advantage in a four-match series. There has been criticism of the nine–ten man style of rugby that we used on occasions, especially during that first Test in South Africa, but it is always easy to criticize in retrospect. At that time, weather aside, we were in the unenviable position of not knowing just how strong the combined South African side would be. They had not toured Britain since the fateful 1970 tour, which was marred by demonstrations, and no one really knew what their potential was. 'They'll be different men when they pull on the green and gold', we were warned by the pundits. It is perhaps sad but true that points on the board are the only things which matter in Internationals and if you find the easiest way to put those points on the board – you carry on doing it.

The following Tuesday, we played Southern Universities, and Newlands was by then completely under water. I was appalled that the match actually took place – it really was dangerous; a player could easily have drowned if caught at the bottom of a ruck. There we had our first taste of South African anti-apartheid demonstrations, with university students running on to the field and attempting to stop the match. What we found unsavoury was not their actions but the way they were dealt with by the police: it was not at all gentle. And these were whites – we shuddered to think what they may have done to black demonstrators.

We then moved north to the High Veld to play Transvaal in what proved to be one of our hardest matches. There was a crisis in the side. The change in climate and altitude combined with the continual rain we had been subjected to in the Cape had resulted in twenty-two out of the thirty players going down with 'flu. Once someone caught the virus it was inevitable that it would spread like wild-fire – we were living in such close proximity to each other, sharing rooms, towels, even beer glasses. By the Saturday of the match there were still six of us of the side who had been picked *in extremis* or so it seemed to us. But we had to play as no one else was any better. I did not dare take my temperature. Bobby Windsor (the Duke) was certainly not his usual amusing self. As for Benny (Phil Bennett) his face said it all when it was decided that it would have to be him, since Alan Old was on crutches and Ian McGeechan was too ill to be considered. We were very soon in trouble against a good Transvaal side, and my legs were feeling very heavy whilst chasing across the field to collect Gerald Bosch's mighty kicks. Having had the advantage of a strong wind, we were only level at half-time and the writing was on the wall. Looking at the rest of the lads I knew they were feeling as bad as I was. Willie-John knew it too. But in spite of all our game improved by playing into the biting wind, and this was the first time I realized how much stamina there was in the side: we were not going to let the team, nor Willie-John down, just because we weren't feeling too good. We eventually won 23–15 and to me, this was perhaps the most important win of the tour. It was a memorable match in some ways, but in others I have very little recollection of the actual run of play. I scored one of only three tries during the whole tour, but to this day I cannot remember anything about it.

The Springbok selectors again misjudged their selection for the second Test. Instead of continuing with their (sound) policy of using their backs to run at the Lions they were over-impressed with the performance of the Transvaal side, and selected many of them for the second Test at Loftus Versfeldt in Pretoria.

Meanwhile, we had spent a few days enjoying marvellous hospitality in Rhodesia and were all recovered from our influenza. We were amazed by the difference between Rhodesia and South Africa. The saddest thing was that even in 1974 the black-white situation in Rhodesia was better than that in South Africa under apartheid but we knew then that there would almost certainly be bloodshed at some stage – possibly even at some of the white homelands we had visited.

Loftus Versfeldt is the South African rugby shrine. To a player from overseas it presents as formidable a prospect as playing at Cardiff Arms Park does to a team from abroad. It is in the heart of Afrikaans-speaking Pretoria, and before the second Test there was the certain feeling in South Africa that here the Springboks would play more as they had in the past against the touring sides.

But it was not to be.

Everything about Loftus is different from Newlands – the high altitude (5000 ft), the climate, the springy turf singed by the sun and the perilously high open stands erected like gigantic pieces of scaffolding. The ground was ideal for running rugby, but, unfortunately for the Springbok selectors, all the running came from the Lions. I remember arriving at the ground, in the bus from the hotel. We were in the middle of one of our favourite touring songs – 'The Flower of Scotland'. Suddenly the bus ground to a halt. Nobody moved. We all sat in our places and carried on singing until we had reached the end. It was symbolic of the tremendous confidence we had in ourselves as a team: singing like that on the way to an important match and not letting anything interfere with the team song was true audacity.

The poor Springboks were in a very different frame of mind. Although many of the local people were confident about their chances, their own coach could not have been. They were virtually imprisoned in a hotel in Pretoria for three days before the Test, and were forbidden to read any newspapers or have any communication with the press. I suppose it was meant to generate some sort of team spirit – after all, there had been about eight changes in the side since the first Test – but I'm sure it only served to lower their morale.

We had gambled on our choice of referee by choosing Cas de Bryn, who had not 'reffed' any of our games till then. Max Baise, after reffing the first Test, had mysteriously been removed from the panel we had to choose from and we weren't particularly happy with the other choices. As it was, Cas de Bryn proved his worth by letting the game flow and we eventually clocked up five tries, including one beauty by J. J. Williams which had resulted from a knock-on by one of our forwards. If the pack did well at Newlands, they did even better on the turf at Loftus and it is a credit to all the forwards that they were able to withstand the extremely fast pace throughout the match. It says a lot for Roger Uttley, a former second row forward, that he was able to make such a success of his move to the flank at the start of the tour. Even though we won easily in the end (28–9) we had to work extremely hard in the first half, especially in retrieving the kicks from Bosch, the 'Boot'. In that rarified atmosphere, even my attempts at kicking to touch could attain forty or so yards – so for the kicking specialists it was paradise.

But in the second half, we were throwing the ball around in such a way that it seemed impossible that we were playing an International – it was more like VIIs, or a charity exhibition match. Benny (Phil Bennett) was brilliant on numerous occasions, running the ball from broken play. Even he became cheeky towards the end as he lay on the ground for some minutes after injuring his ankle in a spectacular try, only to bounce up and slot over the conversion in a matter of seconds.

The image of the sun setting over the West stand, gradually shading more and more of the pitch, with the crowd growing quieter and quieter as Loftus became a 'graveyard' for South African rugby is one I shall never forget.

We were 2–0 up in the series and could not lose. The Springbok selectors came in for a lot of criticism from their own people who, after the second Test, were beginning to take the view that the Lions had plenty to offer, and plenty to teach the Springboks – especially the forwards. There was a growing feeling that great changes would have to be made in apartheid, to allow multi-racial teams to represent South Africa at home and abroad in order to prevent the 'Boks from falling completely from grace in the rugby world. After all, it was the national game and national pride was at stake. We had the feeling that people could accept criticism (in censored amounts albeit) of their government and its policies, but that they could not tolerate criticism of their rugby side.

As for the players being forbidden to see the papers beforehand – 'They definitely won't be allowed to see the papers afterwards,' quipped Bobby Windsor, as ''Boks mauled by Lions' filled the front pages of the Sunday rags.

After the second Test we visited Kruger National Park for a four-day break. It was ideally timed and proved a very relaxing place in which to celebrate our second Test victory – indeed almost too relaxing. We visited two different camps and on the first night, in the absence of any civilized form of entertainment, we amused the other visitors with a game of 'thumper'. This is a sign game where every member has his own particular form of gesticulation, and some of them could be pretty rude. The participant who makes a mistake has to down a can of beer in one. The problem, as with so many of these games, is that one or two people get repeatedly caught making mistakes and, as the alcohol takes effect, they make more and more. My room mate, Billy Steele, had a very unfortunate evening and many of us in retrospect wonder whether he ever quite recovered from it on the tour. We all stayed in 'rondavels', the small round mud huts with grass roofs, and open doors, and were horrified on the following morning to find evidence that a lion (four-footed variety) had been prowling around the camp that night, possibly whilst we were outside in the dark, oblivious to the danger – oblivious to anything.

Mervyn Davies also made his mark on that visit by growing a beard and showing immense feats of strength, strutting around with a crate of beer on his shoulder (to make sure he did not run out) as if it weighed a few ounces. With his floppy hat, sunglasses and cigarette drooping from his mouth, it was a very different Merv from the white-bandaged, serious-looking face we were more used to seeing on the field.

He also had a few experiences whilst we were in Rhodesia. During a lunch on the Zambesi river he had the misfortune to drop his camera overboard. Being the character he is he had to be stopped from leaning over to try and fish it out. As if to teach him respect for the river occupants, a baby crocodile bit him later on in the day, when we visited a crocodile farm. Not a great day for the big man!

I was very close to Merv during the 1974 tour – of all the Welshmen, that is. We had been together in International rugby since winning our first caps together, and felt rather like partners in crime. Our experiences in New Zealand and at London Welsh had been similar, and we were the only two left of the London Welsh mob on the tour.

But, all in all, I suppose I was more friendly with non-Welsh players, and this was due to the way in which Willie-John and Syd had integrated the whole lot of us. The 'family spirit' which remained with us during the whole tour caused a certain amount of criticism from South Africans because there were many occasions when we preferred our own company to that of our hosts. We went out of our way to mix with people at the receptions held after the matches, but these did not take the shape of a formal dinner as they do in Britain, and so we always had time afterwards to make our own entertainment. It was suggested that we were too dedicated to our task of winning to allow us to socialize, but I do not think that was true. It was just that our attitude was different from the teams which had toured South Africa as Lions in the past: if we were going to do well the tour could not be just a glorified holiday.

We were quickly reminded of this, after our spell at Kruger, when we came up against the Quaggas – the South African equivalent of the Barbarians. We had no idea what was in store for us. Originally the side was meant to contain some of the potential young players, and players from areas which did not have a game against us. There was also talk that it would be the ideal game in which to experiment by allowing a few non-whites to play in the same team, and in this way set a precedent for future policies in South African sport. We were therefore very disappointed to find no Morgan Cushe, the much talked about Leopard (Bantu) flanker, nor either of the powerful wingers from the Proteas side we had played against previously. I suppose it was naïve to think that there could be such a move made in the short time available, but we had genuinely believed that the loss of the two Tests had started to worry the South African Rugby Board into making some positive move towards integration. We felt that there were one or two non-white players who were worthy of being considered for Springbok selection, so it would not have been simply a question of including a few in the Quaggas side simply for the colour of their skin.

However, it did not turn out like that. The side selected was very strong indeed – they nearly became the first side to beat us on the tour. A disturbing aspect of this game was the verbal and physical abuse thrown at the referee, Ian Gourlay. It was quite disgraceful, and several of the Lions had to escort him from the field to prevent him suffering serious injuries from the so-called fans. This match emphasized to us that our mid-tour break was over, and that we had to get down to the serious business of training again. One amazing statistic resulting from that Quaggas match was that seventy-five thousand people turned up at Ellis Park, Johannesburg to watch a mid-week game. I suppose it was a great compliment to us and to the game of rugby – but there must have been a lot of absenteeism in the city that day.

Two weeks before the third Test we very nearly came un-stuck again. It often happened that we encountered spirited opposition the week or so before a Test, only to find many of those members of that same opposition finding their way into the Springbok Test side. The Free State and Northern Transvaal matches were no exception, and much of the 'Bok Test side was composed of players from these teams; it made the side almost entirely Afrikaans-speaking, as opposed to that first Test side from the English-speaking Western Province.

Our liaison officer, Choet Visser, was a native of Bloem-fontein, and we were all looking forward to seeing his home-town, despite wise-cracks from people suggesting that 'Bloem was the flattest and dullest place on earth. He had become a close friend and had been very fair to us, at the expense of being called traitor by some of those who did not know him well in South African rugby circles. Those who *did* know him well understood that he was only performing the job allotted to him to the best of his ability. As a man of principle, honesty and integrity, we admired him in much the same way as we admired Willie-John, and although their backgrounds were quite different these two, along with Syd Millar, became very close on tour.

There was a joke amongst the lads, that they formed a secret Mafia with Robert Denton, from the Northern Transvaal Rugby Union (well known for its immense wealth) and a couple of the other Lions – Fergus Slattery and Mighty Mouse McLauchlan. I was only a mere henchman to the 'Don', but honoured to be so. Phil Bennett, who was a tremendous tourist in South Africa, was also very friendly with Willie-John and together they made a great pair. Peter Cooke and Dudley Moore had nothing on those two!

The Free State came the closest to beating us, with the exception, I suppose, of the fourth Test side. The game was hard but we were well in control of it. We were 9–7 down towards the end and, despite intense pressure, just could not score. It was well into injury time before we managed to pull it off. From a scrum in their twenty-five, Gareth broke away and, when held, just flipped the ball inside. J. J. Williams was there to catch the ball and he dived over for the winning try. We didn't need the conversion: the whistle went straight afterwards. But it was a close thing. Again character had saved the day. That, and the indefatigable confidence we seemed to have in ourselves.

The Sunday after the Free State game was spent leisurely, and the Lions were entertained by Choet and his family. It was a welcome break to have a taste of home-cooking and have the company of Choet's grandchildren after all the time spent in hotels. It was no discredit to the Vissers that many of the lads felt homesick for their own families that day, because we were treated as one big family by Choet. He has a marvellous rugby cellar housing an intriguing collection of rugby momentoes and trophies. To this I was proud to be able to add my Lions tracksuit and my dirty old bandage-headband which I had worn in all my games out there. I had needed something to keep my hair out of my eyes when squinting into the sun for high kicks. It was not that my hair was any longer in South Africa; I think it must have been the lack of wind over there which caused me trouble – in Britain the wind does the trick!

From Bloemfontein we moved up to the gold mining area of Kimberly where we hit gold on the pitch by beating the West Griqualand side by 69 points to 16. We were not so lucky when we visited the actual mine. Another tough game the Saturday before the third Test came from Northern Transvaal, where we did not play as well on the Loftus pitch as we had in the second Test.

As before, the Springbok selectors read too much into this game along with the Free State one, and it became clear that they were panicking. A provincial game is very different from a Test match and it is a truism that there are certain players who are tremendous at provincial or club level, but who will never make it at International level. I suppose it all comes back to Big Match Temperament.

Whether the Springboks selected for the third Test had the temperament or not there was very little chance for them to play as well in a side which had chopped and changed so much, as it was for them to play for their provinces in a regular team. The most ridiculous selection was the choice of a No. 8 as scrum-half. The way it was decided was even more crazy: three of the candidates were on show at a training session the week of the Test, and one was chosen purely on his performance that day. Surely this is not the way to select an International scrum-half, especially when it is on the cards that he may be playing behind a beaten pack? We felt sorry for Sonnekus, because it seemed that he was ridiculed by the choice.

So, after an easy win against the Leopards side (comprised only of African players, as opposed to Indians, whites, or those of mixed blood-coloureds) we had a chance to settle the series without dispute. The match was probably the best of the series, with the Springboks being on top for most of the first half – even Gareth was having his kicks charged down by their forwards, pouncing at every opportunity. Just before half-time Ian McGeechan kicked a beautiful ball downfield for it to roll into touch just short of the Springboks line for their throw-in. To our delight, they chose the short line-out, and Gordon Brown moved up to the front. Amazingly, the ball was thrown to the front – all the Broon from Troon (Gordon Brown) had to do was to put his hands up, catch the ball, and fall over the line for a crucial try. So at half-time the Springboks, who had worried us all during the first half, found themselves 7–3 down. Our morale was extremely high and not just because of the score. There had been an incident just prior to Geek's kick in which we had been intimidated by some of the Springbok 'Meanies' as they had been nicknamed, who had been included in the side to sort us out. Willie-John had anticipated this before the match, having seen the names of some of the players selected, and had devised the controversial 'Code 99'.

It had been used a couple of times before, but I'm afraid that it had to be used again at Port Elizabeth. We had decided that if foul play started, and one of our players was in danger, then we would all rush in to break it up and defend him. That way single players would not be isolated as they had been for example in the Sandy Carmichael incident in Canterbury, New Zealand in 1971, and the referee would have to blow up because of all the confusion, before anyone could get seriously injured.

So Code 99 was used with success just before half-time and no one was injured. We had shown that we were not going to be pushed around. To cap it all we had won the ball.

In the second half it was used again after a vicious attack on Bobby Windsor by one of the big Springboks, who left no doubt in anyone's mind what his intentions were. A nasty brawl erupted, with players from both sides throwing punches, forwards and backs included. I was in there too. And since I had further to run to get there than anyone else there was no doubt about my intentions either. It was an extremely distasteful incident, and one I would perhaps have been ashamed of had I ever thought that it was the Lions who had started the business, in the first place. I appreciated the criticism of such tactics and feel now that we did rather overdo the 99 in the third Test. But as I have stated before it was a team defence tactic. Our policy was to go for the ball, and not the man, because apart from anything else games are won by winning the ball – you don't get very far passing a man to your scrum-half.

Thereafter we were able to concentrate on playing positive rugby as we had played it in the second Test. JJ scored a couple of beautiful tries which were as good as anything we had scored in New Zealand, and Phil Bennett again showed that he could demonstrate all the skills by dropping a couple of cool goals. The second try by JJ was especially satisfying for me as it had involved me in a miss-move, which I eventually came back into, and handled twice before sending JJ over the line. It was exciting to find the ball 'passed' inside to me by JJ who had in fact streaked down the touchline unharmed by defenders who thought I had the ball. As I was about to be on the line I turned back to find JJ still outside me; he then cut inside to score under the posts. It confused not only the Springbok defence, but the commentators as well. 'And it's John Williams passing to John Williams, who is now going to pass to John Williams.' Hence the need for JPR and JJ. We were comfortably home 26–9 and winners of the series.

We had made history again. It seemed incredible. We chaired Willie-John off the field: it was the only fitting thing to do. As leader, he deserved all the credit. It was typical of him to insist on being put down – he was not one to take all the glory – and he made his feelings quite clear as he waved up to the Lions sitting in the stands. They too deserved the acclaim, and the tears in their eyes showed how much that gesture had meant to them. We had tremendous celebrations after the game, and Syd Millar actually said we could pack up and go home. It was meant metaphorically, but although there were some tough matches to go, many of us relaxed from that moment. We certainly never played quite the same for the remainder of the tour.

We still had provincial games to play against Border, Natal and Eastern Transvaal before the final Test which was going to be – in tennis terms – a dead rubber. The Natal game had particular interest for me in many ways, not least of which was that Scilla was working in the Addington Hospital in Durban for six months. After all, one of us had to work to pay the mortgage! I was unemployed for the duration of the tour, since I was between 'house jobs'. I could not possibly have absented myself for four months of a six-month job.

Besides, those two six months need to be completed *in toto* to gain the necessary experience and become fully registered with the General Medical Council. It seemed an ideal opportunity for Scilla to travel and work at the same time, especially as her earnings were higher than they would have been in the UK. She was fortunate enough to gain a six-month internship at the 'white' Addington Hospital, working under Professor Adams. We had hoped she might be able to work in the non-white hospital in Durban, but this request was understandably turned down, since its internships went to graduates of the non-white medical school there. After all, we knew that they could not work in the white hospital.

So, she was in Durban – but as far as the tour was concerned, she might have been in London, except that my stamps were cheaper. We were both insistent that she should have nothing to do with the tour. Scilla knew as well as I did what a long tour involved, and it would have been an embarrassment to her, as well as to the other players, to have her around. As it was, I think I saw her twice before the Natal game, when she had travelled to the Transvaal with friends she had made at the hospital.

It was quite exciting, really, because she would book into some hotel which, according to the guide books, was reasonably near to ours, and we would arrange to meet secretly, after the match, in a place neither of us had seen before. Her hotel was usually quite a sleazy dive because although I was staying in five-star hotels most of the time, Scilla could not afford anything similar after travelling all that way.

We looked as if we were having a clandestine affair – no one would have believed us if we had explained that we were actually married. A few of my close friends on the tour, such as Merv, knew that she was in Durban, but no one really minded because her life was quite independent of ours.

When we finally reached Natal at the end of the tour, Scilla was understandably excited and wanted to show me around when I got the odd hour's break from touring duties.

She arranged for us to have dinner at a magnificent restaurant she'd discovered in Durban. We couldn't believe our eyes when we saw who was sitting at the next table – Willie-John, Syd, Fergus and Choet and his wife Joyce. All our undercover plans had been discovered. I introduced Scilla to Willie-John, explaining that she was my wife. He looked at me a bit oddly for a while – he knew that I had a wife in Britain and here was this girl who for all the world could have been South African with a tan and blonde hair. But then he realized that I was serious and seemed amazed to learn that she had been in Durban for three months. I was relieved that he did not seem to mind. I would have been upset had I felt that Willie-John disapproved. He was that sort of man and all the players felt the same about him.

The whole of Natal was looking forward to the game against the Lions as a chance to prove that they were still in the reckoning. Many people in Natal were incensed that their team, and especially their captain, Tommy Bedford, had been over-looked for the Tests. After all, virtually every other team had been represented. So they thought that the ideal opportunity to show the Springbok selectors their mistake would be to beat the Lions, with their running style of rugby. The press were also full of stories of how Natal were going to beat us, so much so that by the time we got to Natal we were fed up with the sound of it.

All except me that is. I could not have picked a worse place to get involved in a controversial incident on the field, nor a worse moment to choose to lose my temper with the hero of Natal, but that is exactly what happened. About half-way through the second half, when the Natal side were holding us extremely well with superb tackling and stamina, I was fielding a high ball in my own twenty-five when I fumbled it slightly and ended up getting bundled into touch by Tommy Bedford with Merv up in support. I think I was annoyed with myself as much as anything at this stage, but then I felt myself being grabbed by the hair, and suffered a hefty kick on my head. I now realize that this was probably accidental. But at the time I was furious and I must admit I lost my temper. I lashed out a couple of times at Bedford, by rabbit-punching him on the floor, and he lay there as if unconscious. I couldn't believe it because I knew that I had not hit him hard. I also knew I should not have hit him at all, but as he lay there, the horror of the situation suddenly dawned. The incident took place close to spectators and I thought the whole crowd was going to attack me. They were shouting and screaming, and one spectator was beating me over the head with a stick. What a scene! I was obviously upset at the time, but there were even worse incidents later in the game – one, I think, involving Fran Cotton. The crowd again went berserk and started throwing *nartjies* (tangerines) on to the pitch, which was common in South Africa, and then beer cans and bottles followed, which was not. Willie-John had to stop the game and call us all together for fear of injury. We went on to score some spectacular tries in the closing minutes of the game and one in injury time, with Mike Gibson coming into peak form since his delayed arrival on tour with us.

But none of that was remembered in Natal. I was described by the press as the biggest thug who had ever toured South Africa, and the reports went on to say that I was well known for my violent nature in British rugby. That seemed unfair – tough, yes, but violent, no. Had I been fortunate enough to be bundled into touch by one of their wingers probably none of the aftermath would have occurred – but the idea that anyone should lay a finger on their hero was unthinkable and I suppose it was.

That evening I had a distressing encounter with Tommy Bedford's wife who marched up to the table I was sitting at with a few of the other Lions, and accused me of all sorts of crimes. This upset me even more as I had spoken to Tommy in the dressing-room afterwards, and it appeared that he had accepted my apology. It all seemed grossly exaggerated, especially when I think of all the tactics and punching used in the scrum and the line-out. Having said that, it does not alter the fact that I was not proud of my actions especially with so many schoolboys watching the match.

Fortunately I was able to put it all behind me for a few weeks as we moved on to Eastern Transvaal the following day. The Lions management showed their integrity by choosing me as captain for the Eastern Transvaal match at Springs. They knew that I had been shaken by the incident in Durban and gave me the best vote of confidence possible. To cap it all, the Eastern Transvaal side had been renowned for hard, punchy matches against previous touring sides, not least the French. I am grateful to the Lions who played under my leadership that day, that I can boast the fact that there was not a single punch or trace of bad gamesmanship during the entire match. I felt that I had cleared my copybook.

But Scilla was not allowed to forget. In fact, were it not for her close friends at the hospital, I'm sure she would have packed her bags and gone home to spend those three months elsewhere. For weeks after the incident she received threatening letters and anonymous phone calls, telling her how awful I was. People would stop her and say, 'Oh you're JPR's wife are you? It's surprising you haven't got a black eye,' or 'What's it like being married to a thug?' The fact that the newspapers were printed locally in Durban, instead of nationally, as many are in Britain, made it worse and the *Natal Mercury* and the *Daily News* just could not let it drop. A cartoon appeared showing me punching a patient (with my doctor's bag) whilst making a housecall. This really upset the doctors at Addington, a group of whom wrote to the newspaper concerned, declaring that if anything similar appeared then the Medical Defence Union would sue the paper for libellous misrepresentation.

It was only when I returned to Durban after the tour that I discovered all these things. Scilla had kept them to herself and had thrown away nearly all the newspaper cuttings so that they would not distress me. Imagine her fury when some kind person sent me an envelope with all the press cuttings –

cartoon and all, with the brief message, 'Just to let you know what we think of you here.'

Eventually I became accepted, at least by the Addington Doctors Quarters (DQ as it was nicknamed) and by a few of the local people. I was so shattered after the tour that I did nothing but sleep and lie on the beach just in front of the hospital for about a week. It is always very hard to adjust to relatively normal living after a long tour, when you have lived out of a suitcase for three months, and been waited upon hand and foot in smart hotels. Not that you could really have described our few months together after the tour, at Addington, whilst Scilla finished her job, as normal living – far from it.

There was a tremendous group of doctors at DQ, many of whom were in the same position as us: trying to see a bit of the world whilst working at the same time. There were doctors from Australia, Germany, Ireland, Czechoslovakia and several like us from the London teaching hospitals. We became involved in all sorts of activities including cricket matches, golf sessions, discotheques on cruises around the harbour and the inevitable *braais* (barbecues) on the beach. There was some work done, but there I must stress that I could not really be classed as one of the doctors. Although I had taken out temporary registration with the South African Medical Council when I arrived in Durban, I discovered that I could not get work as a *locum* in hospitals. This was nothing to do with my rugby incident, but was caused by the fact that the intern system over there is slightly different from that in Britain, and locums are not employed when the other doctors take leave.

I could not work in general practice either, because I was not then fully registered. So I decided that I would concentrate on my tennis again – it was the first opportunity that I'd had to play seriously since those last tournaments in 1970. The climate was ideal for it and there seemed no shortage of courts, since many people seemed to have their own. Once people had overcome their initial anxiety about me, I was invited to play with some very good players at the weekends, and found that I soon slipped back into my old strokes.

After a week or so the idea of becoming a tennis coach was suggested. It seemed impossible at the time, but the more I thought about it the more excited I became at the prospect. Fortunately I was befriended by one of the established coaches in Durban, who was able to incorporate me into his 'school', but I had first to pass a formal coaching exam. There was a lot of scepticism at first from people who were certainly not going to give me the benefit of the doubt, but once I had been put through my paces, it became obvious that, thug or no thug, I did show I was able to hold a racquet – and use it well.

So started a couple of tremendous months when I would spend mornings on the beach, then get into my working clothes (hardly different from my beach attire) and set off for a girls' convent or a boys' prep school, floppy hat and all. The incredible thing was that by working only four or five hours a day I was earning as much as I would have earned in hospital, doing a hundred and ten hours a week. In the evenings I was fortunate to be able to play squash at the Durban Country Club where I had been made a temporary member, though after much protesting from some of the established members. Luckily one of the members had been at St Mary's and had played tennis with me there, so he put in a good word for me.

During those few months it seemed as if the tour was years away. I had deliberately played no rugby as I needed the complete break before I got back into the swing of things around December when the tour resumed. I had caused a few problems by staying out in South Africa, as the All Blacks were due to make a short tour of the UK, including a game against Wales as well as one against the Barbarians. I had kept up correspondence with John Dawes, who was anxious to know if I would be fit for the Wales game, and if I would be back in the country by the middle of November.

Although I assured him that I would be fit, there were many objections to my selection on the grounds that I would not have played a game for five months. This seemed fair, so I planned a ridiculously tight schedule by which I arrived back at Heathrow on the Saturday morning before the usual Welsh mid-week game, and went straight off to London Welsh to play for their sixth side – as a wing-forward. Fortunately I always manage to sleep on plane journeys, (with the right ratio of sleeping pills and alcohol) and so the plan worked quite well, and I think it quietened the critics.

I had a lovely telegram from the lads at London Welsh, wishing me luck against the All Blacks, adding, 'It's not often one of the LW VI side gets capped for Wales.'

There was also controversy over the Barbarians match against the All Blacks. Willie-John had wanted to play a Lions side when he was invited to be captain, since it would have been a chance for the British public to see the side on home ground who had made history in action. But there were objections raised, and in the end he had to make do with only a Lions pack, so I was not picked. That upset me a little because I think the Barbarians still believed that I was not match fit. But the Barbarians side just did not seem to click with W-J's team – the Lions spell had been broken. Watching that match, I thought back to those last few days with the team in Jo'burg.

Back in South Africa the Lions tour was still to be completed. We were unbeaten in the Provincial games and just had the last Test to go. It was obvious that many of the lads were tired and thinking of home. Similar to the New Zealand series and the last Test there, our attitude seemed to be one of making sure we did not lose, rather than going out at Ellis Park to win. I feel that there is a great difference here and one which can dramatically alter the result of the game. Personally, I went on to that field to win, which I hope was obvious by my last dash attempts to cross the line.

I am the sort of person who cannot accept a compromise: in a game, it is all or nothing. The Springboks admittedly played much better than before, with another of my namesakes, John G. Williams taking much possession in the lines-out. But we still felt we had done enough to win the game. When Fergus Slattery seemed to score a try right at the end we thought we had done it – beaten every side we had played in South Africa. But it was not to be, as the referee disallowed the try, ordered a five-yard scrum and blew up before the ball was even out of the scrum. He had to – we would more than likely have scored (again) from that ball instead. So, as it was, the score was 13–13 and we were unbeaten. We could not really blame the referee, because there had been controversial tries all afternoon, including one by Roger Uttley, which showed on photographic evidence to have been grounded by the Springbok, Chris Pope, first.

But, we had achieved what we had set out to do, and at our farewell party, it was a great honour for me to be asked to present our captain, Willie-John, with a silver salver memento from the players. It was a very emotional moment for me, and I can't deny that there were a few tears shed that evening. We were all tired, both physically and mentally, and we all knew just how hard it had been to live with an unbeaten record right to the last. We had played some champagne rugby, and we had played some hard grind, ten-man rugby. We had set all kinds of records, including the one set in Mossel Bay, where we defeated the South Western Districts by 97 points to 0 (setting ten records in the process): J. J. Williams scored a hat-trick of tries in each half, and fly-half Alan Old scored 37 points after missing only one kick at goal out of seventeen attempts. We had played two non-white sides, the Proteas in Cape Town and the Leopards in East London and had seen plenty of promise on the fields there. We knew that things would have to change if South Africa was ever to take part in International rugby again. Already it was obvious that their standards had fallen from lack of competition.

But it was not enough to just promise a multi-racial side to tour abroad – that was the easy way out. It would need integration at club level, so that all the non-white players could get a chance, not just the talented ones who were prepared to act as guinea pigs at a time of change. We hoped that change would come. We hoped that it would come quicker as a result of our tour and we were now confident that it would.

Now, years later, we can see that changes have been slow, and they still have not reached a position which would be acceptable to other countries. But we still hope. South Africa is a beautiful country, and we thoroughly enjoyed its famous hospitality. It would be a pity if it could never be repaid or repeated.

I saw there many things which disturbed me, many which pleased me and gave me hope. Many things annoyed me, many made me angry, but in spite of this, many things made me smile. Of these, the one which sticks in my mind most of all is the road sign on the way to St Lucia in Northern Natal which read: 'Wees op u Vir Seekoeite na Sononder', 'Beware! Hippos crossing the road at night.'

I certainly would never have come across that, had I stayed behind in Teddington.

Fitness and Training

I have always been teased for the serious way in which I approach training. I have perhaps been very aware that the only way I can continue to play my style of full-back game is to be as fit as possible all the time. As soon as I start having to run back for the ball, and having to run the full width of the field to mark a wing, my defensive role is weakened, and I am no longer a full-back.

Many players nowadays turn up to training sessions and expect the coach to get them fit. This, I believe, is the wrong attitude. Fitness is such a personal thing that it should be up to the individual to keep himself fit and to perfect the particular skills he needs for his position. Then he can turn up to a training session in such condition that he can obtain the greatest possible benefit from the coaching. Unfortunately this rarely occurs and half the session is wasted going over what could have been done as homework. So often time is spent going over set moves with little success: players start dropping the ball, others are not quick enough off the mark and the whole thing turns out to be a shambles simply because of a lack of basic fitness. It is only when everyone is fit to start with, as is the case during a long tour, that you realize just how profitable it is to be able to concentrate on teamwork and moves.

I have been lucky in that I never find it a problem to train on my own. When I was having difficulty making the club sessions because of night duty in the hospital, I just had to make up on my fitness training on my own. Somehow I am able to motivate myself, and set myself targets which are every bit as real as if I were racing to catch a speedy wing. I've never really had a vivid imagination, so I'm sure it's not that. Perhaps it's a way of getting things out of my system. Certainly, on tour, I used to take the attitude that the heavier the beer-drinking session the night before, the harder I would push myself the following morning, when everyone else was suffering after-effects. Sean Lynch took much the same view. In fact a long run, working up a great sweat, is a real cure for a hangover! It probably works on the principle that the gallons of water drunk afterwards dilute the alcohol, as well as correcting the inevitable dehydration. I usually train on my own by running five or six miles once a week, plus two sessions, if possible, at the club. I am lucky, now that we are in Wales, that there is such a lot of open space close by and I can run on grass most of the time. Many people decry road-running as training for rugby, because of the strain it puts on the calves. I never really had any problem with that up in London, and certainly would not use it as an excuse: road-running is better than no running. During the run (which I like to go over in the car, checking distances and timing them) I choose different spots for incline training, speed bursts and some body exercises. That way there is a break, and something for me to think about whilst I'm running. I have the greatest admiration for the long-distance runners who cover hundreds of miles a week and still keep themselves motivated. Is it possible to have a completely blank mind and still keep running, I ask myself? Otherwise, what on earth do they think about? It is certainly true that it's easier to set oneself tougher goals if one is training as an individual rather than a team and this, I am sure, is part of the reason why so many players are reluctant to train on their own.

The human body is an amazing machine and readily adapts to activity, regardless of the degree. Thus, irrespective of whatever level of sport one participates at, the body can get fitter simply by being asked regularly to perform more work in training. So training until it hurts does mean it is doing you good, as the body will be more ready to accept that little bit more exercise next time.

Obviously activity must be increased in slow degree, especially at first. Men in their early forties, who have not done any exercise for ten years or more and who previously were good athletes, must not expect to be able to start from where they left off. This mistaken belief has been the cause of many disorders, especially in squash where the game's explosive activity has led to many injuries – even to deaths. If activity is gradually increased over a period of time the body will adapt rapidly. So people should be encouraged to do a little bit, to start with. This is the basis of all 'get fit' programmes where the individual does that much more every session.

I have never been a great believer in piling on lots of tracksuits and sweaters before running, even in the coldest weather, although I know that many of the top athletes do this. The most important thing is to make sure that you don't hang around afterwards before having a hot bath or shower, or the muscles will really stiffen up. It is an interesting exercise, however, occasionally to wear a wetsuit over a tracksuit, just to get an idea of how much fluid one can lose in the form of perspiration. Normally most of it evaporates with the heat of the body whilst running, but when it condenses inside the wetsuit it is surprising how much can be wrung out. It does at least give an idea of the amount of fluid needed as replacement, especially in warm weather, or in hot, humid climates.

Having said all this about running, I can only add that I am delighted with the new upsurge of interest in jogging, both here and abroad. Even if I did not need to get fit for rugby, I think I would still have been a jogger because there is enough medical evidence to show that exercise can play an important part in preventing heart disease of the acquired form.

During the season I need to step up my training runs to two or three times a week, building up to a climax a week or two before the first International. I also play a lot of squash during the rugby season, mainly because it is the most intensive exercise I know and also because it is marvellous for sharpening reflexes.

Training Sessions

When the coach is satisfied that his players have achieved their basic fitness he can start to practise individual skills. The most important part of his job is to make training interesting for everybody, therefore he has to allow players in different positions to concentrate on the skills relevant to them. Usually a coach will have played most of his rugby in one position. If, say, he was a back then he will have a fair idea of the needs of the backs. In that case it is always a good idea to leave the bulk of the forwards' training to an experienced forward playing in the team. If there is more than one 'outside' coach, one for the forwards and one for the backs, then there may often be disagreement about who is actually boss. So it is better to have one overall coach and recruit a manager from the ranks. Carwyn James adopted a similar method in New Zealand, using Ray McLoughlin to coach the forwards and later, when Ray was injured, Willie-John and Ian McLauchlan. Carwyn was able to impart his skill to the backs, confident in the knowledge that the forwards were reaping the benefit of the experience and specialist knowledge of tactics which only come from playing in the thick of a scrum and being exposed to all the tricks of the front-row trade.

Players must be warmed up before any real training takes place, but there are other ways of doing this than by running round the field. One good exercise is to split up into groups of, say, four using fixed areas of ground to move in. Two players can play against two in dribbling the ball for example, touch rugby or mauling, and if they are confined to their sections there is very little danger of overdoing anything before being properly warmed up. All sorts of combinations can be used to limit exertion initially, for instance, using three against one, the three not being allowed to run with the ball, and rotating to occupy the one position. These exercises not only get the players warmed up, but allow them to get the feel of the ball, and practise most of the skills of rugby at the same time. After this first part of the session the players usually split into forwards and backs.

Back Play

The standard of British three-quarter play has dropped since the mid-seventies primarily, I believe, because of lack of the right kind of practice. Many three-quarters nowadays seem to neglect the most important part of back play – passing. Rugby is a handling game and the three-quarters are the ones who should be really expert in the handling arts. My idea of good handling is for the ball to travel from the scrum-half to the open side wing in the shortest possible time and (it should not be necessary to mention this) it must not be dropped nor fumbled. The three-quarters playing the game of rugby league put many of our International and top club sides to shame with their slick passing and handling of the ball, something they maintain has only been perfected by constant practice. To get the ball out to the wing quickly requires certain criteria to be met:

i) the alignment of the three-quarters line should be correct, i.e. not too flat.

ii) the ball should be passed out in front of the player receiving it, so that it does not hit his body at all. This is the 'finger-tip' passing so correctly advocated by Carwyn James. If I appear to mention Carwyn's name a great deal, it is only because he has been right so often; his rugby brain is probably the best in the world.

iii) the player with the ball should take no more than one step with it before passing it on. This again confirms the importance of alignment – if the players are in the right position there is no need to run all over the place to deliver the ball.

This method is contrary to the old method of passing, where the player would give an exaggerated sway as he passed the ball and the ball-taker was encouraged to take it to his chest. By all means take it to the chest when fielding a high ball, but there is no need for this in the general attacking part of the game. It stands to reason that the ball will travel quickest when there are fewest movements of the body. That may sound facile, but if these three points are drummed in before practising such a move and every player is asked to keep all three in mind, it is surprising how many seconds can be knocked off the timing of the ball to the wing. It is those seconds which make the difference between being tackled with the ball and beating an opponent who is then temporarily out of the game. It does require a lot of practice to be able to pass consistently well and fluently, especially when players get tired.

I feel the decline in this speed of pass is probably due to the over-obsession with planned moves. Most great tries result from instinct, rather than planning, as exemplified by Gareth Edwards's great try, started out of defence by Phil Bennett, in the Barbarians *v* New Zealand game in 1973. Also, there has been a change in the type of players in various positions over the last ten years. Centres have now become wing-forwards playing in midfield. These are big strong runners without the deceptiveness of the old players, who relied on their jinking and sleight of hand. Perhaps British play has been too influenced by the 'McRae' style popularized by the All Blacks in the sixties. With bigger, perhaps slower, men midfield the emphasis has been on running straight and on the overworked 'crash ball' up the middle of the field, with the inevitable slowing down of the three-quarter line and phasing out of passing the ball straight out to the wing. This tendency is increasing as more teams pick stronger centres, and opposing teams feel they have to pick at least one crash-tackler in the centre to cope with them.

At the same time, the style of wing three-quarter has also changed. The jinking centre of old has now moved out to the wing, where the extra room gives him more of a chance of using his special skills. The classic example of the change is Gerald Davies who was, up to 1969, an International centre three-quarter but who came back from the Wales tour to New Zealand that year as a world-class wing. The size of wingers in general has decreased in Britain, and they are no longer the big strong runners who ran for the corner without a thought of what would happen if they did not make it. The unfortunate thing is that with the crash-ball going down the centre nowadays the talented wing can run up and down the side-line without touching the ball. And the irony is that in the old days, when the centre had that same sort of talent, he hardly had the ball before it was on its way out to the wing. Things seem to have got a little mixed-up in the change-over! Full-back play has obviously changed dramatically over the last ten years, mainly due to the changes in the kicking-to-touch laws, preventing a direct kick to touch outside the twenty-two metre (twenty-five yard) line. I have been involved in this transition, and although everyone now knows about the full-back coming into the line I feel the main reason it seems easier to block him out now is because the speed of passing is slower. It is not just because defenders are aware that it might happen. If everything is done properly, going flat out, the full-back coming outside the outside centre should have the ball in his hands long before the opposing back row have had time to cover across the field. Then, as everyone knows, the options open to the full-back are many and create what has become known in rugby jargon as the overlap. Half-backs have basically stayed the same, and more than ever, nowadays, they are the match winners and controllers.

FORWARD TRAINING

As a full-back I do not presume to be able to discuss the finer points of forward play, even though I did once play on the flank for Wales and always fancied myself as a frustrated forward. However, there are one or two points to remember when thinking about getting the front eight fit.

Flankers

Firstly, there is the question of the type of stamina they require. With the exception of the back row, forwards need to maintain three-quarter pace (seventy-five per cent, as opposed to the pace of the three-quarters) for most of the game. Therefore they need submaximal speed for long periods. Jogging is excellent for that.

On the whole, the flankers need to spend more time concentrating on speed bursts, if they are going to be able to harrass the opposing fly-half, and be first to the breakdown. Many flankers I have known seem to possess an inborn ability to be fit and fast and no matter how much or how little they train, they will always be first to the ball. Most likely, that's what makes them choose the position. But for every one chap like that, there will be a dozen chaps like me who need to train hard in order to keep up. Flankers also need to be great psychologists, both when 'psyching out' the opposing scrum-half by living dangerously on the off-side in a scrum, and by putting psychological pressure on the opposing fly-half. One great exponent of this was Noel Murphy who, when playing for Ireland, actually shouted to the opposite fly-half all the way through the game! On the same theme, it is interesting to note that many flankers are great readers of the game. They have to play like a back, but within the framework of the forwards.

Locks

Locks have different goals to aim for when they are achieving fitness. Not only do they need to possess all-round strength to support the front row in the set pieces but they also need plenty of jumping ability and powerful arms to rip a ball out of a maul. Obviously plenty of weight-lifting is a help, but it's important to remember that there are different methods of lifting which can strengthen different sets of muscles, e.g. squat lifting, dead lifting, lifting hand weights behind the body etc. So weight-lifting need not be a boring exercise, if a little imagination is used together with guidance from someone with specialist knowledge of muscles, such as a physiotherapist. The spring devices seen in the Charles Atlas advertisements are excellent for increasing upper-arm strength. Was Charles Atlas a good mauler as well, I wonder?

A very good way of improving the legs for jumping is to cycle: this strengthens the calf muscles considerably and can add a couple of inches of bounce to a line-out jump. Timing is of utmost importance in the lines-out and can only really be achieved with lots of practice with other jumpers and a thrower. But it should always be 'opposed' if possible, because there are so many ways of interfering with a jump that even if you have an Olympic medal for the high jump you won't get off the ground unless you can cope with the opposition. A lock is very much a supportive player, often working away quite out of the limelight. His attitude and skills are completely different from, say, those of a number eight or a flanker, and it is worth coaches and selectors sometimes remembering this before they assume that any of the pivot five is readily interchangeable.

Number Eight

The number eight determines his play largely by his stature; not all are lanky line-out specialists like Mervyn Davies. In the scrum alone he has a very important role to play and he has got to be prepared to rotate a scrum, balance it, slow the exit of the ball, whatever the situation calls for. Most of this is gained solely by practice, more often than not by actual match practice, so it's worth remembering to give a number eight the chance of some experience before expecting him to be a specialist in his position.

Props

Good ball requires good scrummaging and it is in this aspect of the game that Britain has improved most over the last few years. There is no doubt that if a side is scrummaging well their whole game is likely to go well. However there is danger in believing that scrummaging is the be-all and end-all. The 1977 Lions in New Zealand proved this when they were by far the better scrummaging side and yet lost the series. Good scrummaging is an important part of a side's skills, but it should only be the foundation of all the other skills.

Weights are the most important accessory of a good prop and much of a prop's training has to be sheer slog on his own. However, as mentioned before, it need not always be boring. It is worth a schoolboy remembering, if he is keen on becoming a front-row forward, that a few sessions on the weights between the ages of about fourteen and seventeen, when the muscles are developing, will pay great dividends later on. Because there are such a lot of circulating androgens (male hormones) at that age the muscles are very receptive to the challenge of weights and thus they develop more readily than they do when a person is older. On the subject of muscle-building, it is to be hoped that the deplorable practice of using body-building steroids never creeps into the game of rugby, amateur or otherwise. Not only are they forbidden by all the international sporting bodies, but their harmful effect on the body has been documented extensively.

Scrummaging machines are of some value but are really no substitute for the real thing. There is no place for 'semi-opposed' scrummaging in training as there is, say, for practising moves. An incident during one of the training sessions on the Lions tour in 1974 demonstrated this: punches were actually thrown between members of the Lions because their personal scrummaging pride was under test. There was no hard feeling between the two members either before or after the incident, unsavoury as it was, and it was no reflection on the tour as a whole – we had the strongest team spirit in 1974 that I have ever experienced. It just illustrates the intensity of the scrummaging during that particular training session and although not an advocate of punching at any time, I would have to give Syd Millar full marks for the motivation of his players. Technique in scrummaging is extremely important, combining positioning of the feet, good binding and low position with as straight a back as possible. It has been shown many times that a small forward with good technique can out-scrummage a more powerful forward with poorer technique. However, just as with everything else, good individual scrummagers still need lots of practice with the rest of the pack before they become part of a good unit.

Mauling

The best way to practise mauling is to have two packs playing against each other, acting as live opposition. However, failing this, six or seven forwards can space themselves out over the length of the field and two players start, one with the ball. They drive into each player in turn, with the next player down the line ripping the ball away. The player being driven into then joins the group and so on until they reach the last player, on whom they form a static maul. This can be repeated up and down the field and combines mauling with fitness: quite a strenuous exercise. The other good thing about it is that mostly there is one person at a time ripping the ball away. The most effective mauling is not achieved by everyone sticking their hands in and trying to grab the ball, but by organizing the pack so that the first one or two who arrive at the maul position do the turning and shielding of the opposition so that the third man to arrive is in a good position to see and rip the ball away. The Welsh pack have been superb maulers for the past four or five years, using Geoff Wheel as the 'rip-off' man, and plenty of preliminary turning work by the Pontypool boys.

Rucking

New Zealanders are still the masters of this, and when performed properly, rucking can be a very skilful art. We in Britain allow too much 'killing' of the ball on the floor, which is where danger creeps in. Unfortunately the offender often goes unpunished, in fact he can often end up gaining a penalty for his own side if the opposition let fly at him on the floor.

When in New Zealand I soon learnt that one had to roll away from the ball on the floor or accept the consequences. These were not necessarily to be kicked deliberately, but often to get heeled out of the ruck with the ball. The New Zealand interpretation of the law in this respect is, I believe, a very good one, as it encourages play to keep moving. However if referees in Britain are not going to clamp down on lying on the ball, then we will never ruck the bull away properly, and it is almost safer to do away with the ruck and blow the whistle straight away. This would be a backward step for rugby. Again the ideal situation for practice is to have two opposing packs, but another exercise is to have several groups of players with one group acting as the ruckers in turn. The other groups line up with the ball at their feet and the rucking group have to run from one group to another, pushing them over the ball. This again combines skill with a lot of physical exercise.

Line-out

The line-out is the biggest headache in rugby. Every country seems to have its own ideas on the line-out laws, and something ought to be done to standardize them. The choice seems to be between 'anything goes' or a return to the double-banking system which at least allows a good jumper a fair chance of reaching the ball. If it is too difficult to spot and penalize players being lifted, why not allow everyone to do it, at least the possibility of penalizing some players and not others would not exist.

The most important person in the line-out is the man who throws in the ball, and certainly there is insufficient time taken practising this. Whether the hooker or a winger throws in it is still a specialist art and should be treated as such. It is so simple for a thrower to practise this on his own by using targets that I cannot understand why it is so neglected.

As far as hookers are concerned, they are a law unto themselves. They always seem to be Jekyll and Hyde characters on and off the field: it must have something to do with being strung up between two tough men and not having any arms left to fend for themselves, something I wouldn't particularly relish either!

BACK TRAINING

Full-Back

Even though the attacking full-back is here to stay, some people get obsessed with this part of his role and neglect the more defensive aspect. I have said over and over again that I believe the full-back's first job is to be the last line of defence, in that he holds a great responsibility to the rest of the team. Forwards don't want to spend their time turning back in case the full-back drops the ball or fails to find touch. Not only is it annoying but it disrupts their whole pattern of play. The most important prerequisites for a full-back are a good eye for the ball and a fair amount of courage. With these two basics he can then practise to perfect his fielding, kicking and tackling. One of his most important roles is to field the high ball, a well-tried method of attack which can be extremely effective if the full-back has shaky hands. Not only is it important to be confident from a defensive point of view about containing these high kicks but often they are also a marvellous way of gaining possession and launching an attack. The options open in such a situation are many. Obviously one cannot kick for touch outside the twenty-two metre line, so in this case the 'up and under' is a very useful ploy. During the fielding of a high ball, the most important thing is to keep one's eye on it until well after it is actually caught, in no circumstances must one look at the opposition bearing down, or the ball is dropped from that moment on. It is not an easy thing to carry out but each high ball must be approached single-mindedly, and everything else must be shut out. Then the arms should be extended to 'cradle' the ball – the hands alone are not strong enough. It is crucial to turn sideways on catching the ball, unless you are able to make a clean mark, as this is self-preservation against the oncoming players. In certain circumstances it may be necessary to raise a knee or stick an elbow out to discourage those players who are keen on the dangerous habit of late tackling.

A method which I have found particularly useful if the opposing pack is pressing is to jump for the ball. Of course this leaves you off balance, but you have a much better chance of catching or even deflecting the ball than do the forwards, who are more likely to be looking at you rather than at the ball. Again, practice makes perfect but it doesn't take much to get a friend to spend half an hour, pumping all kinds of kicks up to you. I was lucky in this respect to have the help of my father, who spent hours on this with me.

Tackling

This needs courage and confidence in your own ability to stop a man. Once you *think* he might get past you, then he's gone. A different approach is needed when training from that used for a winger's tackle on another wing as full-backs generally have to tackle head-on. To do this you must get your head to the side of the man being tackled and use the runner's momentum to carry it out since, being stationary, you have none of your own. Of course you have to have the strength to hold on, but if you have positioned yourself properly, then the weight of the ball-carrier will bring him down. The most difficult tackle for a full-back is on a winger with a fifteen yard overlap who is running flat-out towards you. The ideal is to make the winger do what you want him to. A method I have used with some success is to try and 'psyche' the player. I keep my eyes on him and stare him out. In this way he can become mesmerized and, as he is thinking what to do, I rush at him and hope to catch him by surprise. Sometimes you can get to know which players side-step off which foot and so can read the situation, but this is not always possible with top-class wingers who know that you know, and who can get away by feinting the side-step and going outside or inside, as the case may be. Tackling is no different from anything else; there is no substitute for practice. Sandbags and rubber tyres are reasonable substitutes for the real thing but actual match practice is the best. Theoretically, if a winger has room to move then he should always beat a full-back. The full-back's job is to prove that theory wrong. There is nothing better for me in rugby, than pulling off a really good tackle.

Kicking

This is not the most impressive part of my game; but the most important thing when kicking to touch is to make sure you find touch. There have been many important games lost through nothing else but failure in this. Of course distance is an advantage, both in attack and defence, and there is nothing a pack like better than to see the ball they carefully won sailing down-field over the line. But it is of no use if the ball doesn't find touch and falls straight into the hands of the opposition. So I believe in quality, not quantity. The 'screw' kick is very useful when kicking from narrow angles, but again needs constant practice to perfect. The idea is to place the ball on the top of the foot and to kick 'through' the ball, thus imparting spin. The ball goes straight, then swerves in the latter part of its flight.

The 'grubber' kick is also a good one to add to a full-back's skills, as it can be wonderfully effective when kicking from outside the twenty-two. Although the ball seems to roll in a lucky fashion, it is usually the result of much practice. Another fading art is that of being able to kick with *both* feet. This is extremely important for a full-back; nothing is more embarrassing than being caught on the wrong foot. There are many Internationalists who are good kickers but who only use one foot, mainly because they have never had the confidence to use the other.

213

Falling on the ball

Courage is an important commodity here, but timing also plays an important role. The faller should make sure that his back is between the ball and the opposition, thus lessening the chances of injury.

Attacking

All the above skills are defensive and on top of them comes the ability to attack. For the full-back to enter the line correctly he needs to have his timing just right. The success of such a move lies in him taking the ball at speed, thus imparting impetus to the three-quarter line. Now that it is a well-known ploy to include the full-back in attack, one of the most successful tricks is to use the full-back in the miss move, used so effectively in the third Test against South Africa in 1974.* The ball was won from the line-out by the Lions; I ran up outside our centres but was deliberately missed out of the passing. This left J. J. Williams streaking down the touch-line with the Springboks still wondering why the ball had not been passed to me. As JJ drew their full-back, he passed inside to me – I had been able to keep alongside him as I had not been involved with the ball till then. Just as it looked as if I were going to make it over the line, the cover defence caught up and I flipped a pass inside to JJ, who scored under the posts.

The dummy crash ball is also useful for a full-back to take part in – if it is to be effective at all he has to be so convincing in his run that he ends up getting tackled and taking one, two or even three men out of the field. He has to be pretty strong to cope with that!

Wing Three-Quarters

Wingers and full-backs need to do a great deal of covering for

* The tour is described in detail in Chapter 9.

one another these days, and they should try to develop a good understanding so that each can carry on with his own part in the game without constantly referring to the other. Wings should be capable of dealing both with high balls and the long balls kicked to the corner. The blind side wing should always be aware of 'kicks into the box', thus allowing the full-back to stand further across the field in a better position for the counter-attack. Wingers generally tackle from the side or from the back. They do not, therefore, have the opportunity of 'staring' an opponent out, but there are other ways of applying psychology. If you show your opposing winger, early on in the game, that you can match him in speed then, whether or not you can keep it up for the entire time you have done a lot to lower his confidence. All good wingers have great confidence in their ability to reach the line and score in a one-to-one position. This again reflects the psychology involved in rugby.

In attack, the one thing a wing should try to avoid at all costs is to 'die with the ball'. Concentrate on your strength and practise over and over again, so that you know what you're going to do when you get stopped. For instance, if you have control over your kicking, try the chip ahead, perfected by Grant Batty and J. J. Williams. There is very little a full-back can do in that situation except try to charge the ball down. Alternatively, if you have a natural side-step, work on it until you are confident that you can vary the timing sufficiently to fox the opposition. If a wing is very fast, but has little else in the way of special skills, then the least he can do is to keep his eyes open for support and try to pass inside, or keep on his feet until he has passed the ball. So often a beautiful run ends in nothing because the wing has seen his support too late, or selfishly has hung on for too long.

Centres

As mentioned before, passing is the most important aspect of a centre's play, and it therefore needs perfecting. No matter how brilliantly thought-out a move may be, it will get nowhere if the passing is laboured. Tackling is important and is even better if one can achieve it without allowing the man to pass the ball. But the most important part of all in a centre's tackling is sticking to his man (usually his opposing centre), not attempting to follow the ball around and tackle everyone in sight. That is the job for the flankers.

Outside Halves

Coolness under pressure and the ability to 'do the right thing at the right time' are prerequisites of a good fly-half. They often seem to be instinctive and are not always altered by practice. But tactical kicking is very important and this is something which practice will improve. The fly-half is the general of the side, whether he likes it or not, and he must be prepared to make decisions and follow them through. There is nothing worse than a dithering fly-half, not even one who kicks everything. Apart from that, his build and general rugby skills will dictate the type of game he plays.

Inside Halves

The most important attribute of a scrum-half is to be a competitor. He is a back and yet an extra forward. Courage and strength are vital commodities. Again, tactical appreciation is vital and he will often find himself taking over the role of fly-half on occasions if he has a good kick under pressure. Gareth Edwards proved this in the first Test against South Africa in 1974. His rolling kicks to touch destroyed the Springboks and he became the general of the side for much of the game. Kicking and passing are the two most important skills which can be perfected with practice. Knowing what sort of pass your fly-half prefers is half the battle; a fly-half who likes to stand deep to receive the ball can have his game destroyed by a scrum-half whose pass is short.

For success in most kinds of sport there are I believe six

essential elements. I shall call these the six S's. 1. Skill 2. Stamina 3. Speed 4. Strength 5. Suppleness 6. (P)sychology.

Skill

I have already mentioned my belief that skill is the most important thing in sport. Unfortunately it seems to take second place to overall fitness these days. There is no substitute for skill and all sportsmen should be encouraged to develop and use it at all times.

Stamina

Astrand, the great Swedish physiologist, and others, have demonstrated quite clearly that the ability to perform hard physical work is related to the capacity of the cardiovascular system to take up, transport and give up oxygen to the active tissue of the body. This capacity is often referred to as 'maximal oxygen uptake'. It varies from individual to individual, and to some extent is 'natural'. However, stamina can be improved by training for an extended time at submaximal effort with intervals of rest. This, of course, is the sort of work needed for forwards in rugby who are generally on the go for the full eighty minutes.

Speed

This is desirable for all rugby players but in particular the three-quarters. Training includes sets of sprints at maximum speed. The speed of recovery indicates an improvement in fitness and is essential for three-quarters who may need to run one hundred yards on two consecutive occasions without a break, especially in seven-a-side rugby. Speed of reflexes and speed in making decisions also contributes to success.

Strength

Strength is again needed by all rugby players, but is more important for a forward in his battle to gain possession of the ball for his backs. The strength required by a rugby forward is best achieved by a combination of training methods, all based on progressive work against resistance, and practising speed and movement. Weight training using weights of fifty to seventy per cent maximum and involving fast repetitions will help in this process, especially if combined with the planned use of a scrummaging machine. Strength can also be developed by various forms of circuit training designed to place progressive demands on selected parts of the body. Sit-ups and press-ups, if properly done, still have much to commend them.

Suppleness

Suppleness, or mobility, is the range of movement of a particular joint action. Training for suppleness must never be undertaken when fatigued but may be included in a 'warming-up' session prior to strength or stamina training. Suppleness increases effectiveness, enabling power and strength to be re-applied over a wider range and at a greater speed. It is complementary to strength and stamina and can be maintained by doing an equal amount of active and passive stretching exercises.

(P)sychology

Last, but by no means least. The central nervous system controls and regulates all the activities of the body. It is not known how individuals get 'keyed up' for a big performance. However, everybody is aware of the 'adrenalin-flaring point' which prepares humans and most animals for 'flight or fight'. This is a physiological reaction governed by the autonomic nervous system, but it can be triggered off by psychological means.

All great sportsmen believe in themselves and their capacity for 'fight or flight'. They also have that 'killer instinct' which enables them to come out on top. Top tennis players I have known all say that it is great to win lots of money but it is even greater to *win*, full stop. This competitiveness is something which is instinctive and is not always something which a sportsman can be taught. So psychology can play a large part and the players who are well prepared mentally and physically should be assured of a good performance.

In concluding, I cannot stress too much that there are no short cuts in training. There is no substitute for hard work, and there are no great players who have not had to sacrifice something along the line in their rise to the top.

I I

Sports Medicine

During my medical training I became involved in a number of different types of sport, and so I suppose it was only natural that I should develop an interest in the specialized branch of medicine concerned with sporting injuries. I have learned much from personal experience, through players I have been involved with and indeed through my own numerous injuries.

The more I have heard about friends' experiences the more I have realized how privileged I have been in being able to seek advice and/or treatment from my doctor father and from the specialists and physiotherapists at St Mary's and the other hospitals where I have worked. This has led me to want to do something to make such treatment available to other players, and indeed to all sportsmen, especially those who are amateurs.

There is no special teaching on sporting injuries in medical schools at present and this is why most doctors do not really know the best treatment for the multitude of problems which his sporting patients bring to him. So it is not surprising that the usual answer is, 'Strap it up and come back again in ten days' time.' Whilst this might be acceptable to a working man who is happy to get a 'paper' and sit at home it is totally unacceptable to a person who wants to get fit again for the sport he loves – and if possible in time for next week's game. Of course, that advice may be correct in some instances but not for the majority of injuries.

Is there any difference between injuries sustained at sport and those sustained during 'normal' life? Many doctors believe that they are the same and should be treated as such, but I believe that there are certain injuries which are rarely seen outside the realm of sport – hamstring injuries, cartilage troubles in the knee, cauliflower ears, for instance. Again, doctors generally do not differentiate in their attitudes to treatment. But all sportsmen have one thing in common – they love their sport, and it plays a significant role in their lives. This applies at all levels but perhaps even more so at the 'lower' levels. Sportsmen want to get back to their sport as quickly as possible and this means they have sufficient motivation to put in added effort themselves. There are, it is true, a minority who use injury as an excuse for failure, but they are comparatively few and can usually be spotted and helped by careful discussion. This illustrates an important point: that the doctor has to have time to listen and discuss the injury with the sportsman, so that he gains maximum help from diagnosis, treatment and rehabilitation.

Should sports medicine be a recognized speciality? Many doctors say no, but one can't go on expecting the family doctor to play the role of sports specialist: he is busy enough as it is. Any doctor is going to treat someone whose knee injury only keeps them off the squash court with less of a sense of urgency than he would a miner whose knee injury prevents him from making a living at the pit-face. It's not only understandable, but correct.

Sports clinics may become a necessity, in spite of the lack of funds in the NHS, as more and more people take up sport in their increased leisure time. The forty-hour week is becoming thirty-five hours, and even thirty-two hours. This means for many, more sport, more injuries and more time off work, and the situation is aggravated if they end up being off work for longer than they need because their treatment was incorrect.

The ideal would be to have clinics sponsored by bodies independent of the NHS such as the Sports Council or various other sporting bodies. It would certainly be in the interest of various rugby unions to plough back some of the enormous sums of money made by the exertions of the thirty players and one referee at an International into clinics for use by those and other players.

Such clinics should be situated within easy reach of main towns and cities, and be held on Sundays or Mondays for new injuries sustained over the weekend, with a follow-up clinic some time during the week. The personnel staffing such a clinic should include a fully-trained physiotherapist and a doctor taking special interest in sporting injuries, whether this be from a medical or surgical viewpoint. Preferably they should have some further training in treating such injuries, such as diplomas in physical medicine. There should also be access to radiological methods of investigation (X-rays) and to an orthopaedic surgeon who would be willing to undertake the surgery necessary for ruptured knee ligaments and the like. Unfortunately, many surgeons take the view that sportsmen are wasting their time, since their injuries are 'self-inflicted' . . . that is why it helps to involve sportsmen who also happen to be doctors. Ken Kennedy, who played for Ireland, and also went on the 1974 Lions tour with me, takes an active interest in sporting injuries and the physiology of sport. He qualified some years before me in Ireland but has been practising in London, including some clinics, for a few years. He was very interested in the physiology of high altitude training during the first week of the South African tour and got us to do special breathing exercises and analysed blood tests of the results. Dr Peter Sperryn, also, was an athlete whilst a medical student at St Mary's some time in the fifties, and he now plays a very active part in running clinics, writing papers and being official doctor to the AAA.

The physiotherapist should have the necessary equipment (ultrasonic machines, for instance) either on the spot or readily available for further treatment. These clinics would certainly relieve the vastly overworked casualty departments which at present bear the brunt of dealing with sports injuries, especially at weekends.

In any branch of medicine prevention is better than cure, and sport is no exception. There are three aspects of this:

a. Prevention of injury.
b. Prevention of further injury.
c. Treatment, with adequate rehabilitation.

PREVENTION OF INJURY

1 *Fitness*

This has been referred to earlier in the book, but I believe that even at the 'lower' levels players should do some exercise to improve their physical state before taking to the field. There is no doubt that the fitter one is the less chance there is of getting injured. Most injuries, in fact, do occur at the lowest level of proficiency, and not only result from lack of skill but also the lower level of fitness. Dealing only with rugby, obviously as any season progresses, hard grounds have something to do with this, but hamstring injuries and other soft-tissue injuries are much commoner when players are less fit.

2 *Studs*

In a survey taken comparing injuries among Welsh rugby players in seasons 1969/70 and 1974/5 there was found to be a significant rise in injuries to the head, face and neck. This has since been confirmed by other researchers. Why is this? I believe it is due to the increasingly dangerous studs being used today. It could be that players are over-vigorous in their use, but when I talk to ex-players they say that there is no increase from their day. Certainly plastic studs need only one wearing to sharpen them into lethal weapons, and some of the manufactured aluminium studs are already pointed before they have ever been used. When worn for some time on hard grounds or after 'warming up' on concrete surfaces they present a real danger to the head, face and neck. Most referees inspect players' studs before the game now, but not all with the same degree of thoroughness. It should be stressed to the players that they should keep all their equipment in good order; if they do not they may damage others, not least their own team-mates.

3 *Gum Shields*

I started wearing a gum shield in New Zealand in 1971 after reading an article by a facio-maxillary surgeon (usually a doubly qualified surgeon/dentist) in a paper over there. It was said to give protection to the gum and teeth as well as helping to prevent concussion. I can highly recommend these shields as I'm sure it was because I was wearing one when I broke my upper jaw in 1972 that I still have all my own teeth. Many players now wear them and I feel they are essential. The only problem is that it can take quite some time to get used to wearing them, and it is best to have one fitted initially by a dentist.

4 *Knee Guards*

These are of great use in hot climates where the hard grounds make the threat of grass burns a very real one. In 1974 British Lions used them in South Africa and suffered very few such burns. Even though not a serious injury in itself, a grass burn can keep a player out of the game for a long time, as wounds may easily become infected and take a long time to heal. Vaseline or any other lubricant is also good protection against grass burns on all areas in contact with the ground.

5 *Correct Boots and Clothing*

Low-cut boots are the fashion nowadays and are very light and comfortable to wear. But they give little protection to the ankle, and therefore injuries here are more likely. Boots should be in good condition and not have bits hanging off them, as these constitute a danger to the opposition and to one's own team. Whether players wear the traditional jock strap or briefs beneath their shorts is a question of individual choice, although some authorities are now condemning the time-honoured jock strap which has come under attack for causing the fungal infection *tinea cruris* (jock itch). The main problem with using a jock strap is that it lies damp at the bottom of the bag and probably never gets washed! A dry clean jock strap shouldn't give you jock itch.

6 *Bandaging Weak Joints*

Obviously, if a joint is badly damaged the individual should not be playing. Minor sprains should be bandaged to prevent further damage. Fingers and thumbs are commonly injured and should be strapped prophylactically. Ankles and knees can be supported by Elastoplast or elastic bandages if required.

7 *Shin Pads*

These are worn by members of the front row, particularly hookers, and really do prevent damage to the shins.

8 *Salt Tablets*

These are needed in hot and humid climates. They were used extensively in South Africa in 1974 by the British Lions when not one case of cramp was recorded. I am convinced of the benefit from the use of salt in the prevention of cramp.

PREVENTION OF FURTHER INJURY

Ideally, competent medically-trained personnel should be on hand to treat and advise players on the field of play. Of course that is not always possible, so trainers and coaches should make an effort to attend the various courses now being set up to teach the basics of immediate treatment of players. In these days of substitutes there is no excuse for keeping a player on the field with a serious, or potentially serious injury. If there is any likelihood of any injury being made worse the player should be brought off the field immediately.

1 *Concussion*

As everyone knows, this is a common injury in most contact sports, and rugby is no exception. I feel it is taken far too lightly; every player suffering from concussion should be taken off the field and not allowed to play again for at least a week. If someone is knocked out in a road traffic accident they are admitted overnight to hospital for observation. Why should we take risks in what, after all, is only a game? Like many others, I have been guilty of staying on the field with concussion, and it can be very difficult indeed to persuade a player to go off. Perhaps the referee should at least have the power to send the player off to be examined by a doctor (if available) at the side of the pitch. If in doubt the captain should ask the player to name the opposition and the score. If he hesitates in this, he must come off.

2 *Hamstring Injuries*

These are the bugbear of many athletes: in rugby it is mainly the three-quarters who are affected. No player with a hamstring injury should be allowed to stay on the field, as it will only make the injury worse.

3 *First Aid Room*

Most top clubs have good facilities for first aid. All that is needed is a small clean room with good lighting and suturing equipment, and qualified personnel to authorize transfer to hospital if necessary.

The law-makers and referees must not tolerate illegal play, and support should be given to officials over this rather than criticism. Many referees are afraid to send players off the field because of the consequences of media reaction. This was illustrated in 1977 when Norman Sanson, an admirably strict referee on this issue, sent off both Geoff Wheel and Willie Duggan from the Welsh/Irish International sides respectively.

There was great criticism of this, not only from the press but from the home unions involved. Admittedly the offences were slight compared with, say, the brawling which takes place on an Australian tour, but there was a principle at stake. The game was watched by eighty thousand people at the ground and by many more on television. Since Norman Sanson is renowned for his strictness he could not possibly have displayed laxity and double standards just because it was an International match. Referees also have to be aware of incidents occurring a long way away from the ball which are obviously outside the context of the game. Serious injuries may occur if players are hit or kicked when they are not expecting it. Referees must not tolerate this and should send offenders immediately from the field of play. Although I was retaliating when I displayed anger against Tommy Bedford, I fully realize that I was lucky not to be sent off the field that day – because the incident was off the ball.

TREATMENT, WITH ADEQUATE REHABILITATION

This is in the hands of the specialist and need not be discussed in this book, other than to comment on the great change in the treatment of soft-tissue injuries that has taken place over the last ten years or so. All injuries used to be treated by heat and massage, which seems illogical when there may be bleeding in muscles or joints. Now ice, compression and elevation are employed in an effort to stop any soft-tissue bleeding. This should be carried out in the first twenty-four hours, and when bleeding has stopped gentle massage and heat can be used to disperse blood clots and to promote local blood flow. It is amazing how much more quickly players recover from such injuries by this treatment: I noticed this with the British Lions in 1974 where the recovery was much quicker than in the pre-ice era in 1971.

Treatment of hamstring injuries has changed radically over the years. Whereas ten years ago complete rest for four to six weeks was advocated, it is now thought that this only causes more scar tissue which gives way on resumption of training. After the arrest of bleeding by the application of ice, gentle massage and heat treatment for four to five days should be followed by gentle jogging practice. Then the training may be increased over the next week or so.

Anyone who fractures his nose and is intending to continue playing then is foolish, or incredibly vain if he tries to go to casualty or get admitted to hospital to get it set! The chances are that it will get broken again, and one is then left with the same bony scar tissue, or deviation of the septum. Obviously, if one cannot breathe through either nostril after, say, forty-eight hours, then something must be done.

Any query about a fractured jaw should be referred to a casualty department for immediate X-ray.

Cauliflower ears can be prevented from occurring by having the ear carefully inspected by a doctor shortly after the game, if there is any pain or swelling in the earlobe. They are not always prevented by wearing a scrumcap, as was previously thought, because they are usually caused by friction to the ear, which causes bruising. Players nowadays tend to prefer Elastoplast to pin the ears down and prevent 'cauliflowers' that way. If the doctor thinks there is any effusion, or bleeding, into the rigid lobe, then fluid can be removed simply with a syringe. But it is important to remember that the fluid may recur for days and days, so follow-up is usually necessary.

12

Coming Back Home

It was with great excitement, but a certain amount of trepidation, that I looked forward to my return to Wales. Scilla had had little experience of the Celts, and I had been away in London for eight years. Would it be the same as before? Would I be accepted back after being thought of as a foreigner? How about my career as a doctor? All these thoughts were on my mind as we crossed the Severn Bridge.

I was due to start work as a Senior House Officer (SHO) at the University Hospital of Wales, Cardiff, in September 1976 and, since there had been keen competition for the post, I was determined to show that I had not got the job just because I was a well-known rugby player. It was a twelve-month appointment and we had to do ward rounds at eight o'clock in the morning, which was quite an effort for me. It meant leaving home just after 7 a.m. which I was not used to, so that in my effort to impress I could conduct my own rounds first to make sure that everything was in order for the consultant.

It did, however, have the advantage of getting the rounds over, before the day proper started in the operating theatre. I spent six months doing general surgery, and was soon performing my own thyroid and gall bladder operations, under the patient and encouraging eye of Mr Hilary Wade. *His* father had also been a surgeon in Cardiff, and it was interesting that *my* father had performed his surgical house job under him, back in the 1940s. Then after ten weeks on the cardiac surgery team, I went over to the Cardiff Royal Infirmary, which copes with all the emergency and trauma surgery from the Cardiff area. This was all great experience and I was kept really busy both in casualty and theatre. During this time, I had made my début back with Bridgend, and was involved with squad training sessions a good few months earlier than usual, as Wales was due to play against the touring Argentinian side. I knew I was not at peak fitness, nor were most of the Welsh team; we only just beat the Pumas with a last minute penalty awarded for a dangerously high tackle on me by the giant Travaglini. The press were quite critical of both Gareth and me and began calling for our retirement – but we both knew what a heavy season we had in front of us, and having been around for so long we knew all about 'pacing' ourselves.

During my year of general surgery, I had to think seriously about planning my future, since I was by then completely committed to a career in surgery. I therefore applied for a surgical registrar rotation job for three years, starting in July 1977. The interviews were in May, and since the rotation was to be a major stepping stone towards the final FRCS examination, this was one of the reasons why I was unavailable for the 1977 Lions tour to New Zealand. It would have been very difficult for me to apply for the job, then tell the consultants that I could not attend the interview nor would I be able to work for the first two months of the appointment. I also had my family to consider and I could not afford four months of unpaid leave at that particular time since Scilla, with a month-old baby, could not possibly be the sole breadwinner as she had been for the 1974 tour. So, after much deliberation, and discussion into the early hours, I decided I could not sacrifice so much, especially as I had already been on two Lions tours at the expense of my medical career.

My first match back for Bridgend was something of a disaster. It was against Saracens up in London. While playing for London Welsh, we had never experienced much difficulty in beating Saracens. However, playing as a Welsh club in London on a weekend away from home in the bright lights was something entirely different – and we lost. The critics gave me a roasting, but what did they expect? I had only been back with Bridgend for a short time, and it takes time for players to get used to a newcomer, especially since many of them seemed a little wary of me. Only one or two players were still in the side which I had played for in the early days – so, it was really as if I was starting completely from scratch.

Since then I have learnt that Bridgend, like all Welsh club sides, have poor playing records in London and indeed the Midlands. Like some wines they 'do not travel well'. The reason for this is difficult to imagine but I think it is mainly psychological, since I do not believe that travelling those distances can take that much out of a side from a physical point of view. I have tried all sorts of means of overcoming this amongst the players, but have come to the conclusion that it is a fact – and nothing will change it.

Another factor, which is real and not psychological, is that the London Society referees do not let the Welsh players get away with some of the things they do in Wales. I first noticed this while playing for London Welsh: the Welsh players were used to playing the ball on the floor (in creating a ruck as in New Zealand) and couldn't understand it when they were repeatedly penalized for it in London. This having happened, I believe that the Welsh players became inhibited by feeling, unreasonably, that the London Society referees were against them.

After that initial match, Bridgend settled down as a team and I started to make a good contribution to their game. This was not only by my play, for the treasurer was delighted at my return – it put an extra five hundred to a thousand admissions on the gate.

At this time, we were living in Llantwit Fardre, near Pontypridd in a hospital house. Scilla was working in the Paediatric Department at East Glamorgan Hospital and so we were able to use hospital accommodation until our house in Llansannor was ready to move into. It was a very convenient arrangement, but unfortunately owing to the previous occupants, the whole house smelt of curry. The only room unaffected was the bedroom. So we moved everything upstairs, including the television, and spent most of our time up there. When the curtains were closed on a Sunday afternoon (for viewing 'Rugby Special') the neighbours must have thought we were newly married.

We were able to move into the house we had bought in the Vale of Glamorgan in mid-November (1977) and again the circumstances of the move were fairly hectic. On the Friday afternoon I had driven down to Swansea to take part in the show 'This Is Your Life' – for Mervyn Davies. Rob Leyshon came with me, since as registrar in neurosurgery at the time, he had looked after Merv in the University Hospital for Wales (UHW) when he suffered his brain haemorrhage. This was quite a get-together, as, in tribute to Merv, many of our friends came down from London, including most of the 1971 Lions. All the old London Welsh crowd packed tightly into a Mini and John Dawes drove us on to the stage to remind Merv of those days travelling down the A4 for squad sessions. I arrived back in the early hours of the morning having celebrated a great reunion and in poor shape for the removal of our furniture from cold storage into our new house. On top of all this I was due to play against Neath in Bridgend in the afternoon. Somehow, everything was accomplished, including a narrow win against Neath, for that Saturday night we sat amongst cardboard boxes and jumbled furniture, in the freezing cold, celebrating the day with champagne and smoked salmon. This was a ritual, for when we moved into our first house in Teddington, a thoughtful friend had stuffed a carrier bag into our hands, saying we might find it useful later when we couldn't find the kettle amongst the boxes. We didn't know what was inside until midnight when we sat down for a breather, and popped the champagne cork: a very much appreciated gesture.

Our house-warming party was delayed until 26 December – it turned out to be a great day – we had planned it so that many of the London Welsh crowd would be able to drop in on their way down for the matches in Llanelli and Swansea (Boxing Day was a day later that year). We had found a great local pub, the Hare and Hounds just a few miles away, and had bought a couple of barrels of their excellent Worthington BB for the party. It was much appreciated by our guests who started to drop in at lunchtime and (some) came and went until the early hours of the morning. It took us till the following year – all five days – to recover. Little did we know what a great year 1977 would turn out to be. It was Jubilee Year for the Queen and many exciting things happened to us as well.

Lauren, our daughter was born on Easter Sunday, following my game for the Barbarians against Cardiff who were celebrating their centenary that year. I had scored a try and had been thrilled to play in the same side as those two great flankers Jean-Claude Skrela and Jean-Paul Rives, especially as we had beaten Cardiff (always a pleasant experience to a Bridgend man). Scilla had known that something was happening earlier in the evening but had enjoyed a meal out with some of the other wives, and thought it would pass off – typical doctor! When she saw the state I was in she suggested that we should go home first for some coffee, before going back in to Cardiff to UHW. She eventually woke me at 3.30 when she thought I was sober enough to make my entrance into the hospital where I was working on the cardiac surgery team – it would never do to make a spectacle of myself one night, when I would be operating on heart valves the next. I was ushered into the doctors' room by a sympathetic midwife, who thought I was just overcome by the idea of becoming a father, and allowed another couple of hours' sleep, before they woke me for the birth at 8.15 a.m. I was so amazed by this little bundle of life which was handed over to me to look at, that my hands were shaking. 'Careful, don't drop her, she's all slippery,' cried the midwife, then suddenly became embarrassed as she remembered that I was JPR. As if I would drop her!

"IT'S J.P.R'S NIPPER!"

This cartoon appeared in the *South Wales Echo* when
our daughter Lauren was born, on Easter Sunday 1977

A few months later we were invited on to the Royal Yacht
Britannia, when the Queen visited South Wales as part of her
Jubilee celebrations. When we saw that the reception was due
to start at 9 p.m. we were surprised that it was so late. It was
only when we saw the television coverage of her engagements
in Wales that day that we realized why. Before arriving back at
the Cardiff Docks where the *Britannia* was anchored for the
night, the Queen had visited Swansea, Cardiff Castle, Caer-
philly, and numerous other places on the way, meeting and
chatting to people. It was an incredible schedule, and I had to
admit to myself that my life could no longer be called hectic
compared to hers. As all the guests boarded the yacht, the
crowd lining the docks gave out cheers to all those people they
recognized. There was a cheer for me, a huge one for Merv,
who had not long been home from hospital after his operation,

and then there was another big cheer. 'Oh, I expect that is Barry John,' said someone in front of me. I turned round expecting to see BJ and found that it was Jim Callaghan, the Prime Minister. Knowing what a fan of Welsh rugby he is, I'm sure he was not insulted by that comparison.

We were hosted on board by the Royal Navy, who were delighted to see Merv and me, as many of them were keen rugby supporters, and plied us with lots of champagne. Near the end of the reception, the Queen came over towards us. She recognized Merv and had quite a chat with him, then, with the guidance of John Morris, the Secretary of State for Wales she came over to me and mentioned Merv's accident, knowing that I was a doctor. She asked me if I worked in UHW, as she had opened it five years previously, and then talked quite a bit about the hospital. I was amazed by the informality and knowledge of her conversation. She put me so much at ease that I thanked her for the reception, saying that we had really enjoyed it – we didn't get much chance to go out now, I said, because of our newly-born daughter. As soon as I had said it I felt dreadfully embarrassed, and could see Scilla frowning at me: it wasn't quite the thing to say to one's sovereign, but the Queen was completely unaffected and kept up the same vein of conversation by asking whether the grandparents were baby-sitting!

Straight after the reception, we were invited to a frigate nearby in the docks, where the captain turned out to be a friend of ours, Lee Merrick, who had played for Richmond when Merv and I were playing for London Welsh.

We had just left that party, and were heading off home through the docks, when the car suddenly stalled, and nothing it seemed was going to persuade it to start. There we were, absolutely lost, in the least salubrious part of Cardiff, with not a soul about, feeling absolutely helpless. It just did not seem possible that only a few hours before, I had been talking to the Queen about baby-sitters and sipping champagne on the Royal Yacht.

Later that year, while on duty at the Cardiff Royal Infirmary, my bleeper went off and the switchboard operator informed me that I was in the Queen's Silver Jubilee Honours List. I had been awarded the MBE for my services to rugby, and the following morning on the ward round, there were a lot of envious consultants: they knew, as I did, that I could eventually achieve the same letters after my name as they, if I worked at it, but no matter how many degrees they might have, not many had honours like that bestowed upon them.

The trip to Buckingham Palace in December for my investiture marked the end of a truly memorable year.

1978 started with a bang, in more ways than one. I was on my way to the Welsh Probables *v* Possibles at Cardiff one Saturday morning in January, when my car crashed into an oil tanker on one of the narrow lanes near Llansannor. It was lucky that my Capri had a long bonnet, otherwise I really would have been in trouble, as the whole of the front caved in completely. I was a bit shaken up at the time, but typically, my only thought was that I should not be late for the trial. I managed to use someone's phone to tell Scilla to come and pick me up in her little Fiat. I didn't tell her why and the look on her face when she saw the wreckage made me realize how lucky I had been, lucky also that she and Lauren had not been in the car as well. I still thought that there was nothing odd in going to play a game – after all I had received fewer bruises than I normally get on a Saturday afternoon. I think I even scored a try in the trial. But it caused quite a sensation in the press. Later Gareth Edwards was heard to say: 'If I know John, he probably just expected the tanker to move over: you'd expect the car and the tanker to be a write-off, but JPR would be in one piece for certain.'

It was also used by the Welsh poet Tom Bellion to write a very flattering (and funny) poem about my apparent indestructability – 'JPR Collides with Tanker – The Tanker Has Spent a Comfortable Night and is Expected To Recover' goes the title.

The captaincy of the Bridgend team for their centenary season was decided before the Welsh team left for Australia in May 1978. This was a very nerve-racking experience as the position meant a lot to me. I had had a taste of captaincy both at London Welsh and the previous season with Bridgend when the captain (Lyndon Thomas) was injured for several months. There were two candidates – Meredydd James, a prop, who had been playing for Bridgend for some time, and myself. We knew it would be a close decision and a lot of canvassing went on before the big day. At Bridgend the players pick the captain, and after a close count I was thrilled to hear I had been chosen. However, in spite of the excitement I was under no illusions about the coming season, especially when we were given a fixture against the 1978 All Blacks.

There was little break from training on my return from Australia and the lads really trained hard for about six weeks before the season started with our centenary VIIs. These were sponsored by Alcan Metals for the first time. It was a great event and sides came to play from Europe – France, Ireland, Italy – as well as Cardiff, Melrose, Moseley and Bridgend. Public School Wanderers made up the eight, being a mixture of players from different countries. There were two sections and everyone played each other in their section, a different arrangement from that normal in VIIs. We didn't want sides who had travelled long distances to play only one round and get knocked out for the rest of the tournament.

After some great matches Cardiff and Bridgend qualified for the final. This was a tense affair with the lead changing hands several times before Cardiff eventually clinched it in extra time. We were disappointed not to win but not too upset, as the day had been a great success. The local Bridgend support had been tremendous and we had launched our centenary in fine style.

September was a very hectic month for us with special games against the Irish Wolfhounds and the Welsh Residents XV, as well as our usual heavy fixture list. We managed to survive September with only one defeat; our most impressive display was the heavy defeat of Pontypool, which luckily for us was televised. This was just the start we needed, although I must admit the weather was very kind to us – we had to rely on hard, fast grounds for our open fifteen-man game. We suffered the odd defeat, but generally managed to play the game we wanted to.

The Wales *v* New Zealand game was approaching and two leading contenders for captaincy, Phil Bennett and Terry Cobner, decided that they no longer wished to be considered for international rugby. This, on top of the retirement of Gareth Edwards and Gerald Davies, was a great shock to all Welsh rugby followers. It also left Wales without a captain. I suddenly realized I was in with a chance, with Derek Quinnell being the other contender. He was captain of West Wales against the All Blacks, and after that game I knew that it was inevitable I would be chosen. Had anyone told me I would be captain of Wales at the beginning of the season I wouldn't have believed him. I was delighted to hear the news but ruefully admitted to myself that I was only captain by default.

So, with a 'new look' Welsh side I was taking on the strength of New Zealand at the National Stadium. What a thrill, and what a challenge! Nobody thought we had a chance, but that day we proved ourselves. The lads played magnificently only to be robbed in the last few minutes of the game by a controversial line-out penalty. We went into a 12–4 lead in the first half and were totally on top. I wondered at the time whether it would be enough. We pressurized the All Blacks' line for twenty minutes in the second half, but wasted opportunities of scoring, and this was to prove disastrous.

We were still 12–10 in the lead, with a few minutes to go, when we were penalized at a line-out and Brian McKechnie kicked the match-winning goal. I couldn't see what had happened so could not comment on the incident. But I was a little upset that Roger Quittenden, the referee, who had seen barging at every line-out that afternoon, should see fit to hand the game to the All Blacks. I felt more upset when he told me that Wales were the most disciplined side he had ever 'reffed', so it was not as if he had been looking for offenders. When I saw it televised the following day I could not believe it. It was disgraceful and there is no doubt in my mind that Andy Haden should have been sent off for 'ungentlemanly conduct'. He 'fell' out of the line-out before the ball had left our hooker, Bobby Windsor's, hands. On top of that Frank Oliver did not contest the ball and Geoff Wheel was penalized for barging – an appalling decision. When the others fell away, poor Geoff Wheel, who had been contesting the ball, suddenly found all his support gone and put his arm across to balance himself. Still, we could not change the result and once again a Wales *v* New Zealand match was surrounded by controversy. Perhaps New Zealand feel that Bob Deans had been avenged.

The spirit of our players shone through that night and we accepted the defeat in magnificent style. I admired the young-sters so much. They came into the team in the shadow of their great predecessors and yet played as if they'd been there all their lives. They took the bitter disappointment with consider-able maturity. I'm sure they will do Wales proud for years to come.

I decided after this match the best thing would be to return to playing club matches and I turned out for Bridgend two days later against Neath. The Bridgend players played their hearts out as if to avenge my disappointment. We enjoyed a good victory. The build-up was now growing for our Bridgend game against the All Blacks. Only Munster had lowered their colours and they were proving as hard to beat as their pre-decessors, though not so brilliant. I admired their friendliness off the field, knowing how difficult but how important it is to have good public relations on long tours. In fact, after the Welsh game I congratulated their manager, coach and captain on their success on and off the field, and thanked them for restoring some of the friendship lost between the two countries over the previous five years.

Bridgend had to play Neath at Neath five days before our game against New Zealand, and the weather was atrocious. I was worried in case any of our players should be injured. In the event I was the only person to injure myself, but my knee responded well to treatment and our preparations went well for the 'big' game.

No major touring side had ever graced Brewery Field.

Our only misfortune was the terrible weather conditions. It had rained continually for five days and all pitches in South Wales were turned into quagmires. Our field is usually very good, but even this was under water on the day of the game. Our team had been picked on the previous Sunday and we had a full day's squad training as our final preparation. The weather was a bitter blow to us, as we intended to throw the ball around and run at it. But we still felt we were in with a fair chance: as we were at least a club side and a very good one at that. I remember running on to the field and being so excited to see seventeen thousand spectators packed into our 'modest' ground. In spite of the rain the stands and surroundings looked superb.

We started off tremendously, but then unfortunately missed an easy goal kick which would have been very important to us psychologically. I asked Steve Fenwick to take it, knowing his big match temperament, but our outside-half wanted to take it instead and Steve felt he should be allowed to do so. I now feel in retrospect I should have insisted on Steve taking it.

Then it happened!

I was involved on the edge of a ruck in the All Blacks' twenty-five-yard line when they won the ball on the opposite side from where I was lying pinned down with my head out of the ruck. I was about five or so yards away from the ball when I felt a kick in my face. The first one didn't do much damage but when the second one came I knew it was bad. I could feel the studs near my right eye, then my cheek bone clunked. As I had broken this previously it was stronger than normal and held firm. Then the studs moved down to my upper jaw which was protected by my gum shield. This flew out but my teeth were intact. Something had to give and I was left with a horrendous hole in my cheek all the way through to my tongue. I knew I had to go off the field, as blood was pouring out at a terrific rate. One of the branches of the facial artery was severed and I think I lost about two pints of blood before the stitches were completed. My father was there immediately, along with a dentist, inserting stitches inside my mouth, and together they patched me up quickly. My brothers had also rushed down to the medical room to help and tried to dissuade me from returning to the field. But they knew, as my father knew, that it was impossible to stop me. Unfortunately, during this time the All Blacks had scored seven points against our fourteen men and this, in the end, was to prove vital to the result. I probably shouldn't have returned, but I knew how much my players relied on me and this was shown on my return. We came back to 10–6 at half-time and were in with a real chance. Unluckily the wind blew up during the second half and even though we tried we found it difficult to get out of our half. With a silly try near the end we lost 17–6, but felt none-theless that we were the 'real' winners, as we came off with far more glory than the All Blacks did.

Not having seen the incident I was kind to the New Zealanders in my speech that evening and once again congratulated them on their form. But I was hurt that nobody had come to apologize or ask me how my face was. Still, it must have been an accident, I thought.

When I saw it on television the following day I was nearly sick. My assailant raked me once and then came back for a second go when he saw who it was. It corresponded with my recollection but I was amazed to see the referee so near. The evidence was irrefutable and I needed to say nothing – it was plain to see. In spite of pressure from everyone I wanted the incident to be closed; I didn't feel prolonging it could do anyone any good. When I saw the culprit come on as a sub-stitute in the game against the Barbarians the following

Saturday it was the final straw and it seemed truly to be a kick in the teeth to Bridgend, Wales, Great Britain and rugby as a whole. Amidst boos from the crowd he lifted up his arms in a triumphant gesture as if to say, 'Yes, I did it to JPR but there's nothing anyone can do about it.' It made the management as guilty as the player, and after all the complimentary things I had said about them I think I deserved better treatment than that. They either chose to ignore the incident or condone it. In view of all their speeches about wishing to play rugby football so that their sons and youngsters would want to take up the game, I am afraid that they lost a lot of credibility in my eyes after that.

It was a sad day for rugby and will take a lot of repairing. Every player, and I am no exception, has done things they have regretted on the field, but I can honestly say that I have always apologized to the player concerned after the match. It is imperative that the authorities must no longer condone thuggery, or the game will degenerate and cease to be the same game which has brought pleasure to so many people over so many years, not least to me.

Acknowledgements

I am grateful to the following for permission to reproduce the photographs and cartoon in this book:

With my father during the Junior Tennis Championships at Penarth in 1965 (*Hill's Welsh Press Ltd*)

With Gerald Battrick on the Centre Court at Newport in 1967 (*Western Mail and Echo Ltd*)

Winning the Junior Wimbledon title in 1966 (*Sport and General Press Agency*)

The announcement of my first cap, against Scotland, in 1969 (*Thomson Newspapers Ltd*)

Our wedding day, 1973 (*Boards of Buxton*)

My first try against England in 1970 (*Sport and General Press Agency*)

The winning tackle (against France) that ensured our grand slam of 1976 (*Colorsport*)

On the rampage in New Zealand in 1971 (*New Zealand Herald*)

Touring New Zealand, 1969 (*Sunday Times*)

With the Lions in South Africa, 1974 (*John Rubython*)

During the first Test against South Africa, 1974 (*Evert Smith, Evening Post, Port Elizabeth*)

The Tommy Bedford incident in South Africa (*Natal Mercury*)

Tending an injury on the field of play (*Colorsport*)

An attempted break during the fourth Test in South Africa (*Colorsport*)

More skirmishes in South Africa (*Doug Lee, Sunday Express, Johannesburg*)

On duty at Cardiff General Hospital (*Sunday Times*)

Bridgend v New Zealand, 1978 (*Dennis Stephens*)

Cartoon: JPR's nipper (*courtesy of Gren of the South Wales Echo*)

Chronological Table

1964	Under-15 Welsh Schoolboy cap (3 appearances)
1966	Junior Wimbledon Tennis Title
1967	Welsh Secondary Schools cap (3 appearances)
1968	Welsh Rugby Union tour to Argentine
1969	Full Welsh cap

     48 appearances: 1969–78

     28 additional appearances, not receiving full Welsh cap, against Fiji, Canada etc.

     No. of appearances in Welsh 15 jersey: 75

     No. of appearances in Welsh 7 jersey: 1

     Welsh tour of New Zealand, Australia and Fiji

1971	British Isles Rugby Union tour of New Zealand (14 appearances including all four Tests)
1973	Welsh tour of Canada
1974	British Isles Rugby Union tour of South Africa (15 appearances including all four Tests)
1975	Welsh tour of Japan
1978	Welsh tour of Australia

1949	Born 2 March
1953–9	Attended Laleston County Primary School
1959–60	Bryntirion Prep School
1960–6	Bridgend Boys' Grammar School
1966–7	Millfield School
1967–73	St Mary's Hospital Medical School
1968	1st MB
1970	2nd MB
1973 (Apr)	Conjoint: MRCS, LRCP
(Nov)	MB, BS
1973–4	House Surgeon, St Mary's Hospital, W2
1974	Tennis coach, South Africa
1974–5	House Physician, Hillingdon Hospital, Uxbridge, Middx.
1975–6	Anatomy Lecturer, St Mary's Hospital Medical School
1976	Casualty Officer, Battle Hospital, Reading, Berks.
1976–7	Senior House Officer, Surgery Dept., University Hospital for Wales
1977–79	Rotating Surgical Registrar, UHW

Index

Index